Late Punic Epigraphy

Edited by
Karel Jongeling and Robert M. Kerr

Late Punic Epigraphy

An Introduction to the Study of Neo-Punic and Latino-Punic Inscriptions

Edited by
Karel Jongeling and Robert M. Kerr

Mohr Siebeck

Karel Jongeling, born 1947; studied Semitic languages in Groningen; 1984 Ph.D.; has lectured North-West Semitics and Welsh in Leiden since 1979.

Robert M. Kerr, born 1968; studied Semitic languages and comparative linguistics; is currently working on his doctoral thesis on late Punic.

ISBN 3-16-148728-1

Die Deutsche Bibliothek lists this publication in the Deutsche Nationalbibliographie; detailed bibliographic data is available in the Internet at *http://dnb.ddb.de*.

The book was printed by Gulde-Druck in Tübingen on non-aging paper and bound by Buchbinderei Held in Rottenburg.

Printed in Germany.

Preface

The present volume purports to give an introductory overview of late Punic epigraphy, i.e. a representative selection of relatively comprehensible Neo- and Latino-Punic texts. On the one hand, the present authors intend to pick up where Gibson's *Textbook of Syrian Semitic Inscriptions* left off, on the other to broaden the selection offered by Donner and Röllig in *Kanaanäische und Aramäische Inschriften*, whilst at the same time also reflecting the results of research carried out during the past decades. That this work is limited in scope to late Punic epigraphy bears witness to the ever increasing specialization within the field of Semitic epigraphy referred to by Röllig in the fifth edition of *KAI*. Nonetheless, we hope that this work will be of use to all those with an interest in North-West Semitic, namely philologists, linguists and theologians. Although we necessarily presume that the reader will have a working knowledge of classical Hebrew, Phoenician and/or Arabic, historians interested in the (Western) Mediterranean region during the first centuries before and after the Common Era may also find this work of some use.

The work itself is intended for classroom use, ideally in the second term of an introductory course on North-West Semitic epigraphy, although it may also of course be used for private study. The commentary accompanying each inscription has been limited to what is necessary to comprehend the respective text. Those who wish to pursue the discussions in more detail are referred to the selective bibliography. We assume that the student will avail him or herself of the mandatory lexical and grammatical tools whilst using this text-book, namely Hoftijzer-Jongeling's *Dictionary of the North-West Semitic Inscriptions* (Leiden 1995) and the third edition of Friedrich-Röllig's *Phönizisch-Punische Grammatik* (Rome 1999). We note further that the Neo-Punic texts are given in Latin transcription, whilst the separate Neo-Punic and Latino-Punic glossaries contain both common and proper nouns together for ease of consultation. In addition, only those lexemes which in our opinion have a more or less certain interpretation are included in these glossaries, and variant spellings are not always listed exhaustively to prevent overburdening the work.

The authors gratefully acknowledge the financial support provided by the *Research School CNWS* of Leiden University, which enabled them to travel to Libya and examine many of the Punic texts there. We are also grateful for the friendly assistance of Dr. Ali Khadouri, President of the *Libyan Department of Antiquities* and Dr. Mustafa Turjman, of the same department. We also express our gratitude to the *British School at Rome* for their kind permission to use the illustration of *IRT* 827/Lepcis Magna LP 3. Finally, we wish to thank Mohr Siebeck for their willingness to publish this volume, and the friendly co-operation of the responsible editor Dr. Henning Ziebritzki, the production manager Ms. Tanja Mix and their colleagues, in seeing it to press.

Leiden, August 2005

Karel Jongeling
Robert Kerr

Table of Contents

Bibliographical Abbreviations

Aaf	Antiquités Africaines
AAH	Acta Antiquae Hungaricae
AarchH	Acta Archaeologica Academiae Scientiarum Hungaricae
AÉ	L'Année Épigraphique
AI	Africa Italiana
AION	Annali Istituto Orientale di Napoli
AJ	The Antiquaries Journal
BAC	Bulletin Archéologique du Comité des Travaux Historiques et Scientifiques
BASOR	Bulletin of the American Schools of Oriental Research
Bu Njem	see MARICHAL 1992
B&O	Bibbia e Oriente
CB	Cahiers de Byrsa
CIL	Corpus Inscriptionum Latinarum, pars octava, Berlin, 1863-.
CIS	Corpus Inscriptionum Semiticarum, pars prima, Paris, 1880.
CRAIBL	Comptes Rendus à l'Académie des Inscriptions et Belles-Lettres
DISO	see JEAN – HOFTIJZER 1965
DNWSI	see HOFTIJZER – JONGELING 1995
DS-NELL	Dutch Studies on Near Eastern Languages and Literatures
EH	see BERTHIER-CHARLIER 1955
GLECS	Groupe Linguistique des Études Chamito-Sémitiques
HdO	Handbuch der Orientalistik
IAM	see FÉVRIER-GALAND-VAJDA 1966
ICO	see AMADASI 1967
ILAf	see CAGNAT-MERLIN-CHATELAIN 1923
ILS	see DESSAU 1892-1916
IPT	see LEVI DELLA VIDA–AMADASI GUZZO 1987
IRT	see REYNOLDS–WARD-PERKINS 1952
IRTS	see REYNOLDS 1955
JA	Journal Asiatique
JAOS	Journal of the American Oriental Society
JBL	Journal of Biblical Literature
JNES	Journal of Near Eastern Studies
JRS	The Journal of Roman Studies
JSS	Journal of Semitic Studies
JTS	Journal of Theological Studies
KAI	see DONNER – RÖLLIG 1966-1969
KAI^5	see DONNER – RÖLLIG 2002
KSINA	Kratkie Sobščenija Instituta Narodov Azii
LA	Libya Antiqua
LS	Libyan Studies
MAIBL	Extraits des Mémoires présentées par divers savants à l'Académie des Inscriptions et Belles-Lettres
MEFR	Mélanges de l'École Française de Rome

NP	Neo-Punic inscriptions as listed by SCHRÖDER 1869: 63-72 and HARRIS 1936: 160-161
NSI	see COOKE 1903
n.s.	nova serie
OA	Oriens Antiquus
OJA	Oxford Journal of Archaeology
OLA	Orientalia Lovaniensia Analecta
OML	Oudheidkundige Mededeelingen van het Rijksmuseum van Oudheden te Leiden
PBSR	Papers of the British School at Rome
PPG	see FRIEDRICH – RÖLLIG 1999
Punica	see CHABOT 1916-1917.
QAL	Quaderni di Archeologia della Libia
RANL	Rendiconti della Academia Nazionale dei Lincei
RB	Revue Biblique
REPPAL	Revue des études phéniciennes, puniques et des antiquités libyques
RÉS	Recueil d'Épigraphie Sémitique
RHR	Revue d'Histoire des Religions
RIL	see CHABOT 1940-1941
RSF	Rivista di Studi Fenici
RSO	Rivista degli Studi Orientali
SEL	Studi Epigrafici e Linguistici
SO	Studia Orientalia, Helsinki
SM	Studi Magrebini
SPC	see BERTRANDY – SZNYCER 1987
TRE	see ELMAYER 1997
VO	Vicino Oriente
VT	Vetus Testamentum
ZDMG	Zeitschrift der Deutschen Morgenländischen Gesellschaft

Introduction

§ 1 Neo-Punic and Latino-Punic

Late Punic as understood in the present work is a catch-all term to denote those inscriptions post-dating the Roman conquest and destruction of Carthage at the end of the Third Punic War in 146 BC. In modern academic usage, Punic (from the Latin) generally refers to the Phoenician language as attested in the (former) Phoenician colonies in the Western Mediterranean, esp. North Africa, whilst Phoenician (from the Greek) refers to this language as attested in the Lebanese motherland and Eastern colonies. Punic, in the course of time, gradually underwent its own development as ties with the motherland weakened and as it came into contact with the indigenous languages of colonised regions, and later, in the phase under consideration, with the Latin superstrate (cf. Afrikaans vs. Dutch or South American vs. European Spanish). Phoenico-Punic is a Semitic language belonging to what is traditionally known as the Canaanite branch of North-West Semitic. Its closest relative is classical or biblical Hebrew (although it does share some features only well-attested in post-biblical Hebrew such as the compounding of prepositions and the use of prolepsis) while there are some isoglosses with South Semitic (e.g. the verbs *kwn* and *p ᶜl*).

Apart from glosses in classical texts, the late Punic corpus consists of what are generally speaking known as Neo-Punic and Latino-Punic inscriptions. Although some scholars use the term Neo-Punic as a synonym for late Punic, these two terms are actually not synonymous. The former, as mentioned, applies to the last recorded phases of Phoenico-Punic in general, whilst neither Neo-Punic nor Latino-Punic refer to a language classification based on linguistic criteria, but rather to the script employed to write these texts.

In the first case, Neo-Punic refers to a development of the Phoenician script. This script, occasionally attested before the Roman conquest of the Carthaginian territories (e.g. N 5 from Carthage and the odd letter or word in Punic inscriptions), was originally the cursive ductus vis-à-vis the more formal Punic script, whose development began already in an earlier period, as a few remnants of ostraca show. In the case of North Africa, Neo-Punic seems to have become the lapidary standard after 146 BC, although the Punic predecessor is sometimes still attested (possibly Djebel Massoudj 1; although Neo-Punic texts tend to be dated to after the fall of Carthage, this is by no means always certain) and then spread throughout the Mediterranean region (and in one case in Wales) in a more or less uniform style. In several instances, namely in towns that allied themselves with Rome early on, a 'monumental' form of this script evolved (e.g. at Lepcis Magna, where for a time in the first century AD, Punic seems to have enjoyed a status comparable to Latin in public epigraphy), whilst in Sardinia (that had been conquered by Rome during the Second Punic War), a separate development took place. Linguistically speaking, the language of the Neo-Punic texts is to all intents and purposes that of the texts written in Punic script. Nonetheless, the Neo-Punic inscriptions show several striking optical differences, namely the tendency to spell phonetically using *matres lectionis* (cf. §3a) and the large number of non-Semitic names, many of Libyco-Berber origin. Both of these features have their roots in the spread of the Punic language amongst the aboriginal peoples of North Africa.

In the case of Latino-Punic, an entirely different (though distantly related) script was adapted, namely the Latin alphabet (reflecting however the contemporary colloquial pronunciation of North Africa). The adoption by one language of a script hitherto used for another language (cf. the use of the Hebrew square script for Jewish languages, Karshuni, Coptic etc.) is not in itself unusual and can usually be attributed to exclusion from traditional education in the language being written. The seventy or so texts comprising the Latino-Punic corpus emanate from Tripolitania and date roughly speaking to the third and fourth centuries AD. They are a striking witness to the survival of Punic as the spoken idiom by those who were only superficially in contact with Rome. Mention should also be made here of the Punic texts in Greek script (Greco-Punic) from El-Hofra/Constantine in Algeria, which although earlier, display similar phonetic features. At first sight, these 'transcribed' texts appear rather strange due to their (Greco-) Latin 'disguise.' Nonetheless, based on what can be gleaned from them with any certainty, they render Punic comparable to that of the Neo-Punic texts. Their primary linguistic importance (especially with regard to classical Hebrew) is that by nature of the script employed, they are fully vocalized.

§ 2 The survival of Punic

In the preceding, mention was made that 'Late Punic' dates to after the Roman destruction of Carthage in the Third Punic War 146 BC. The geographical spread of these inscriptions in North Africa attests to the continuing widespread use of Punic in the region. The latest dated North African Neo-Punic inscription is Lepcis Magna N 19, dating to 92 AD. The Latino-Punic texts date from either the first century (cf. Zliten LP1) or second century (cf. Lepcis Magna LP1) AD. and continued to be written on into the fourth century (cf. ad Bir ed-Dreder LP2). The survival of Punic as attested by the inscriptional finds, is correlated by the evidence given by Classical sources. For example STRABO (63/4 BC-AD 24) mentions (17.3.15) that the Phoenicians 'acquired all of Libya [i.e. Africa] where man can live without pursuing a nomadic existence' and that (*loc. cit.*) 'they had three hundred cities in Libya', the region of Phoenico-Punic, i.e. the Libyphoenican, influence stretched (17.3.19) along the coast from 'Carthage to to Cephalae [modern Misurata] ... to the mountainous territory of the Gaetulians [in the south]' (cf. e.g. PROCOPIUS *Wars* 4.11.21f., *Buildings* 6.3.9f.). Libyphoenician, might then be seen as a synonym for Punic (vs. Syro-Phoenician). On this culture, SALLUST (86 BC-AD 34) noted (*Jugurthine War* 78) that with regard to the inhabitants of Lepcis Magna 'the language alone has been altered by their intermarriages with the Numidians; their laws and customs continue for the most part Sidonian' (cf. too St. JEROME, *In Galatas* II 'the Africans (*afri*) had altered the Phoenician language'). This comment would seem to be in line with the epigraphic finds, such as the numerous dedications to Semitic deities (e.g. Hr. Maktar N 39, El-Hofra GP1 et passim) and which also accounts for the presence of Libyco-Berber names in the onomasticon.

Although it is clear that the North African region was saturated by Cartheginian culture in the centuries preceding the Roman conquest of the region, the apparent longlivety of Punic, or rather Libyphoenican culture in the region has caused much debate. Punic seems to have become entrenched in Africa and would also seem to have been one of the few foreign languages apart from Greek which the Romans took some knowledge of. At the close of the Punic wars, PLINY (*Natural History* 18.22) notes that the Carthage's libraries were given to the African petty kings that had helped Rome, indicating that Punic must have had some status among them as a language of education and culture (cf. too the use of Punic on the coins by these kings who owed their sovreignty to Rome, SCHRÖDER 1869: 282ff. and MANFREDI 1995). At the same time, PLINY notes that the Roman senate bestowed 'honour' on but one Punic author, namely Mago, by having his work on agriculture translated into Latin. Interestingly enough (*idem* 18.23), this undertaking was headed by one Decimus Silanus, of a senatorial family (*vir clarissimae familiae*), who was seemingly an (experienced?) expert at the task (*in quo praecessit omnes*). Another important source to the knowledge of Punic in Rome at the time are the Punic dialogues in PLAUTUS' *Poenulus*. Nonetheless, the *topos* of 'Punic books' can be followed for several centuries and is an interesting testimony to the survival of Punic. SALLUST in his excursus on Africa (*op. cit.* 17. 7), used as a source *punici libri* of or by Hiempsal II(?) which were 'interpreted' for him. SOLINUS (first half of the third century AD) too refers to Punic books of Juba II(?) concerning the source of the Nile (*Collectanea rerum memorabilium* 32.2) as does AMMIANUS MARCELLINUS (fourth century AD; *History* 22.15.8). Finally, St. Augustine (AD 354-430, i.e. roughly contemporaneous with some of the Latino-Punic inscriptions) in 391 (*Ep.* 17.2) mentions that much wisdom has been preserved in *punici libri*, a fact seemingly well-known by the learned men of the day.

Although Punic is referred to several times elsewhere -(cf. MILLAR 1968: 130f.): cf. STATIUS (AD 45-96; *Slivae* 4.5.45f.) in a poem to Septimius Severus (a forefather of the emperor? –cf. *IRT* 412f.), who (surprisingly) didn't have a Punic accent (cf. ADAMS 2003: 237); APULEIUS (AD 123-170; *Apologia* 98.8f) who riduculed his stepson who 'never speaks except in Punic or something in Greek which he imitates from his mother - he doesn't want and isn't able to speak Latin';

ULPIAN's (†AD 228) comments on the permissibility of Punic in judicial situations (*Dig* 32.11, 45.1.1.6) and an anecdotal reference to the emperor Septimius Severus' eloquence in Punic (*Epit. De Caes* 19.8) and his sister's inability to speak Latin (and presumably just Punic, *Historia Aug. v. Sept. Severus* 15.7; note the family was of equestrian rank *idem* 1.2)- our primary source on the survival of Punic is St. Augustine (see esp. COX 1988 for a detailed exposition). Both St. Augustine and his son Adeodatus had some knowledge of Punic: even if it was not their mother tongue, it was at least their mother's tongue (i.e. his knowledge was at least sufficient to quote a proverb and to recognize a Hebraism). In his works, St. Augustine makes numerous mentions of the Punic language, which was still very much alive in his days (cf. e.g. *Ep.* 17.2). Basically speaking, he frequently took recourse to Punic to clarify the meanings of transliterated Semitic words found in his Latin Bible (e.g. *messias, mammon*), which makes it quite clear that we are dealing with a Semitic language closely related to Hebrew (cf. e.g. *Evang. Ioh.* 15.27 'for in fact these Hebrew, Punic and Syriac (Aramaic) are related and neighbouring languages'). Along with these glosses, St. Augustine makes mention of rural parishes on large estates in which the tenants (*coloni*) spoke Punic for the most part (cf. *Ep.* 66.2 where translation into Punic was needed). An interesting example are the events narrated in *Ep.* 209: St. Augustine found it necessary to install a bishop at the formerly Donatist *castellum* of Fussula, at some distance from his own diocese at Hippo. One of the prerequisites for the candidate was that he must be 'instructus' in Punic (cf. ADAMS 2003: 238, this seems to imply someone who had learnt Punic in later life –cf. St. Irenaeus who learnt Celtic for missionary purposes). Additional information is provided by *Ep.* *20, which relates the same events from a somewhat different perspective and in which the senior Catholic cleric in Africa, the *primas Numidiae*, attended and participated in a parochial meeting carried out in Punic. Although it would seem that Latin did enjoy more status, Punic seems to have been the vernacular of the common people, especially that of the more inland Donatist communities, the elite were not exclusively Latinate. It is interesting to note that when in a sermon preached at Hippo on the coast, St. Augustine (*Serm.* 167.4) quotes a Punic proverb in Latin 'since not all of you know Punic', which is reminiscent of the areal spread of Arabic and Berber in the present day Maghreb: generally speaking Arabic is dominant along the coast, whilst Berber becomes increasingly more common into the interior.

Previously it has been asserted that by Punic, St. Augustine indiscriminately referred to a native African language, i.e. Berber (e.g. FREND 1942, 1952), and that he was largely Latinate (e.g. BROWN 1967: 22; the latter also overemphasizes the role of Latin in Christian North Africa, *idem* 1968). As we have seen in the preceding, Augustine was in fact referring to a Semitic language. Interestingly enough, he also refers to Punic as *afer*, i.e. African, e.g. *Ep.* 17: 2 'considering that you are an African, and that we are both settled in Africa, you could not have so forgotten yourself when writing to Africans…' *Afer, africa* were Punic loans in Latin (cf. the lexica) and refer originally in classical literature to the (former) Cartheginian territory (as does Greek Αφρικη, vs. Λιβύη) as opposed e.g. to the

Mauri and the *Numidiae*. Again, in one case St. Augustine reports that peasants (*rustici*) who were Punic speakers (*punice respondentes*) referred to themselves as *Chanani* i.e. 'Canaanites' (*Epistulae ad Romanos expositio inchoata* 13). Indeed Punic was a linguistic entity with which the Romans at least had some familiarity with, and of which we might presume that there was some knowledge of, as e.g. the Punic passages in the *Poenulus* (supra) only make sense if there was some knowledge of Punic, and loan-words into Latin (such as possibly *ave*, cf. QUINTILLIANUS 1.6.21) have a credible Semitic etymology (cf. ad Nawalia LP 1). This stands in stark contrast to Libyco-Berber of which the Romans seemingly had no first-hand knowledge (cf. e.g. *City of God* 16.6 and POMPONIUS MELA *Chron.* 1,8.41; Libyan loanwords, such as *mapalia/magaria* seem to have entered Latin via Punic). Libyan today remains something of an enigma (cf. GALAND 1990), and it is uncertain whether we are dealing with a single language or a dialect continuum. Although it does appear to be distantly related to modern Berber languages, our actual knowledge of it is scanty (cf. e.g KOSMANN 1999: 17). Most of the Libyan inscriptions too (cf. *RIL*) are difficult to date with any certainty, although bilingual Latin and Punic (cf. Bordj Helal N 1, Ain el-Kebch N 1) texts do give a rough indication.

The classical references cited in the preceding show a flourishing Punic culture in North Africa well into the fourth century. Although some of these references have been doubted (e.g. PROCOPIUS, cf. VÁRHELYI 1998: 393), the sum total taken together does make a strong case. Based on what we know of the Vandal period and the following Byzantine reconquest, there is no reason to suppose a dramatic decline in Punic culture, except possibly where estates (with Punic tenants, cf. St. Augustine supra) were destroyed during hostilities, e.g. with Libyan tribes such as the Luwata (cf. CORIPPUS). Indeed, Romanization in the North Africa was but minimal and indigenous culture seems to have continued to flourish under Roman suzerainty (cf. e.g. GRAHAME 1998).

In the past (e.g. VÁRHELYI *art. cit.* 395, MACMULLEN 2000: 46) some issue has been made of the fact that the several hundred late Punic inscriptions amount to little in comparison with the 30.000 or so Latin inscriptions from the region. The issue in our opinion is not the number of inscriptions, but the fact that the late Punic ones were written at all. The numerical data only indicate that epigraphy in the Punic language was not as widespread as in Latin, which would seem to be confirmed by the use of Punic by tenant farmers and the disdain for its use in higher Roman circles noted in the classical sources (supra). Most of the late Punic inscriptions follow Latin epigraphic custom: cf. the funerary inscriptions, the dedicatory inscriptions on buildings etc. Of special interest here are Qalat Abi s-Siba N 1, in which a Latinate formula is used in the Punic (*resta viator et lege ...*) but not in the much shorter Latin text, and Gasr el-Azaiz LP 1, in which a Latin technical term (*centenarium*) seems to have been imitated (*naṣiba*). A comparison of late Punic epigraphy with Punic epigraphy seems to indicate that the latter was generally much more restricted in genre (mostly to votive and funerary inscriptions), and we note to that in the East 'public epigraphy', such as royal inscriptions is lacking until the Persian and Hellenistic eras (and note Israel, where it is lacking completely). In Roman times, Punic seems to have been vital enough to imitate Latin genres, which is borne out by the bilingual texts from Lepcis Magna in a 'monumental' Neo-Punic ductus (e.g. N 16, 18, 19), that seem to indicate that in the first century AD, that it was still necessary to use Punic to get one's message across (note too Lepcis Magna LP 1). At the same time, outlying regions such as the Tripolitanian pre-desert, where there was admittedly not much epigraphy, the Latino-Punic inscriptions outnumber the non-official Latin ones.

With regard to the Latino-Punic texts, it has often been noted that they are an oddity with 'miscellaneous and rather haphazard switches into Latin' that 'would tentatively suggest that in the last days of Punic, when a language shift was well under way and literacy of the traditional kind dead, those attempting to write the old language in the new script found it difficult to avoid convenient switches into the now dominant language Latin' (ADAMS 2003: 245). Although these texts are but few and more often than not difficult to read, another interpretation of the data is possible. The presence of several ostraca and the seemingly systematic spelling do not necessarily point to a dying language, especially since most of the loans from Latin are technical terms. In addition, where these texts can be read with some certainty, they render what would seem to be grammatically correct Punic (pace e.g. VÁRHELYI 1998: 394 it is wrong to speak of 'debased Punic', without defining what this is, esp. vis-à-vis non-debased Punic). One might also question how common 'traditional literacy' in the 'old script' ever was. One is reminded of the situation in Egyptian, where traditional literacy was a monopoly of the traditional temple elite. The adaption of the Greek alphabet, along with numeous Greek elements helped establish a new elite and reinvigorated written Egyptian. Might such a scenario also be applicable to Punic in North Africa?

§ 3 Late Punic orthography and phonology

This section of the book, discussing several points of grammar can be kept necessarily brief, since as mentioned in the preface, we assume that the student will have a working knowledge of a (esp. North-West) Semitic language and since we also presume that the student will make use of the third edition of FRIEDRICH-RÖLLIG's *Phönizisch-Punische Grammatik*. Especially with regard to late Punic, this edition has been expanded considerably vis-à-vis its predecessors. The grammar of the late Punic texts does not generally speaking differ too much from earlier stages of Phoenico-Punic, the major differences are restricted to phonology.

The first modern treatment of the Phoenico-Punic material, including the Neo-Punic texts known at the time was SCHRÖDER 1867. Although still useful, especially with regard to Punic words in classical sources, it was largely superseded from a descriptive point of view by HARRIS 1936. Also of some use is VAN DEN BRANDEN 1967, which although idiosyncratic, employs the Phoenician script throughout and thus acquaints the student with the relevant writing system right from the beginning. SEGERT 1976 provides a concise overview of Phoenico-Punic grammar based largely on FRIEDRICH-RÖLLIG 1970. Another good introduction, especially for the earlier stages of the language is CUNCHILLOS-ZAMORA 2000. In many cases, our readings and interpretations are different from those presented by Charles KRAHMALKOV in his recent *Dictionary* (2000) and *Grammar* (2001). Although we have considered KRAHMALKOV's works, in this book we will not enter into a discussion with them. In our commentary we explain our readings, based where possible on the illustrations provided, those who so wish may compare them with KRAHMALKOV's readings and interpretations (see also our reviews of the works, resp. JONGELING-KERR 2002, 2003).

§ 3a Neo-Punic vowel notation

At some stage in the development of Punic prior to the advent of the neo-Punic script as the lapidary norm, certain historically attested consonants, namely the laryngeals and pharyngeals, ceased to be pronounced, which is corroborated by the Greco-Punic texts from El-Hofra (cf. *Megillah* 24b for a parallel development in post-biblical Galilean Hebrew). This is in all likelihood due to substrate influence initiated by the spread of the Punic language among the indigenous Libyco-Berber population of North-Africa, whose names are so frequent in Late Punic epigraphy: re. a comparison of BENZ' book, largely on names from Punic texts, in which the majority of attested names are of Semitic origin, with JONGELING's work on Neo-Punic names, in which more than half are non-Semitic (both Libyan, and Latin). The graphemes representing these quiescent consonants, along with the half-vowels *w* and *y*, in a similar but separate development to classical Hebrew, came to be used as vowels, a feature sporadically attested already in Punic texts. In Neo-Punic however, due to the aforementioned extinction of traditional scribal practice, phonetic spelling employing *matres lectionis* became the norm, initially it seems to first have been used to render foreign words and names. This seems to have been a uniform development throughout North Africa. It would seem that the gutturals disappeared mostly without leaving any discernable phonetic residue, which is confirmed by Greco and Latino-Punic spellings. A basic overview of neo-Punic vowel letters is given in the following table (cf. *PPG* §§100-109):

Transcription	Hebrew	Arabic	Neo-Punic Vowel
ɔ	א	ا	/o/, /e/, /u/
h	ה	ه	/a/,
w	ו	و	/u/
ḥ	ח	ح	/a/
y	י	ى	/i/
ᶜ	ע	ع	/a/

With regard to the use of vowel letters, the following points should be noted:

ʾ the weakest of the gutturals, seems to have been the first to loose its consonantal value. As such it was originally used to indicate the presence of a vowel. It is mainly used to indicate */o/* in Semitic words. Further, it is also used to indicate an */e/*, especially to indicate the *–e* ending of the Latin vocative (the form in which Punic borrowed personal names).

h originally a voiceless guttural like the preceding. Its use as a vowel letter is less common, possibly regionally determined. It too seems to indicate any vowel. In Sardinia (Bitia N 1), where a separate development must necessarily have occurred, the *–h* is used for the borrowed *–e* ending in Latin personal names.

w a vocalic bilabial glide, which when used as a vowel indicates the */u/*, mostly attested in Latin names and loanwords. Unlike classical Hebrew, it does not normally indicate */o/*, although this use is attested a few times.

ḥ also once a voiceless guttural. Its use as a vowel is seldom. When so used, it indicates */a/*.

y a vocalic palatal glide, as a vowel it denotes */i/*. It is not used for */e/*.

ʿ once a voiced guttural. It is the usual grapheme to represent */a/*.

The following points should be noted: the use of vowels is frequent, but by no means mandatory nor systematic, except possibly when transcribing foreign (esp. Latin) names and loan-words. Unlike classical Arabic, there is no regular rendition of long vowels, and as in Hebrew, vowel length is not indicated. In general, Neo-Punic 'plene' spellings are reminiscent of those of post-biblical Hebrew (e.g. *ḥydš* 'renovate' (piel), *ṣypwr* 'bird'), without however the latter's regularity. Occasionally traditional spellings with the expected guttural in its expected place are found, but these must rather be seen as historical spellings. Sometimes too, an admixture of the two spelling systems is attested, namely the historical consonant along with the consonant representing the required vowel (e.g. respectively *šmʾ*, *šmʿ* and *šmʾʿ (/šamo/)* 'he heard' or the historical *ʾbn* vs. the phonetic *ʿbn (/abn/)* 'stone').

§3b Latino-Punic Spelling

The spelling of Punic with the letters of the Latin alphabet presents some problems, which are partially attributable to the purely phonetic transcribed 'disguise', but mostly due to our ignorance of late Punic. Late Punic had lost its gutturals and pharyngeals, but whereas Neo-Punic historical spellings aid the identification of lexemes, this is not applicable in Latino- and Greco-Punic. Generally speaking, what can be gleaned from these texts with any certainty shows a fairly standardized spelling. The Latin vowels equate the use of vowel-letters in Neo-Punic. As in Latin, vowel length is not indicated, although an innovation should be noted, namely the use of *Y* in Latino- and υ in Greco-Punic to indicate a reduced vowel (schwa). In addition, there are two additional graphemes regularly employed for phonemes foreign to Latin, namely *ꞩ* and *Σ*. The former, a ligature (*s* + *t*), regularly indicates voiceless velar sibilant (/*ṣ*/) in Semitic words (e.g. *mynꞩyft* (neo-Punic *mnṣbt*), 'funerary monument') and in names of Libyan origin. The second symbol, reminiscent of a Greek uncial sigma, is usually interpreted as voiceless sibilant /*š*/ due to its alleged similarity with the ancient tifinagh sign Σ which can have this phonetic value. The only certain Semitic word given by *PPG* (§§45b, 48e) however is the enigmatic *ΣUMAR*, supposedly ptc. G ms. <√ *šmr* (although it is not listed §§ 139f.); we would read differently (cf. comm. ad Bir Shmech LP1). The only other attestations are in Libyan words and names, excepting instances of the demonstrative pronoun *ΣY*. The former, based on our present knowledge, are not helpful. The latter however are interesting, especially since the symbol in question is reminiscent of the cursive Latin *Z*, a grapheme (otherwise) unattested in our corpus. It should be noted that neither symbol is unique to Latino-Punic, as they are also found in Latin texts to spell foreign names and loanwords (*ꞩ IRTS* 8a: 3 and in an unpublished text from Wadi Gargar; Σ at Bu Ngem).

In some cases, these vocalised texts provide additional support for phonetic shifts attested elsewhere in transcriptions, such as *a>ā>ō*, e.g. the transcriptions qal 3 ms *ναδωρ*, *σαμω* (El Hofra GP 1), *avo* (e.g. ad Sirte LP 1), cf. *PPG* §78. In other cases, the phonetic transcription does offer some surprises, such as the systematic rendition of the perfect qal of $p^{c}l$ as *fel* (3 sg. m., e.g. Gasr Doga LP 1), *fela* (3 sg. fem., Ghirza LP 1), *felv* (3 pl. m., e.g. Bir Shmech LP 1), cf. *PPG* §75b, p. 39.

§ 4 The character of the texts

Most of the late Punic inscriptions are short stereotyped inscriptions. Generally speaking, the late Punic texts belong to the following genres: votive inscriptions, epitaphs and building inscriptions. Texts belonging to the two former genres tend to make use of stereotype formulae, which is a crucial aid in interpretation. Longer texts that depart from the well-known short formulae (e.g. Bordj Helal N 1), such as some of the longer neo-Punic building inscriptions (e.g. Cherchel N 2) tend to be very difficult to interpret because they are not stereotype. To some extent the funerary and the building genres converge. On the one hand, the construction of large mausolea was a major building activity (cf. e.g. Cherchel N 2), whilst on the other, some buildings such as 'fortified farms' were designed to be an eternal dwelling for the families of the petty rulers (cf. ad Gasr el Azaiz LP 1).

§ 5 Note on Neo-Punic palaeography

Basically the form of the Neo-Punic graphemes is a cursive development of the Punic script as we know it from many inscriptions from Carthage and elsewhere in North Africa, but which had its origin in Phoenicia and the Eastern colonies. It seems that this cursive style developed along the same lines everywhere in North Africa, while at least one text from Sardinia suggests that outside the Carthaginian range of influence, the development could differ. Because of the nature of the script and the very few datable Neo-Punic texts, it is impossible to date texts according to the shape of the signs.

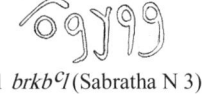

1 *brkbʿl* (Sabratha N 3)

It is almost certain that the cursive was developed for the use on e.g. ostraca and papyrus, where smooth movements resulted in more flowing lines. Also the number of strokes used for one sign is decreased, sometimes considerably as e.g. in the case of the *ḥ*, which originally needed five strokes, but in its cursive form only three, or even one as in the ostracon from Al-Qusbat. The cursive style used on stone in the Neo-Punic texts is not always easy for the reader. However, the type of script used in Tripolitania for official texts may be described as a monumental form of the cursive script in which most signs are well differentiated from each other (cf. e.g. the following texts in the present collection: Lepcis Magna N 1, Breviglieri N 1). Closely related to this script is the form for private use as found on several tombstones (cf. e.g. Lepcis Magna N 2, 24, 29). In the illustrations, it is easy to see how the signs are lined at their tops, some coming down half-way, as is the case with *d, z, y, m, ʿ, š*, while *ʾ, b, g, h, w, ṭ, k, n, s, p, ṣ, q, r, t* use the whole

2 *rb mḥnt* (Breviglieri N 1)

depth of the line (fig. 1), *ḥ* sometimes having a length between the two groups mentioned (fig. 2).

Only *l* extends above the line (fig. 1). In a few instances, the line from which the signs are, as it were, suspended, is also incised in the stone (cf. Qalat Abi s-Siba N 1). Several signs have forms that resemble each other more or less, even in the monumental script, however, in the texts written and cut out by less experienced writers and lapicides, these signs are sometimes not really differentiated at all. The following problems are most frequently encountered:

ʾ - m when the size of the signs is not taken into account, *ʾ* and *m* sometimes have the same form, or they only differ because of the small down-stroke at the top right of the ʾ-sign (no distinction between ʾ and *m*, and the distinction by means of a small down-stroke in the top right-hand corner both occur in Guelma N 22).

b - d - r in the monumental script have different forms (for *b* and *r*, see fig. 1 and 2, for *d* and *r*, see fig. 3), however, in the more cursive form, all three signs may be represented by a down-stroke reaching down half-way (see fig. 4); the more elaborate and the shortened forms of these signs sometimes co-occur in the same text (see fig. 5);

3 *ʾt ndʿr* (Sabratha N 3)

4 *ndr ʾš ndr* (Hr. Maktar N 1)

5 *ndʿr ʾš nʿdr* (Tunisia OU N3)

h-ḥ-h have the same form as the first part of *ḥ* in one of its variant forms, the first one having the form of a mirrored capital R, the other one having the same form, followed by a short, or sometimes long down-stroke, however, in most instances *h* is formed by one continuous line, while *ḥ* in most instances is formed of three strokes (see figs. 6, 7, 10) that may even resemble three times the sign for a short *b*, *d* or *r* (see fig. 8).

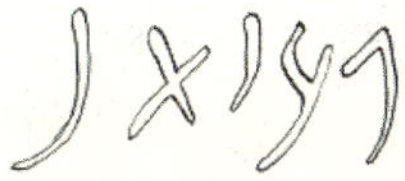
6 *ḥmn* (Tunisia OU N 1)

7 *ḥmn* (Hr. Maktar N 41)

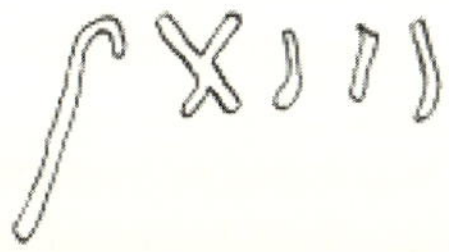
8 *ḥmn* (Hr. Maktar N 51)

z - š *z* and *š* are in many instances irregularly formed, and especially in the texts from Guelma, it is often difficult to differentiate between them (see e.g. Guelma N 1 and 3).

n - t *n* and *t* are both formed by a long down-stroke, in many texts differentiated by a small stroke at the top (mostly for *t*, see e.g. Hr. Sidi Khalifat N 1), but in several texts undistinguishable, or differentiated otherwise, as in Lepcis Magna N 44 where *t* is slightly curving to the left, while *n* is completely straight (see fig. 9).

9 *ʾšt ḥnbʿl* (Lepcis Magna N 44)

s - ṣ *s* and *ṣ* differ in the form of the down-stroke on the right, the *s* having a down-stroke turning to the right, the one of *ṣ* turning to the left (see fig. 10), but in many texts this down-stroke on the right is not curving to the left or the right (cf. fig. 11, perhaps not a very trustworthy drawing).

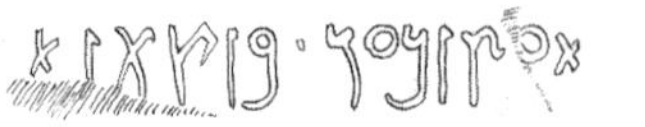
10 *mʿsnkʿw btṣʾtm* (Breviglieri N 1)

11 *ḥsm btṣ* (Hr. Djerou N 1)

An overview of the form of the Neo-Punic signs, also in relation to their Phoenician and Punic predecessors is to be found in the script tables accompanying *PPG* and in PECKHAM 1968. For the convenience of the user, we have added our own overview of the Neo-Punic signs.

As a palaeographical discussion of the Latino-Punic texts must be dealt with in the context of (North African) Latin epigraphy, which would more than exceed the scope of the present work, we will refrain from any detailed discussion.

§ 6 About this book

This concise edition of late Punic texts contains, as mentioned in the preceding, a selection of relatively comprehensible texts, suitable to serve as an introduction to this field of Semitic epigraphy. Where possible, we have included drawings and would urge the beginner right from the outset to study these along with the respective transliterations (and for the Neo-Punic texts with the appended palaeographic table).

Each text contains a select bibliography for further study, mention where (other) illustrations may be found along with a transliteration, a translation and a concise commentary. Where we disagree with other interpretations, this is mentioned in the commentary along with our motivation. For reference purposes we have also included both glossaries and a list of all Neo-, Latino- and Greco-Punic inscriptions known to us in the appendices.

The beginner will soon note that many of these texts are still controversial with regard to their interpretation. We hope that this modest work will encourage further studies in this often neglected branch of Semitic epigraphy.

Neo-Punic Texts

Egypt

Memphis

Memphis N 1

Bibliography: *CIS* 97, lines 3-4.

Illustrations: CIS tab. xv.

Text:
1) knttʾ bn ʾpkn
2) ʾmdrn bn ʾmdrn

Translation:
1) *knttʾ* son of *ʾpkn*
2) *ʾmdrn* son of *ʾmdrn.*

Remarks:
In an Egyptian temple in Memphis numerous Punic and some Neo-Punic graffiti were found. The latter comprise some names that would seem in all likelihood to be of Berber origin.

Greece

Delos

Delos N 1

Bibliography: BERGER 1887.

Text:
1) ʿzrbʿl
2) kṭʿ

Translation:
1) Azrubal
2) *kṭʿ*

Remarks:
The word or name *kṭʿ* remains unexplained. Unfortunately no illustration of this text seems to have been published.

Libya

El-Amruni

El-Amruni N 1

Bibliography: LEVI DELLA VIDA 1964b: 305-306; VATTIONI 1980-1981; FERCHIOU 1989; ADAMS 2003: 217-219; *KAI* 117.

Illustrations: LIDZBARSKI 1898, Taf. xvi, 5 (drawing); FERCHIOU 1989, plate xvi (photograph).

Text:
1) lʿl[ʾn]ʾ rʾpʾm š ʿpwlʾẙ
2) mʿk[šm]ʾ rydʿy bn ywbzʿlʿn
3) bn ywrʿ [t]ʿn hmtʾby bʿnʿ tʿnb
4) rʿ ʿšt[ʾ] ʿl pwdnš wšʾwʾwʾ
5) rʾ wmʿk[šm]ʾ bʿn[m]

Latin parallel:
1) D*is* M*anibvs* Sac*rvm*
2) Q*vintvs* Apuleivs Maxssimvs
3) qvi et Ridevs vocaba-
4) tvr Ivzale f*ilivs* Ivrathe N*epos*
5) vix*it* an*nis* lxxxx Thanvbra
6) conivnx et Pvdens et Se-
7) vervs et Maxsimvs f*ilii*
8) piissimi p*atri* amantissimo s*va* p*ecvnia* f*ecervnt*

Translation:
1) To the Rofoim Gods of Apuleus
2) Maximus Rideus, son of Yubzalan,
3) son of Yuratan, the Metabian, Tanub-
4) ra his wife built (this) together with Pudens, and Seve<ve>-
5) rus and Maximus, their sons.

Remarks:
Both inscriptions, the Latin and the Punic one, were found among the debris of a large mausoleum in El-Amrouni at the end of the 19th century. For a reconstruction of the mausoleum, cf. FERCHIOU 1989. CLERMONT-GANNEAU 1895: 159-160, 164, was the first to read *rʾpʾm* in the first line and to relate this word to *Manes* in the Latin text. The preceding word has been a matter of debate. The available space requires something like *lʿl[nm] ʾrʾpʾm*, as given by RÖLLIG sub *KAI* 117, or, possibly, *lʾl[nʾ] ʾrʾpʾm*; the reading accepted by most commentators, cf. e.g. FERRON 1964-1965: 73. This means, however, that the *ʾ* preceding *rʾpʾm* must be the article. CLERMONT-GANNEAU 1895: 159-160, however, has argued that the article is not to be expected in connection with *rʾpʾm*, because this word functions as a proper noun. Our reading, as given supra, is based on the supposition that two signs are needed to fill the gap, and that CLERMONT-GANNEAU is correct in his supposition that *rʾpʾm* was probably used without the article. The name *rydʿy* in l. 2, equivalent with *Rideus* in the Latin text, has provoked a lot of discussion. BERGER 1895: 73, 75, notes that the name seems to be of Latin formation, however, unknown in Africa. FERCHIOU 1989: 57, 60, also notes that the name is not attested in the well-known collections of names from North Africa, mentioning, however, *Ridai* in a Latin text from Dougga (*CIL* viii 27173: *Rosa Asian/anicis Ridai F / uxor car / ap so*; cf. however JONGELING 1994: 120 for the names *Ridai, Riddei, Ridea*). According to FERCHIOU, the name might be a Latin transcription, or even a translation of a Punic word (cf. also ADAMS 2003: 218, n. 426). This reasoning seems only acceptable when one can point to a Semitic name or word that might be the prototype of this Latinized *Rideus*. BERGER 1895: 75, reads the name at the end of l. 2 as *ywb[z]ʿlʿn*, noting that for the uncertain sign the reading *ṭ* or *ʿ* is also possible. He then accepts the third possibility, because he supposes the name to be of Semitic origin, containing the element */baal/*. How one is to relate this name to the Latin equivalent *Iuzale* remains unexplained. As we know that the grapheme *b* was sometimes used for a sound different from a voiced labial stop, the reading *ywbzʿlʿn* for */yuvzalan/* seems the most appropriate one. The incorrect reading has influenced FERCHIOU 1989, who speaks of *Iuzala*, 'written *Iudzalan* (or *Iubaalan*) in Neo-Punic.' ADAMS 2003: 217-218 reads *ywbzʿlʿn*, giving the same transcription in his translation followed by *Iubalaan* (sic) between brackets. VATTIONI 1980-1981 reads the two names in lines 2-3 as *ywb[?]ʿlʿn bn ywr[ht]ʿn* followed by the epithet *hmnʾby*, which he translates 'sopran-nominato.' RÖLLIG, sub *KAI* 117, supposes that *ʿl* in line 4 means 'in the name of' and points to a difference in the formulae used in the Latin, resp. the Neo-Punic text. It seems easier to suppose that *ʿl*, at least in this text, has the meaning 'together with.' *bʿnʿ* is for */bānā/*, rather than */banō/* as supposed by RÖLLIG, ibid. *bʿnm* in line 5 may be for 'their sons', as both parents are mentioned in the text, or 'his sons, relating to the deceased, or even 'her sons', relating to the mother just mentioned.

Breviglieri (Ras el-Hadagia)

Breviglieri N 1

Bibliography: LEVI DELLA VIDA 1927: 95-96, 6; LEVI DELLA VIDA 1951: 65-68; *RÉS* 662; *KAI* 118; *TRE* 6; *IPT* 76.

Illustrations: LEVI DELLA VIDA 1951, fig. 8; *IPT*, fig. 14 (drawing); *KAI*, Taf. viii; *IPT*, tav. ix (photograph).

Breviglieri N 1

Text:

1) l^{ɔ}dn l^{ɔ}mn m^{ɔ}š ^{ɔ}lm šp^{c}r st wmqdš bt^{ɔ}y wḥrp^{ɔ}t ^{ɔ}š b^{ɔ}n^{ɔ} w^{ɔ}yqdš
2) bšt rb tḥt rb mḥnt bšd lwbym lwqy ^{c}yly l^{c}my^{c} n/tksp bn
3) š^{c}sydw^{c}sn/t bn n/tmrr ^{ɔ}š bbn^{ɔ} m^{c}snk^{c}w btṣ^{ɔ}tm btm

Translation:

1) To the lord to Ammon, this divine statue of a bull and the sanctuary of his rooms and the porticos (are the those) which built and consecrated
2) in the year of the proconsul in the land of Libya Lucius Aelius Lamia *nksp*, the son of
3) Shasidwasan, the son of *nmrr*, who is among the sons of Masankaw, completely at his own expense.

Remarks:

Lucius Aelius Lamia was proconsul from 15 to 17 AD. Note the circumlocution to describe the Roman proconsul: *rb tḥt rb mḥnt*. The use of the pl. cstr of *bn* to indicate a tribe or people, as in *bn^{ɔ} m^{c}snk^{c}w* is a well-known construction in Hebrew and Arabic. *šp^{c}r* can be explained as the nota relationis *š* followed by *p^{c}r*, which may mean '(young) bull', although it has previously been explained as an unknown word indicating the material used in making the statue. Taking it as a whole, however, *šp^{c}r* might be the name of a deity, possibly also to be found as a name element in the personal name *š^{c}prgm*, attested in texts from Hr. Maktar. *bt^{ɔ}y* is explained as a pl. + suff. 3 sg. m. of *bt*, 'house, temple', by most commentators, cf. *PPG* §240, 11. This spelling, however, is unexpected as was remarked by RÖLLIG, *KAI* a.l., noting that the expected form would be *bty^{ɔ}*. Perhaps *bt^{ɔ}y* is to be divided into *b*, prep., and *t^{ɔ}y*, a sg. or pl. form of *t^{ɔ}*, 'chamber, room', attested e.g. in Hebrew.

Hr. Gen Rieime

Hr. Gen Rieime N 1

Bibliography: LEVI DELLA VIDA 1949; *KAI* 128; *TRE* 34; *IPT* 29.

Illustrations: KAI, Taf. viii (drawing); *IPT*, tav. xviii, 29 (photograph).

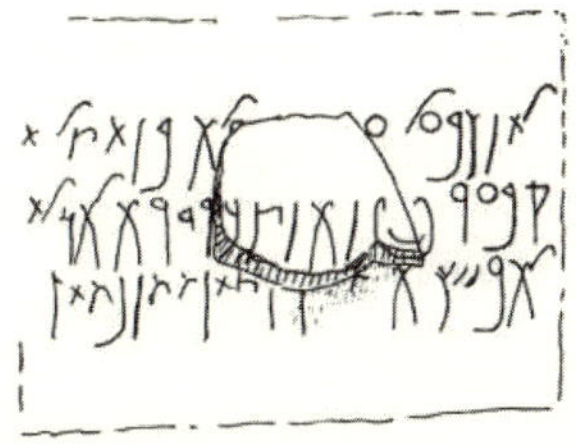

Text:

1) lmtnb^{c}l ^{c}[ ]^{c}/d/b/rl^{ɔ} bn mslm
2) qb^{c}r ṭ[n^{ɔ} sk]r dr^{ɔ} l^{ɔ}wlm
3) l^{ɔ}b ḥw^{ɔ} š̊[^{c}]n̊t̊ šmnšš npš mt

Translation:

1) For Mutumbal the [ ] son of Maslam.
2) The tomb was erected as a memorial of his family for ever
3) for the father who lived 86 years …

Remarks:

This tombstone has been re-used as a round millstone, which has resulted in a big hole in its middle, causing a lot of damage to the text, and the loss of much of the rest of this beautifully carved memorial. In line 2, LEVI DELLA VIDA-AMADASI 1987, sub *IPT* 29, suppose that there is enough room for three letters, a name, between *ṭn^{ɔ}* and *skr*, as tentatively suggested by RÖLLIG, *KAI* 128 a.l.: "Die Lücke ist durch die Ergänzung noch nicht ausgefüllt. Stand noch ein Name darin?" It is, however, very well possible to fill the gap without the insertion of a personal name (cf. the illustration). Both readings, *ṭnᵓ skr* and *ṭnᵓt skr* (cf. AMADASI, *IPT* 29 a.l.) seem to be possible, cf. the drawing. *šmnšš* is best explained as the result of assimilation: < *šmnm šš*. The concluding words, *npš mt*, are translated as 'monument of a deceased one' by LEVI DELLA VIDA 1949 (cf. RÖLLIG sub *KAI* 128, ELMAYER sub *TRE* 34) and LEVI DELLA VIDA-AMADASI sub *IPT* 29, pointing to the possible occurrence of the same word *npš* in Ain Zakkar N 1. As the reading *npᵓš* is Ain Zakkar is very improbable, support for this interpretation is not really strong. Then, we find that in many funerary inscriptions the concluding remarks relate something about the deceased, one should suppose something in the same range as *tm bḥym*, or, comparing Latin texts of this type, something comparable to *O(ssa) T(ibi) B(ene) Q(uiescant)*, 'may your bones rest in peace.' In case *mt* is the indication of the deceased, it might be the equivalent of *ossa*, and *npš* might be a verbal form meaning 'rest' or something comparable.

Lepcis Magna

Lepcis Magna N 1

Bibliography: LEVI DELLA VIDA 1927: 92-93, 1; REYNOLDS 1951: 118-119; LEVI DELLA VIDA 1967a: 395-409; VATTIONI 1971: 242-246; TEIXIDOR 1964-1980: 215; GARBINI 1974b: 6; GARBINI 1986: 11-12; *NP* 1; *IPT* 9; *TRE* 1; *IRT* 349; *CIL* viii 7.

Illustrations: GESENIUS 1837, tab. 27, lxiv (drawing); REYNOLDS 1951, pl. xx, 1; *IPT*, tav. iii 9 (photograph).

Text:
1) ᵓt/n lmlkt hmqm ᶜl m[

Latin text:
1) ... Vespasian]i f. Dom[itian ...(erased!)
2) ...]Avg. Svfe[

Translation:
1) ... for the work of the place on ...

Remarks:
One of the earliest Neo-Punic texts that was made known in Europe in the modern period. LEVI DELLA VIDA 1967a discusses the possibility of interpreting *hmqm ᶜlm* as a priestly function, in which *mqm* should be explained as a part. yif. of the root *qwm*, 'the one who raises' (for the title *mqm ᵓlm*, 'the one who raises the god', cf. *DNWSI* s.v. qwm_1, but he favours the explanation of *mqm* as 'place', as is also done by VATTIONI 1971, cf. also GARBINI 1986). ELMAYER sub *TRE* 1 reads: *št lmlkt hmqm ᶜlm*, which he translates: 'this for the work of the sanctuary for the divine.' The reading *št* (or *st*) is, however, hardly possible.

Lepcis Magna N 2

Bibliography: LIDZBARSKI 1898: 434-435, 3 Ba; *NP* 2; *TRE* 2; *IPT* 10.

Illustrations: LIDZBARSKI 1898, Taf. xvi, 2 (drawing); *IPT*, tav. iii 10 (photograph).

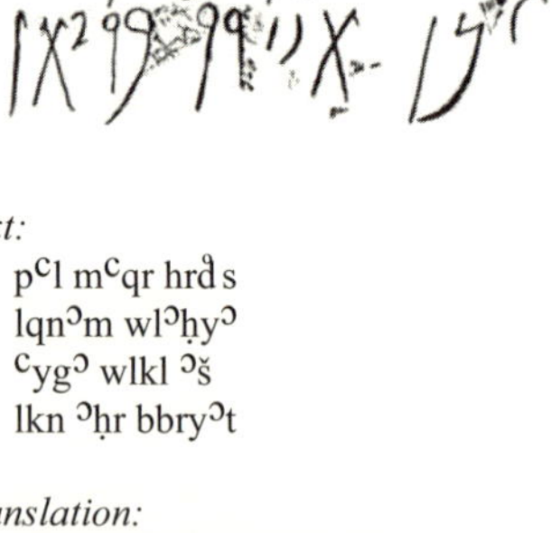

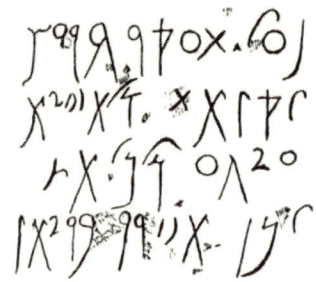

Text:
1) pᶜl mᶜqr hrd̊s
2) lqnᵓm wlᵓḥyᵓ
3) ᶜygᵓ wlkl ᵓš
4) lkn ᵓḥr bbryᵓt

Translation:
1) Macer, the *rds*, made (this)
2) for himself and his brother

3) Aygo and for everyone
4) to be later in *the family*

Remarks:
The older reading $r^{c}s$ instead of *rds* in line 1 might be the masculine counterpart of $r^{c}š^{c}$ in Ain Zakkar N 1. LEVY 1857: 90 read $r^{c}ṣ$ explained as 'lord.' Cf. also ELMAYER sub *TRE* 2, who describes $r^{c}s$ as 'ethnic? rank or office?', without a definitive solution. However, LEVI DELLA VIDA-AMADASI, sub *IPT* 10, notes that the photograph rather favours the reading *rds*, and it seems better to accept this reading, although this word also remains an enigma. *qnᵓm* has been explained as a personal name by several older commentators, cf. e.g. LEVY 1857: 90, who read *qtᵓm* and connected this, according to him tribal, name with the name of the well-known Berber tribe of the *Ketama*. Later BERGER 1889 supposed this word to be a representation of the Egyptian divine name Chnum (cf. also LIDZBARSKI 1898: 3673 s.v.). GELB 1929-1930, reading *qnᵓm*, also explains this word as a personal name, derived from the root *qnᵓ*. LEVI DELLA VIDA 1927 has connected *qnᵓm* with Syriac *qənōmā*, 'person.' This solution has since been accepted by most commentators, cf. e.g. FÉVRIER 1952b: 223, LEVI DELLA VIDA-AMADASI, *IPT* sub 10 and *PPG* §124a. At the end of line 3 LEVI DELLA VIDA 1927 reads *wlwlᵓš*, but, as LEVI DELLA VIDA-AMADASI notes sub *IPT* 10, that the reading *wklᵓš* is more attractive, according to the photograph in *IPT*, yet the earlier drawing clearly shows *w*. The same holds true for the last letter: only the reading *š* is acceptable. LEVI DELLA VIDA tried to find the Latin name *Valens* in this text. ELMAYER, sub *TRE* 2, accepts LEVI DELLA VIDA's reading, but he explains *wlᵓš* as a colloquial form of *wldy*, 'his children', which is impossible. The most probable explanation for the second half of line 3 seems to be: *w-*, copula, + *l-*, preposition, + *kl*, noun 'all', + *ᵓš*, noun, 'man', or nota relationis. The last line remains of uncertain interpretation. *lkn* can be explained as the preposition *l-*, followed by the infinitive of the verb *kwn* as supposed by e.g. LIDZBARSKI 1898: 294, LEVI DELLA VIDA 1927: 94, and later commentators, but as long as the rest of the line is uncertain, this interpretation is doubtful. *ᵓḥr* may be used absolutely, meaning 'later', according to LEVI DELLA VIDA ibid., while he has supposed the meaning 'safety, tranquillity' for *bryᵓt*. ELMAYER sub *TRE* 2 translates *bryᵓt* by 'good health', which is, of course, possible, but gives a somewhat strange impression in a tomb inscription. The idea that someone claims a tomb made by him for himself and his descendants is attested elsewhere, cf. e.g. Wadi el-Amud N 1.

Lepcis Magna N 4

Bibliography: SCHRÖDER 1869: 259; ADAMS 2003: 216-217; *NP* 4; *TRE* 5; *IPT* 12; *IRT* 655; *CIL* viii 16.

Illustrations: SCHRÖDER 1869, Taf. x 1; *IPT*, fig. 6 (drawing).

Text:
1) brkt bt b^{c}lšlk ᵓm $ql^{cᵓc}$y hrbᵓ

Latin parallel:
1) Byrycth Balsilechis filivs mater Clodi medici

Greek parallel:
1) βυρυχθ βαλσιαληχ θυγατηρ μητηρ κλωδιου ιατρου

Translation:
1) Berekht, the daughter of Balshillekh, the mother of Clodius the doctor.

Remarks:
βαλσιαληχ almost certainly is a mistake for βαλσιλληχ. When ADAMS 2003: 216 gives this text with reconstructed accentuation, he inadvertently presents this dubious α as the accented one. Note that the name *Balshillekh* is inflected only in the Latin version, not in the Greek one. ADAMS 2003: 216-217, notes that the use of Greek by Punic speaking people is mainly restricted to doctors (cf. also Hr. Aouin N 1).

Lepcis Magna N 5

Bibliography: SCHRÖDER 1869: 259; *NP* 5; *TRE* 4; *IPT* 13; *IRT* 654; *CIL* viii15.

Illustrations: SCHRÖDER 1869, Taf. x 2; *IPT*, fig. 7 (drawing).

Text:
1) bd^{c}lqrt hmqrty ql$^{c\supset}$y hrb$^{\supset}$

Latin parallel:
1) Boncar Mecrasi Clodi-
2) vs medicvs

Greek parallel:
1) βω[νχαρ μεχρασι κλωδι
2) ος ιατρος]

Translation:
1) Bodelqart, the Mekrathi, Clodius, the doctor.

Remarks:
Note that the spelling of the name Boncar in the Latin parallel text makes it difficult to suppose that *bd^{c}lqrt* is a misspelling of *bd-mlqrt*, as supposed by LEVI DELLA VIDA-AMADASI, cf. *IPT* sub 13.

Lepcis Magna N 6

Bibliography: DUSSAUD with CUMONT 1926; LEVI DELLA VIDA 1927: 97, 8; *TRE* 8; *IPT* 14.

Illustrations: CUMONT 1926, p. 158; *IPT*, fig. 8 (drawing).

Text:
1) [^{c}b]dmlqrt bn ḥnb^{c}l hp[.]q̊ẙ p^{c}l$^{\supset}$ lbny$^{\supset}$ ^{c}m̊yq
2) lmbmḥy$^{\supset}$

Translation:
1) Abdmelqart, the son of Annobal, the … made it for his sons …
2) during his lifetime.

Remarks:
The original of this text seems to be lost. Only the drawing made by the French traveller GIRARD (end of the 17th century) remains. This drawing was published by CUMONT 1926 and again in *IPT*. According to LEVI DELLA VIDA-AMADASI 1987, sub *IPT* 14 (and cf. the drawing) the text contains two lines, although according to LEVI DELLA VIDA 1927 it consists of three lines, the second one starting with *p^{c}l$^{\supset}$*. The first name may be completed as *[^{c}b]dmlqrt* or as *[b]d-mlqrt*. The function or tribal indication (?) mentioned after the name *ḥnb^{c}l* looks a bit like *hpnqy*, but DUSSAUD (with CUMONT 1926) does not dare to suppose that someone is mentioned with the epithet 'the Punic one' in a text from Lepcis (cf. LEVI DELLA VIDA 1927: 27 n. 2). ELMAYER sub *TRE* 8 reads *hp[ṭ]q̊ẙ*, which he translates as 'magistrate.' *p^{c}l$^{\supset}$* was read by DUSSAUD (with CUMONT 1926) as *b^{c}l$^{\supset}$*, citizens of, which is justly corrected by LEVI DELLA VIDA 1927. ELMAYER follows the earlier reading *b^{c}l$^{\supset}$* and translates this word as 'chief.' Then follows a word read *lpty$^{\supset}$*, for 'Leptis', by CUMONT. But as the Punic name of this town is *lpqy*, this is impossible, as more or less noted by DUSSAUD and mentioned by LEVI DELLA VIDA 1927, who read *lbny$^{\supset}$* 'for his sons.' ELMAYER, sub *TRE* 8, reads *lpny$^{\supset}$*, which he explains as *lpny*, 'first' > 'notables.' The sign read as *n* looks rather like $^{\supset}$, so one must suppose that an extra line, originally not belonging to the text has been added later. Supposing this to be correct, one must presume that following the last word of line 1, at least one complete personal name has been lost. The name following *bny$^{\supset}$* has been read *$^{c\supset}$yq* by LEVI DELLA VIDA 1927, a reading accepted in *IPT*, although according to our interpretation of the drawing, *^{c}m̊yq* is more probable (note that DUSSAUD with CUMONT 1926 also read *-m-*). The same reading is advocated by ELMAYER, sub *TRE* 8, *^{c}myq*, translated by him as 'valley.' The last line was read by CUMONT and DUSSAUD as *l$^{\supset}$pml[ṭ]y$^{\supset}$*. This was explained as a loan from Greek: επιμελητεια, 'office of an administrator.' ELMAYER, sub *TRE* 8, takes only the first part of this word, *l$^{\supset}$pml[ṭ]*, and he explains this as Greek επιμελητης, 'custodian.' The reading *lmbmḥy$^{\supset}$* seems to be without much doubt. For the compounding of prepositions, cf. also Lepcis Magna N 18.

Lepcis Magna N 10

Bibliography: LEVI DELLA VIDA 1927: 105-107; LEVI DELLA VIDA 1944: 5-6, 8; *KAI* 129; *TRE* 13; *IPT* 18.

Illustrations: LEVI DELLA VIDA 1927: 105, fig. 8; *IPT*, tav. v 18 (photograph).

Text:
1) lᵓdn lᵓl qn ᵓrṣ bnᵓ w
2) ᵓyqdš t ᶜksndrᶜ wt ᶜrpt st
3) btṣᵓtm btm qᶜnddᵓ bn qᶜnddᵓ
4) bn ḥnᵓ bn ᶜbdmlqrt k šmᶜ qlᵓ brkᵓ

Translation:
1) For the lord, to El, the creator of earth, has built and
2) consecrated the *exedra* and this portico
3) completely on his own expense Candidus, the son of Candidus,
4) the son of Anno, the son of Abdmelqart, because he heard his voice, blessed him.

Remarks:
The epithet *qnᵓrṣ* has been explained both as 'the creator of earth', or as 'the lord (the possessor) of the earth.' *DISO* differentiates between two verbs *qny*$_1$, 'to create,' and *qny*$_2$, 'to possess', although *DNWSI* and other dictionaries suppose one verb that can be translated with different shades of meaning, as e.g. GESENIUS 1915 (cf. also the literature mentioned sub *DNWSI qny*$_1$). It may be that the distinction felt by modern scholars did not have a counterpart in the minds of those using these words two thousand or more years ago. *ᵓl qn ᵓrṣ* has been equated with *Poseidon / Neptunus*, cf. LIPIŃSKI 1995: 392; cf. also AMADASI 1984: 193-194.

Lepcis Magna N 16

Bibliography: LEVI DELLA VIDA 1938: 104-109; *KAI* 121; *TRE* 30; *IPT* 24; *IRT* 321, 322-323.

Illustrations: IPT, tav. xiv 24a, 24b (photograph).

Text Lepcis Magna 16a:
1) ḥnbᶜl myšql ᵓrṣ mḥb dᶜt htmt zbḥ špṭ ᵓdr
2) ᶜzrm bn ḥmlkt ṭbḥpy rᵓps btᵓrm btm pᶜl wᵓyqdš

Text Lepcis Magna 16b:
1) ḥnbᶜl myšql ᵓrṣ m
2) ḥb dᶜt htmt zbḥ špṭ ᵓdr ᶜzrm bn ḥmlkt ṭbḥpy rᵓps btᵓrm btm pᶜl wᵓyqdš

Latin parallel (IRT 321):
1) Imp*eratore* Caesare Divi f*ilio* Avg*vsto* pont*ifice* max*imo* tr*ibvnicia* pot*estate* xxiv co*nsvle* xiii patre patr*iae*
2) Annobal Rvfvs ornator patriae amator concordiae
3) flamen svfes praef*ectvs* sacr*orvm* Himilchonis Tapapi f*ilivs* d*e* s*va* p*ecvnia* fa*ciendvm* coer*avit*
4) idemq*ve* dedicavit

Latin parallel (IRT 322-323):
1) imp*eratore*] Caesare Divi f*ilio* Avg*vsto* pont*ifice* max*imo* tr*ibvnicia* pot*estate* xxiv
2) co*nsvle* xiii patre patriae
3) Annobal ornator patriae amator concordiae
4) flamen svfes praef*ectvs* sacr*orvm* Himilchonis Tapapi f*ilivs* Rvfvs d*e* s*va* p*ecvnia* fac*iendvm* coer*avit*
5) idemq*ve* dedicavit

Translation 16a:
1) Annobal, who adorns the country, who loves the complete knowledge, sacrificer, sufet, lord of
2) the *ᶜzrm*-offering, the son of Imilco Tapafi Rufus, made it according to plan at his own expense and consecrated it.

Remarks:
For the reading *btᵓrm* in line 2 instead of *bn ᵓrm*, 'the son of *ᵓrm*' as advocated by LEVI DELLA VIDA-AMADASI, cf. e.g. *IPT* a.l. (cf. also RÖLLIG, sub *KAI* 121), see FÉVRIER 1954b: 77. The explanation of *myšql* as a yiph. part. of *šql* remains uncertain; *PPG* §147b, supposes a development */mašqīl/* > */mišqīl/* as a result of vowel harmony, which is not impossible; the semantic development is said to have been *to lay out money for* > *to adorn*. *ṭbḥpy* is the name of an important family or clan in Tripolitania in the Roman period, cf. e.g. AMADASI 1983b. The name is attested in several other Latin inscriptions: *Tapapius*, *IRT* 273, 319, *Tapafius*, *IRT* 745, and in a Latino-Punic one: *Typafi*, Libya OU LP1.

Lepcis Magna N 17

Bibliography: LEVI DELLA VIDA 1942: 29-32; ADAMS 2003: 227-228; DI VITA-EVRARD 2004; *KAI* 127; *IPT* 25; *IRT* 294.

Illustrations: IPT, tav. xv, 25; DI VITA-EVRARD 2004: 319, 320 (photograph).

Text:
1) mʾš z ṭynʾ lʾdn šdrpʾ b̊d̊ mlqrt bn mtnbʿl šdby
2) mš̊ p̊ r̊ [---.]hb̊ qr špṭm̊ ṭnʾ̊t [.
3) ṭ[----]wššm wšnm
4) [-------. dnʿ]r̊ yʾ ḥmšm wšlš

Latin parallel:
1) Libero Patrvm sac*rvm*
2) Boncarth Mvthvmbalis f*ilivs*
3) Sydby iiii-vir M*acelli* ex mvltis
4) lxii qvibvs adiecit de svo liii

Translation:
1) This statue has erected for the lord Shadrafa Bodmelqart, the son of Mutumbal *šdby*
2) …………sufetes
3) …………and sixty two
4) …………denarii fifty three

Remarks:
The name *šdby* has been read *šmkyʾ* by LEVI DELLA VIDA 1964b: 308, LEVI DELLA VIDA-AMADASI 1987: 62, who maintain that it is an equivalent of the name read as *sobti* in the Latin text. The explanation of *sobti* as a Latin rendering of Punic *špṭ* (cf. e.g. RÖLLIG, *KAI* sub 127) is less probable, as the normal rendering by *sufes* was well-known in Lepcis, as it is attested frequently in both Latin and Neo-Punic texts from Lepcis Magna. The reading accepted is the one proposed by DI VITA-EVRARD 2004: 319-320. The word order of the first clause has been described as abnormal by ADAMS 2003: 228. However, although perhaps unusual, the word order does not seem to be incongruous with the grammatical possibilities of Phoenico-Punic.

Lepcis Magna N 18

Bibliography: LEVI DELLA VIDA 1949: 400-404, 31; VOLTERRA 1952; FÉVRIER 1952b; FÉVRIER 1961: 6; *KAI* 124; *TRE* 31; *IPT* 26; *IRT* 338.

Illustrations: IPT, tav. xvi (photograph).

Text:
1) gʿy bn ḥnʾ lmbšm gʿy bn bnm mʿqr t ʿmdm w
2) t hmʿqʾm ygn wt hmḥz rbd lmbmlktm btm bʿlytn
3) qmdʾ ʾš ʿlʾ bbnm ʾt mʿqr bn gʿy bktbt dbrʾ
4) hbt š gʿy bn ḥnʾ kʿs lpʿl wḥtm

Latin parallel:
1) Ti*berio* Clavdio
2) Drvsi f*ilio* Cae-
3) sari Avg*vsto* Ger-
4) manico pon-
5) [tif*ici*] max*imo* trib*vnicia*
6) potest*ate* xiii
7) imp*eratori* xvii co*nsvli*
8) v cens*ori* p*atri* p*atriae*
9) M*arcvs* Pompeivs Silva-
10) nvs co*nsvl* xvir s*acris* f*aciv*nd*is*
11) proco*nsvl* patron*vs*
12) dedicavit
13) Q*uinto* Cassio grato pr*aetore*
14) proco*nsvle* Cretae et
15) Cyrena[rv]m leg(ato)
16) propr*aetore* Africae
17) C*aivs* Annonis f*ilivs* nomi-
18) ne [C*ai*] Annonis f*ilii* n*epotis*
19) svi colvmnas cvm
20) svperficie et forvm
21) d*e* s*va* p*ecvnia* d*edit*
22) Balitho Annonis
23) Macri f*ilivs* Commodvs
24) testamento adopta-
25) tvs f*aciendvm* c*vravit*

Compare also the parallel text *IRT* 615:
1) senatvs p*opvlvs*q*ve* lepcitanor*vm*
2) c*aio* macri f*ilio* c*ai* annonis
3) n*epoti* phelyssam ob colvm
4) nas et svperficie*m* et fo
5) rvm stratvm honoris
6) cavssa decrevervnt
7) balitho [m]acri f*ilivs* [c]o[m]
8) [modvs …

Translation:
1) Gaius, the son of Anno, in the name of Gaius, his grandson Macer the columns and
2) the place let repair, and the forum he had paved according to their work at his own expense; Baliton
3) Commodus, who entered among the sons with Macer, the son of Gaius, through the means of a document concerning the affairs of the house of Gaius, the son of Anno, let it be made and completed it.

Remarks:
Note the compound preposition *lmb* in line 1, also attested elsewhere in Phoenician and Punic. The expression *bn bnm* shows that the Punic vocabulary did not conatin a specialized word with the same meaning as Latin *nepos*. For *mḥz* in line 2, cf. the study of AMADASI 1982. *ᵓš ᶜlᵓ bbnm ᵓt ... bktbt dbrᵓ hbt š* is an interesting translation of the Latin *testamento adoptatus*, literally 'who went up with / among the sons ... in the document on the matters of the house of ...' It is also possible to divide *ᵓš ᶜlᵓ bbn mᵓt* 'who went up as a son together with ...' (cf. VOLTERRA 1952, FÉVRIER 1952b). *kᶜs lpᶜl* is also best explained as a translation of the Latin expression *faciendvm cvravit.* On the possible reading *bnm*, cf. also JONGELING-KERR 2002: 178.

Lepcis Magna N 19

Bibliography: LEVI DELLA VIDA 1949: 404-406; AMADASI 1979; AMADASI 1980: 31-32; GARBINI 1986: 12; *KAI* 126; *TRE* 32; *IPT* 27; *IRT* 318, 347.

Illustrations: IPT, tav. xvii (photograph).

Text:
1) bn ṭybry q[lᶜwdy sᵓsty]
2) ᵓdr ᶜzrm z[bḥ lᵓlm]
3) wᵓspᶜsyᶜnᵓ [š]p̊ṭ̊
4) zbḥ ᵓlk[l ḥy]t mḥb ᵓrṣ m̊
5) ḥb bnᵓ ᶜm myšql ᵓrṣ
6) mšlk bnᵓ ᶜm mḥb dᶜt htmt
7) lmy lpny ᵓdrᵓ ᵓlpqy wᶜm ᵓlpqy
8) lpy mᵓsᵓ ᵓbtm wmᵓsm bnt/m
9) ytnᵓ lᶜbd bṣpᵓt kl ḥytm
10) mzbḥ wpᵓdy
11) pᶜl lmbmlktm btm

Latin parallel:
IRT 318
Text a:
1) [ ]
2) [Avgv]sto
3) [sac]rvm
4) Å̊s̊p̊ [r]enas
5) proco*nsvl*
6) dedicavit

Text b:
1) ornator patriae
2) amator concor-
3) diae cvi primo
4) ordo et popvlvs
5) ob merita maio-
6) rvm eivs et ipsivs
7) lato clavo sem-
8) per vti concessit
9) aram et podi*vm*
10) de s*va* pec*vnia* f*acienda* c*oeravit*

IRT 347 *Text:*
1) Imp*eratore* Caesare Divi Vespasiani f*ilio* Domitiano Avgvsto Germanico pontif*ice* max*imo* trib*vnicia* potest*ate* xi imp*eratore* xxi co*nsvle* xvi censore pe[rpetv]o patre patriae
2) Ti(berivs) Clavdivs qvir*ina tribv* Sestivs Ti*beri* Clavdi Sesti f*ilivs* praefectvs sacrorvm flamen divi Vespasiani svfes flamen perpetvvs amator patriae amator civivm ornator patriae amator concordiae cvi primo ordo et popvlvs ob merita maiorvm eivs et ipsivs lato clavo semper vti conce[ssit]
3) podi*vm* et aram d*e* s*va* pec*vnia* f*acienda* c*vravit*

Translation:
[Tiberius Claudius Quirina Sestius]

1) the son of Tiberius Claudius Sestius,
2) the lord of the ^{c}*zrm*-sacrifices, sacrificer of the divine
3) Vespasianus, sufet,
4) sacrificer for ever, the one who loves the country,
5) who loves the sons of the people, the one who adorns the country,
6) saviour of the sons of the people, lover of the complete knowledge,
7) the one to whom before the mighty ones of Lepcis and the people of Lepcis
8) according to the merits of his fathers and his own merit(s)
9) they permitted the use of the purple striped toga for his whole life,
10) an altar and a podium
11) made according to the work to be done, at his own expense.

Remarks:
For *myšql* in line 5, cf. the remark sub Lepcis Magna N 16. For the reading of the beginning of l. 8, *lmy lpny*, cf. AMADASI 1979: 31-32 (cf. id., 1980: 32, LEVI DELLA VIDA-AMADASI 1987: 68), instead of the earlier reading *$^{\supset}$š lpny*, proposed by LEVI DELLA VIDA 1949, and accepted by e.g. RÖLLIG, sub *KAI* 126 (cf. however *KAI*^{5} where RÖLLIG has adopted the reading of AMADASI 1979). The translation of *m$^{\supset}$s*, 'merit', is based on the Latin parallel. At the end of l. 9 LEVI DELLA VIDA-AMADASI 1987: 69, propose to read *btm*, used adverbially to strengthen the preceding suffix in *m$^{\supset}$sm*, 'his own merit' (Latin: *merita ... ipsivs*), as the possible existence of a contruction *m$^{\supset}$sm bnm* 'his merit, namely of their son', is indeed less likely; the problem felt by LEVI DELLA VIDA-AMADASI 1987: 69, in the fact that *btm* is used again at the end of the text with another shade of meaning is minor, the meaning of *btm*, 'completely', may differ according to the context.

Lepcis Magna N 20

Bibliography: LEVI DELLA VIDA 1949: 407, 33; *TRE* 33; *IPT* 28.

Illustrations: IPT, fig. 10 (drawing), tav. ix, 28 (photograph).

Text:
1)]s^{c}byn$^{\supset}$ ṭbḫ̣ [py

Translation:
1) Sabinus Tapafi

Remarks:
The reading *ṭbḥpy* is certain, for this name cf. Lepcis Magna N 16.

Lepcis Magna N 24

Bibliography: LEVI DELLA VIDA 1963: 472; *TRE* 44; *IPT* 33.

Illustrations: LEVI DELLA VIDA 1963, tav. iv; *IPT*, tav. xx, 33 (photograph).

Text:
1) $^{\supset}$mtb^{c}lhṣry

Translation:
1) Amatbalaṣuri

Remarks:
The name, of course, means the 'handmaiden of the Tyrian Bal.'

Lepcis Magna N 25

Bibliography: LEVI DELLA VIDA 1963: 472; *IPT* 34.

Illustrations: LEVI DELLA VIDA 1963, tav. iv; *IPT*, tav. xx, 34 (photograph).

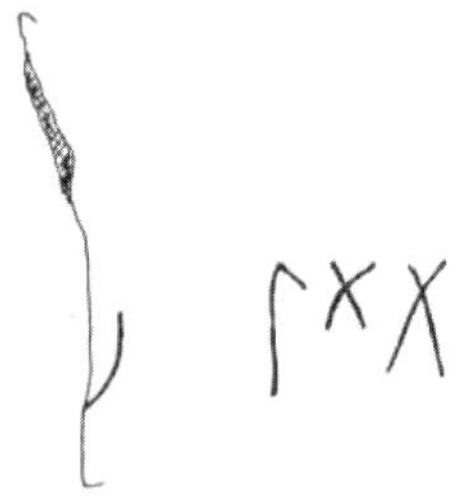

Text:
1) $^{\supset}$mt b[…

Translation:
1) Amatba…

Remarks:
The name may be completed *^{ɔ}mtb^{c}l* or, as in the preceding text, *^{ɔ}mtb^{c}lḥṣry*. Note however, the wide gap between *^{ɔ}mt* and the following character.

Lepcis Magna N 29

Bibliography: LEVI DELLA VIDA 1963: 472; *IPT* 38.

Illustrations: LEVI DELLA VIDA 1963, tav. v; *IPT*, tav. xx, 38 (photograph).

Text:
1) bqy dd/r^{c}y

Translation:
1) Boccius Didai

Remarks:
The reading of the second name is uncertain, but *dd^{c}y* may be compaired to names as *dida, didda, dideiia, didia, didius* and others as attested in Latin inscriptions from North Africa, cf. JONGELING 1994: 40-41.

Lepcis Magna N 44

Bibliography: LEVI DELLA VIDA 1963: 476; *IPT* 53.

Illustrations: LEVI DELLA VIDA 1963, tav. viii; *IPT*, tav. xxiii, 53 (photograph).

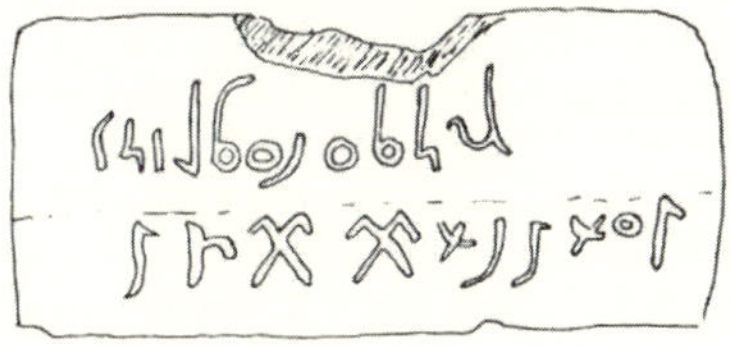

Text:
1) n^{c}mtpm^{ɔ} ^{ɔ}št
2) ḥnb^{c}l ^{c}rks

Translation:
1) Namefamo, the wife of
2) Annobal *^{c}rks*.

Remarks:
The name or epithet following the name of the husband of Namefamo remains unexplained.

Lepcis Magna N 52

Bibliography: LEVI DELLA VIDA 1963: 478; *TRE* 45b; *IPT* 61.

Illustrations: LEVI DELLA VIDA 1963, tav. x; *IPT*, tav. xxv, 61 (photograph).

Text:
1) m^{c}rg^{c}ryṭ[^{c}]

Translation:
1) Margarita.

Remarks:
The name, in this form, is from the Greek μαργαριτης, 'pearl'.

Lepcis Magna N 54

Bibliography: LEVI DELLA VIDA 1963: 479; *IPT* 63.

Illustrations: LEVI DELLA VIDA 1963, tav. xi; *IPT*, tav. xxvi, 63 (photograph).

Text:
1) n^{c}mtgd^{ɔ} ^{ɔ}št mšdygn/t^{ɔ}

Translation:
1) Namegiddo, the wife of Mashdigano.

Lepcis Magna N 64

Bibliography: AMADASI 1983a: 794; *IPT* 74.

Illustrations: *IPT*, tav. xxix, 74 (photograph).

Text:
1) srwy slpqy pl^{c}wṭ^{ɔ}

Translation:
1) Servius Sulpicius Plautus

Remarks:
Note the three Latin names in a Neo-Punic text. Both the number of names, reflecting the Roman *tria nomina*, and their form point to strong Roman influence.

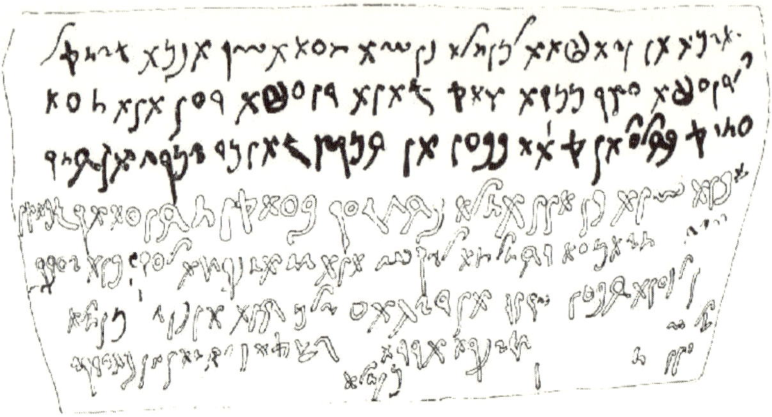

Al Qusbat N 1

Al Qusbat

Al Qusbat N 1

Bibliography: LEVI DELLA VIDA 1964: 4; VATTIONI 1966: 38-39; LEVI DELLA VIDA 1967b: 257-259; GARBINI 1986: 13; TEIXIDOR 1964-1980: 16-17; Tri: 51; *TRE* 51; *IPT* 86.

Illustrations: LEVI DELLA VIDA 1964, tv. i; *IPT*, tav. xxxii, 86 (photograph).

Text:

1) [ ]mykᵓ ᵓtnym ṭmᵓ lkn šlm ptḥᵓ šᶜmᵓ ḥrᵓb kᵓ wyšql[ᵓ]
2) ldnᶜṭᵓ ᶜsr kkrᵓ ṣmq wᵓ/mt/nᵓ dnᶜṭᵓ bᶜt ᵓtᵓ šᶜm
3) ᶜšẙ q bhlᶜlᵓt qᵓm bbᶜt ᵓt hkrs wᵓtkd ykr̊ẙ ᵓt hšd
4) š̊ bnᵓ ḥnᵓ bn mtn ᵓšlmbhgwᶜr bᶜmqt šhtᶜmᵓr wkmst
5) šḥ[ᶜ]t šymkrᵓ bhšlšm lyrḥ mnᵓ ḥmš prṣm lᶜbr bn/tᵓ yᶜbr
6) [ ]n/t lpᶜnᵓ hbᶜt ẘ b/dn/tr̊ ᵓt dygᵓ/mᶜ ylk htm ᵓt pr̊ ẙ [ ] kn šlm
7) šlḥ [ ]ṣyprm ᵓrrm [b]h̊ m̊ qm b [ ] mn/t [ ]n/t bgydry
8) ytn̊ [ ] šᶜ̂ [ ]n̊/t̊ [ ]kn šlm

Translation:

1) Accounts (?) of *ᵓtnym* … … and they shall weigh
2) for Donatus 10 talents of dried fruits and … Donatus … at the time …
3) …. in the list, the vase and the amphora … the field
4) of the sons of Hanno the son of Mutun, … …
5) …, which they will sell on the thirtieth of the month, … five prṣm …
6) … before … the total …
7) … birds … …
8) …

Remarks:

This difficult text is the only published Neo-Punic ostracon to date, and it makes it abundantly clear how much we depend on formulae and well-known words to be able to read and explain Neo-Punic texts. Although several words may be recognized in this text, its overall meaning remains unexplained.

[ ]mykᵓ looks like a plural cstr. of a masc. noun. LEVI DELLA VIDA-AMADASI 1987: 132, propose *smykᵓ / tmykᵓ*. Both roots are known from biblical Hebrew, *smk*, 'to support', *tmk*, 'to hold.' *t/smyk*, therefore, might mean something like 'account.' Although possible, the solution is mainly based on the context and not really supported by the etymology. *ṭmᵓ* is explained by LEVI DELLA VIDA-AMADASI 1987: 132, as a loan from Greek or Latin (τομος / *tomus*), meaning 'section', which seems hardly acceptable. Perhaps the word should be related to the root *ṭᶜm*, the nominal form *ṭaᶜam* in Hebrew

meaning not only 'taste, flavour', but also 'understanding, decree.' In that case it could be explained as a qal perf. 3 pl. 'they have decided' > 'it is decided', or as a passive form of which *]mykʾ* is the subject. The following *lkn* is attested elsewhere as the inf. qal of *kwn*, which seems at least possible in this context. *šlm* may be derived from the root *šlm*, 'to pay', but its precise derivation is difficult to decide. Note that Hebrew offers two words, *šelem* and *šillem*, both meaning 'requittal.' *kn šlm* occurs again at the end of lines 6 and 8, but the context does not help. *ptḥ* is easily related to the root *ptḥ*, 'to open.' The context remains obscure, however. *šᶜmʾ* is explained by LEVI DELLA VIDA-AMADASI 1987: 132, as a pl. cstr. of *šym*, 'place of deposit', a derivation of the root *śym*, 'to place.' The next word, *ḥrʾb*, is related to Hebrew *ḥoreb*, *ḥorbāh*, 'dryness, dry country', and interpreted as 'dry provisions,' ibid., which seems more ingeneous than probable. *kʾ* is the adverb 'here', or the conjunction 'because', depending on the highly uncertain context. The last word of this line *wyšql[ʾ]*, should the reading be correct, is probably best explained as a form of the verb *šql*, 'to weigh', however, the explanation of the form with prefixed *w*- as an inperfect consecutive is less likely, as this form is still not attested with any certainty in Phoenician nor in Punic, cf. *PPG* §266, 1, who only mention a few examples, all of them uncertain. It is not impossible, of course, that the verb is used in the yiphil in Punic, and that the form *yšqlʾ* is a perf. 3 pl. For *ṣmq* one may compare Hebrew *ṣimmūq*, 'dried raisins', but this word is also used for 'dried olives'. LEVI DELLA VIDA-AMADASI 1987: 133 n. 1, note that dried olives as such are not mentioned in the classical sources. The word is derived from the root *ṣmq*, 'to be dry,' and perhaps may indicate other dry fruits. The next word, when read *ʾtʾ*, may be the preposition *ʾt* followed by the suff. of the 3rd person, or, when read *mnʾ*, a perf. 3 pl. of the verb *mny* , 'to count, to pay.' *bᶜt* may be the same word as *bᶜt* in several Punic texts, meaning 'tariff, list.' The last word of this line may be *šd*, 'field', but because of the difficult context one cannot be certain. In the rest of this line, only the words *ʾt hkrs wʾt ksd* stand out. VATTIONI 1966: 38, translates 'the vase and the amphora', which seems at least a possibility. However, LEVI DELLA VIDA, 1967b defends his original explanation, where he equates *krs* with Greek χρησις, translating 'profit', and explains *ʾtkd* as a itpael perf. 3 sg. m. of *ʾkd* or *wkd*, 'to decide,' cf. also LEVI DELLA VIDA-AMADASI 1989: 133-134. This explanation is also accepted by GARBINI 19-86: 13. The combination of *krs* and Greek χρησις, which normally means 'use', seems rather improbable. In the next line, following the first uncertain sign, *bnʾ ḥnʾ bn mtn* seems rather certain. LEVI DELLA VIDA reads the personal name as *mtnʾ*, followed by the marker of relativity *š* and the prepositions *l* + *m* + *b*. Though possible, the name *mtn* being far more common than *mtnʾ*, it seems more attractive to connect the *ʾ* with what follows. It is possible to find a form of the root *šlm*, or one may think of the nota relationis in the form *ʾš*. The words *bᶜmqt šhtᶜmʾr* are explained by LEVI DELLA VIDA as 'in the valley of the palm.' LEVI DELLA VIDA notes the problem that *ᶜmq*, 'valley', is only attested as a masculine word in Hebrew and elsewhere in Phoenician. *tᶜmʾr* may very well be the equivalent of Hebrew *tāmār*, however, the combination 'the valley of the palm' does not sound realistic somehow. As a geographical indication, one would perhaps rather expect a construct state connection *ᶜmqt htmr*, as is the case in e.g. *šd lwbym*. The explanation of *kmst* as *k* + *mst*, the second word equalling Hebrew *missāh*, the whole expression meaning 'in accordance with', thus LEVI DELLA VIDA-AMADASI 1987: 134, is possible, but without foundation in the unintelligible context. Several words in line 5 are recognizable. *prṣ* is interpreted as a certain coin by LEVI DELLA VIDA-AMADASI 1987: 134. They relate the word to the Hebrew root *prṣ*, 'to incise', and further to Aramaic *prs, prš* and later Hebrew *prṭ*. These comparisons, of course, only draw attention to the fact that the vocabularies of most Semitic languages contain three-radical roots based upon the two-radical root *pr* meaning something like 'to break', 'to tear', 'to divide.' In the rest of the text only a few words occur that may be related to known roots. The first word of line 7 may be derived from the root *šlḥ*, as LEVI DELLA VIDA supposes. However, the combination *š* + *lḥ* is at least a possibility. In line 7 it is difficult to find a meaning for *ṣyprm* other than 'birds', and in case the reading is correct *h̊m̊qm* may be for 'the place.'

Sabratha

Sabratha N 16

Bibliography: ROSSI-GARBINI 1983; GARBINI 1986: 17; SZNYCER 1988: 195-196; ADAMS 2003: 228-229; DI VITA-EVRARD 2004.

Illustrations: ROSSI-GARBINI 1983; DI VITA-EVRARD 2004: 317 (photograph);

Text:

1) ndr lbᶜl . bšᶜnṭsty [y]ẘn̊t̊ḥn . bn ᵓgᵓdr . ks dḥᵓ [k šmᶜ] ᵓt qlm

Latin parallel:

Domno . Sapvrno . vico M[---]no . v*oto* . s*vs-cepto* . Iv[--]hn . [A]giadvris . F[il]ivs . f*ecit*.

Translation:

1) Has vowed to Bal of *bšᶜnṭsty* Iunatan, the son of Agiadur an ablution bowl, because he heard his voice.

Remarks:

The addition to the appellative *bᶜl*, *bšᶜnṭsty*, is of uncertain interpretation. It may the name of a place, or the prepostion *b* followed by a place name, if the Latin text, *Domno . Sapvrno . vico M(?)[*, is to be trusted. ADAMS 2003: 229, notes that *v.s.* in the Latin text should be interpreted as v*otum* s*olvit*, a normal expression in this type of text (cf. also SZNYCER 1988: 196). In view of the Punic *ᵓgᵓdr* we can restore *[A]giaduris* in the Latin text. DI VITA-EVRARD 2004: 318, proposes to read *vico A[ntistia]no* in the Latin text, and to explain *bšᶜnṭsty* as the prep. *b*, followed by the nota relationis *š* and the name *Antisti*, or rather, to read *bšd nṭsty* 'in the region of Antistius.' The combination *bš* preceding a geographical name seems rather uncertain. However, the other solution leads to an incomplete spelling of the name *Antistius*, which also seems awkward. *ks dḥᵓ* may be translated as 'ablution bowl' in view of the Hebrew verb *dḥh* which in the hiphil means 'to rinse off, to wash.' *dḥh* may very well be a masc. derivation of this root, although a fem. *dḥt* > *dḥᵓ*, where ᵓ indicates /ō/, cannot be excluded.

Sabratha N 17

Bibliography: ROSSI-GARBINI 1983: 104-107.

Illustration: ROSSI-GARBINI 1983: 105 (drawing).

Remarks:

This text is difficult to read and explain. ROSSI-GARBINI 1983: 105-107, presents the following reading: 1) lᵓ *ᵓdr mtn ᶜl bt ḥm* 2) *pt dḥᵓ ḥmṣ* 3) *ysk [*, which GARBINI translates '1) O, may the gift for the girl / house of heat be strong, 2) the vulva may be made swollen, 3) …' Several of his proposed readings are improbable, as e.g. the first sign, which is quite different from the *l* in the second half of line 1. The reading of *ṣ* at the end of the second line is at least extremely doubtful, while the reading of the first sign of the third line as *y* is also improbable. We recognize the following signs: 1) *b/d/r ᵓ ᵓ b/d/r b/d/r* space *m b/d/r n* space *ᶜl b/d/r t ḥ m* 2) *p t ḥ m* space *b/d/r p m š k/n* 3) *t n s k ḥ* (?)

Tarhuna

Tarhuna N 1

Bibliography: ROSSI-GARBINI 1983; GARBINI 1983; GARBINI 1987; SZNYCER 1988: 196-197; AMADASI 1992: 101-103; GARBINI 1992; SZNYCER 1994; *TRE* 54.

Illustrations: ROSSI-GARBINI 1983, tav. vi; AMADASI 1992: 104 d (drawing); GARBINI 1983, tav. vi; SZNYCER 1994, fig. 1 (photograph).

Text:

1) mnṣbt š pᶜbyt
2) bt gᶜrᶜp mᵓ ṭ
3) nᵓ qwynṭᵓ
4) btm

Translation:

1) Stele of Pabit,
2) the daughter of Garap, which ere-
3) cted Quintus,
4) at his own expense.

Remarks:
Although the text of this inscription seems quite clear, much discussion has already been published on it, mainly because ROSSI-GARBINI 1983 supposed it to be a dedication to the goddess *Caelestis*. This proposition is still accepted by ELMAYER, sub *TRE* 54. The correct reading of the third line was established by SZNYCER 1988, 1994. The problem remaining, as SZNYCER 1994: 31, 33, remarked, is the reading of the two Libyan names. ROSSI-GARBINI 1983 read *n*^{c}*byt* in line 1, a reading accepted by AMADASI 1992, ELMAYER sub *TRE* 54. For *n*^{c}*byt,* one may compare NBT, *RIL* 1076, 1083. However, GARBINI 1992 reads *r*^{c}*byt* and SZNYCER 1994 reads, without further comment, *k(?)b/ryt.* The stone is now displayed in the Museum in Tripoli and the study of the original has convinced us that ELMAYER, sub *TRE* 54, is right in reading *p* as the first sign of this name, although we do not accept his combination with the preceding sign, when he reads *sp*$^{\supset}$*byt* as a name. Equally difficult is the reading of the second Libyan name. ROSSI-GARBINI 1983, combining with part of the following word, read *gdb*^{c}*nm*$^{\supset}$*ṭ.* ELMAYER, sub *TRE* 54, reads *gdbp m*$^{\supset}$*ṭn*$^{\supset}$ as a double personal name. Later this name was read *gdb*^{c}*n* by AMADASI 1992. We are convinced, after studying the original, that the reading *g*^{c}*r*^{c}*p* is the most probably one. The first ^{c} has a very small deformation which makes it look somewhat like *d,* but one would expect a longer shaft for this letter. For the use of *m*$^{\supset}$ with relative function, first noted for this text by AMADASI 1992, cf. Hr. Djerou N 1. The verbal form in line 2-3 has been read *ṭyn*$^{\supset}$ / *ṭn*$^{\supset}$ by SZNYCER 1988: 197. The *y,* however, read at the end of line 2 is quite different from the one in line 1. Because outside the written area several holes are to be found of more or less the same depth as this presumed grapheme, we suppose that this is a hole not intended as a part of the text. The reading of the last word in this text is also problematic. Looking at the certain examples of *n* (in *mnṣbt* and *qwynṭ*$^{\supset}$) and *t* (in *mnṣbt*), one gets the impression that the reading *btm,* as proposed by ROSSI-GARBINI 1983, is more probable than *bnm,* 'his son', the reading advocated by SZNYCER 1988: 197, although this is perhaps easier as far as the context is concerned.

Wadi el-Amud

Wadi el-Amud N 1

Bibliography: LEVI DELLA VIDA 1964: 57-60; VATTIONI 1966: 39; LEVI DELLA VIDA 1967b: 259-260; GARBINI 1986: 13; TEIXIDOR 1964-1980: 100-101; *TRE* 38; *IPT* 79.

Illustrations: LEVI DELLA VIDA 1964, tav. xxxia; *IPT*, tav. xxx, 79 (photograph).

Text:
1) b$^{\supset}$r mqn$^{\supset}$t $^{\supset}$tm$^{\supset}$ $^{\supset}$š p^{c}lm
2) m^{c}ṣwkn l$^{\supset}$by$^{\supset}$ ymrr bn g^{c}ṭyṭ
3) hmṣly wl$^{\supset}$mm zwṭ bt g^{c}tydn hn/tglby
4) wl$^{\supset}$bny wl$^{\supset}$šty ^{c}sly^{c}n/t bt yn/tkd^{c}sn bn
5) ṣywk hn/tglby ḥš l$^{\supset}$rbtnm npl$^{\supset}$ btṣty bn/ty
6) bḥytnm wbḥyt bn$^{\supset}$m $^{\supset}$ršm w$^{\supset}$y$^{\supset}$ṣdn

Translation:
1) Tomb; absolute property, which made
2) Masaukan for his father, Yamrur, the son of Gatit,
3) the *mṣly,* and for his mother Zut, the daughter of Gatidan, the *nglby,*
4) and for his son and for his wife Aslian, the daughter of Yankedasan, the son of
5) Siwak, the *nglby* -alas for the four of them. It was made completely at his own expense,
6) during their life and the life of his sons Arisham and $^{\supset}$*y*$^{\supset}$*ṣdn.*

Remarks:
For the first word VATTIONI 1966 proposes the reading *b*$^{\supset}$*r.* LEVI DELLA VIDA 1967b defends his earlier reading, *qb*$^{\supset}$*r,* cf. also GARBINI 1986: 13, however, there is not enough room for the supposed *q.* The spelling of *qbr* with $^{\supset}$ in the second syllable would also be surprising. *b*$^{\supset}$*r* with this meaning is also attested in Zliten LP1 as *bvr*. In line 5 *ḥš* is a problematic word. LEVI DELLA VIDA 1964: 59, relates the word to the root *ḥwš/ḥšš,* which in Hebrew means 'to sigh', the substantive being used as an exclamation, 'woe, alas.' ELMAYER, sub *TRE* 38, supposes a lapsus for *mš,* 'statue', which seems less probable. The same author proposes to explain *l*$^{\supset}$*rbtnm* as the preposotion *l,* followed by a variant form of *rbtnm,* which he then erroneously explains

as a singular *rbt* + suff. 1. pl. c. + a redundant plural morpheme. The *m* in *bḥytnm* in line 6 has been added a little above the line, between the shafts of the *h* in *hn/tglby* in line 5. The spelling *l^{ɔ}bny*, which is best translated 'for his son', is interesting. One may suppose a development comparable to the one in Arabic: */bVn-/* > */bn-/* > */Vbn-/*, which leads to a hypothetical pronunciation */*ləbniyu*/.

Wadi el-Amud N 2

Bibliography: LEVI DELLA VIDA 1964: 60-62; *TRE* 39; *IPT* 77.

Illustrations: LEVI DELLA VIDA 1964, tav. xxxivc; *IPT*, tav. xxix, 77 (photograph).

Text:
1) mnṣbt m^{ɔ} p^{c}l^{ɔ} bn̊ [^{ɔ}m]
2) l^{c}bn^{ɔ}m nymr^{c}n ẙ [
3) bn^{ɔ}m n/tšn/tylšn/tpl ^{ɔ}ršm

Translation:
1) Stele which his sons made
2) for their father Nimiran …
3) … Arisham.

Remarks:
For the use of *m^{ɔ}* as a relative pronoun, cf. the remark sub Hr. Djerou N 1. The *bn^{ɔ}m* in line 3 may be a derivation from the verbal root *bny*, 'to build', or a form of *bn*, 'son', construed by a suffix.

TUNISIA

Ain Zakkar N 1

Bibliography: CHABOT 1936-1937: 170-171; FÉVRIER 1955: 63-64; HOFTIJZER 1961: 344-348; FÉVRIER 1964-1965: 93-95; JONGELING 1984: 9f.; GARBINI 1986: 37; FERJAOUI 1996: 25-35; JONGELING 1996b: 157-158; JONGELING 1997; *KAI* 136.

Illustrations: CHABOT 1936-1937, 171; the same drawing reprinted with FÉVRIER 1955; FERJAOUI 1996, pl. 3-4 (photograph).

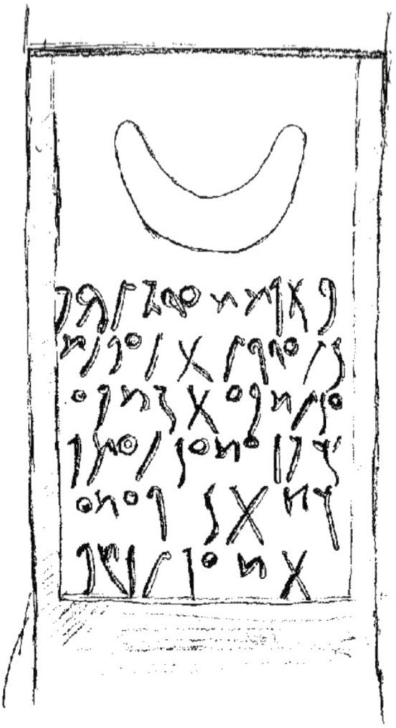

Text:
1) bm/^{ɔ}rš š ^{c}dyt hk
2) nt ^{c}drt mt^{c} bt š
3) ^{c}nt šb^{c}m wšb^{c}
4) wkn^{c} š^{c}nt ^{c}sr
5) wšmn r^{c}š^{c}
6) mš^{c}rt nṣb

Translation:
1) Boraš, the client of Adyat the priest-
2) ess important, she died at the age of
3) seventy-seven years
4) and she had been ten years
5) and eight *r^{c}š^{c}*
6) Mašarat erected it.

Remarks:
Line 1 starts with *bmrš* or *b^{ɔ}rš,* as supposed by FERJAOUI. Earlier readings are highly improbable. FERJAOUI translates: 'in *^{ɔ}rš*.' JONGELING 1997 supposes *b^{ɔ}rš* to be a personal name, related to the following name by means of the marker of relativity *š*, probably to indicate the relation of a client to his/her former master. This may explain why in this text the geneology of the de-

ceased is not mentioned. At the end of the line and the beginning of line 2 *hk̊nt*, 'the priestess', has been read. The reading is difficult, as the second sign, of course, looks more like *n*, while the third sign looks more like *b* than anything else. We adopt the reading, however, for want of a better explanation. HOFTIJZER 1961 reads *hnkt*, relating the word to the well-attested *hnkt* in the formula *hnkt* ^{c}*bnt* (cf. the remark sub Kef-Bezioun N 1), yet, as the following word can hardly be read ^{c}*bnt*, this is not acceptable. The following ^{c}*drt* is certain, at least as far the reading is concerned, which makes the reading and interpretation of *mt*^{c} *bt* as 'she died at the age of' seem highly probable. Although most commentators divide the text otherwise, the reading as presented above seems probable. *r*^{c}*š*^{c} indicates the function the deceased had fulfilled for 18 years (cf. also the remark on *rds* sub Lepcis Magna N 2). *mš*^{c}*rt* is a name known from Libyan texts as MSRT/MŠRT.

Bir bou Rekba (Thinissut)

Bir Bou Rekba N 1

Bibliography: VASSEL 1920: 475-477; *RÉS* 942, 1858; *KAI* 137.

Illustrations: VASSEL 1920: 476 (drawing of the end of lines 1 and 2).

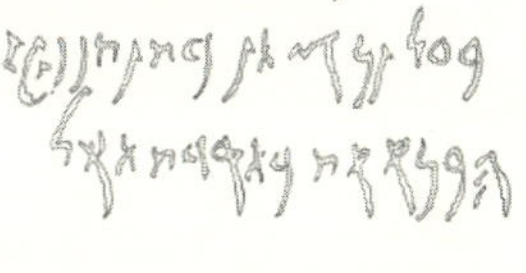

Text:

1) l$^{\supset}$dn lb^{c}l wltnt pn b^{c}l mqdšm šnm $^{\supset}$š p^{c}l b^{c}l tnsmt bšt špṭm
2) ḥmlk wḥmlk bn $^{\supset}$nkn kn$^{\supset}$ ^{c}l mlkt hbn$^{\supset}$ $^{\supset}$š bmqdšm $^{\supset}$l
3) $^{\supset}$pšn bn gdsn wb^{c}lḥn$^{\supset}$ bn mskr w^{c}l mlkt hmṭḥ
4) prnkn bn mndkn wyšd$^{\supset}$ bn $^{\supset}$nkn b$^{\supset}$ h$^{\supset}$lnm $^{\supset}$l ^{c}lt h
5) mqdšm $^{\supset}$l b^{c}sr wšb^{c} lyrḥ mp^{c} lpny hšt z np^{c}l nbl
6) nskt $^{\supset}$rb^{c} ^{c}lt hmqdšm $^{\supset}$l spm šnm wzbrm šnm wnntn
7) $^{\supset}$t hkhnm $^{\supset}$t $^{\supset}$rš bn $^{\supset}$nkn w$^{\supset}$t bd^{c}štrt bn ypš

Translation:

1) To the lord, to Bal and to Tinnit Fane Bal; two holy places which the citizens of *tnsmt* made in the year of the sufetes
2) Imilk and Imilk, the son of Ankan; were over the building work that was in these holy places
3) Apšan, the son of Gadsan and Balanno, the son of Miskar and over the plastering work
4) Parankan, the son of Manadkan and Yašdo, the son of Ankan. These gods went into
5) these holy places on the seventeenth of the first month Mappa of this year. Were made vessels of
6) cast metal four for these sanctuaries, two bowls and two vessels and they were presented
7) to the priests, to Arish, the son of Ankan and to Bodashtart, the son of Yapash.

Remarks:

DUSSAUD, with BERGER 1908, concludes from the use of the preposition ^{c}*lt* in line 4, that the gods in question must have been of a celestial nature, because they descended upon the sanctuaries. LIDZBARSKI, however, remarks that one cannot draw conclusions from the use of ^{c}*lt* that may have been used with the same meaning as $^{\supset}$*l* or even *l*. *nntn* in line 6 is to be explained as a nifal of *ntn*, parallel root to *ytn*. For the date mentioned in line 5, cf. BERLINER 1916. Note that the unknown word *zbr* indicates some sort of vessel; it is used parallel with *sp*, and both *zbr* and *sp* are hyponyms of *nbl*. Note that in Arabic, a word *zubra*, 'a piece of iron', is attested. Could this be related to the *zbr* in this text, due to the use of *nskt?* The $^{\supset}$*t* repeated several times in the last line, must be the preposition 'with' rather than the nota objecti.

Bir Tlelsa

Bir Tlelsa N 1

Bibliography: LIDZBARSKI 1915: 287-290; DUSSAUD 1917: 165-167; FÉVRIER 1949a: 25-26; SZNYCER 1980; JONGELING 2004; *KAI* 138.

Illustrations: LIDZBARSKI 1915: 288; SZNYCER 1980, pl. ii, b (photograph).

Text:
1) lbʿl ʾdr - htqdš
2) bʿlšylk bn mʿrqʾ ʿwyʿny
3) t hmzbḥ š hmqnt š ʿbr ʾ
4) š ʿgʿ š bšm hmlkt btm km
5) bktʿb ṣlm btʾrm btm
6) - ḥydš wʾyqdš -

Translation:
1) To the mighty Bal has consecrated for himself
2) Balshillek, the son of Marcus Avianius,
3) the altar of cattle, of cereals o-
4) f cakes, of perfume; the work completely as
5) in the design, according to its plan, at his own expense
6) he renewed and consecrated.

The description of the altar is normally transcribed as *hmzbḥ šhmqnt šʿbrʾ šʿgʿ šbšm.* However, because of the strange representation of the feminine ending (*-t, -ʾ, -ʿ*), we think it is better to divide as we have done here. The word *ṣlm* in line 5 has been variously read and explained. Most commentators read *slm*, whereby FÉVRIER thinks of a variant form of *šlm*, 'perfect'; LIDZBARSKI, 1915: 288f., proposed to interpret this word as the plural of an unknown *sl*; LEVI DELLA VIDA 1964: 309, supposed *slm* to be the sg. + suff. 3 sing. m. of a word *sl* meaning 'entrance' or 'pallisade.' It seems, however, most probable that the word is the direct complement of the preceding *ktʿb* (the reading *km/ʿ knʿ* at the end of line 5 and the beginning of line 6 as proposed by LIDZBARSKI 1915, and followed by RÖLLIG, *KAI* a.l., is highly improbable). RÖLLIG, *KAI* a.l., has remarked that it is possible to read *ṣlm*, 'statue', instead of *slm.* As the form of *s* and *ṣ* are in many instances not really differentiated in the Neo-Punic script, and this is the only occurrence of this sign in this text, this is an attractive proposition, as it leaves us with a word that is at least well-known in Nort-West Semitic. The expression *ktb ṣlm* probably indicated something like 'a blue-print, a design.' The expression *btʾrm btm* occurs also elsewhere, viz. in Lepcis Magna N 16, where it is also followed by a form of the ifil of *qdš: ḥnbʿl ... btʾrm btm pʿl wʾyqdš,* and in Lepcis Magna N 13, where, however, the context is broken. In both texts, *IPT* and *KAI* read *bn ʾrm* instead of *btʾrm*, but the combination with *btm* both in Lepcis Magna N 16 and Bir Tlelsa N 1, and the fact that the name *ʾrm* is not attested elsewhere, makes the reading proposed by FÉVRIER 1954: 77, very attractive. FÉVRIER 1977 points to the concurring use of *mktb* and *tʾrt* in the Milkpilles epitaph. Note of course, also the concurring use of the ifil of *qdš* and *tʾr.* It is probable, therefore, that the derivations of the roots *ktb* and *tʾr* have different but complementary meanings. The suffix *-m* in *btʾrm* is interpreted as a pronominal element referring to the subject of the verb by *PPG* §332 in Lepcis Magna N 16. It seems to us that it rather refers to *ktʿb* mentioned just before it. It is interesting to note how the syntax of this text remains uncertain. Several scholars have taken *Balshillek* in line 2 as the subject of the verbs in line 6, moving this line in their translation to a position near to the subject, cf. e.g. DUSSAUD 1917: 167, SZNYCER 1980: 41, *PPG* §332. Others have combined *Balshillek* to the preceding *htqdš*, cf. e.g. RÖLLIG, *KAI* a.l. Also because the hithpael of *qdš* in classical Hebrew is almost always used with reflexive meaning (pace *PPG* §149), we think that this explanation is probably correct. The supposed Latin influence on the syntax of this text, cf. *PPG* §332, should therefore be reconsidered.

Bordj Helal

Bordj Helal N 1

Bibliography: ÁLVAREZ DELGADO 1964: 213-214; MASSON 1977: 41-43; SZNYCER 1977a: 47-57; JONGELING 1996a: 78; *NP* 125; *RIL* 72; *KAI* 139.

Illustrations: RIL pl. xii 1; SZNYCER 1977, pl. ix photograph).

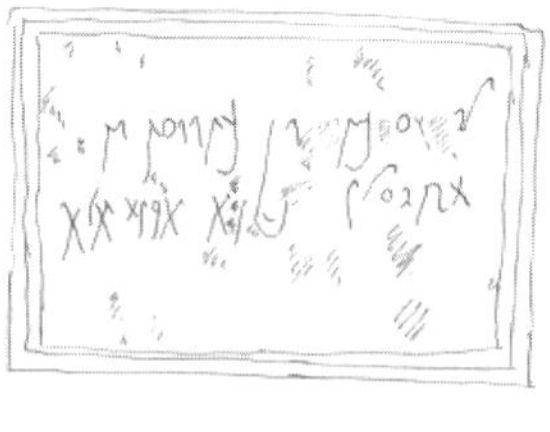

Text:
1) ly[g]wʿkny bn knrdʿt bn
2) msyʿln ṭnʾ ʾbnm ʾlʾ

Libyan text:
1) YGWKNH
2) WKNRDT
3) NNBYH

Translation:
1) For Yagwakani, the son of Kanardat, the son of
2) Masyalan were these stones erected.

Remarks:
MARCY 1936: 85, reads *ṣ* in the name *msyʿln*. Note that all editions previous to SZNYCER 1977 read the first personal name in line 1 as *ygwʿkn*. SZNYCER's reading is to be preferred, especially since the Libyan version of the name ends in a vowel (H). This is the only Neo-Punic text in which, apparently denoting a funeral monument instead of a headstone, the plural *ʾbnm* is used instead of the singular.

Carthage

Carthage N 5

Bibliography: CIS 949.

Illustrations: CIS ii tab. xii (photograph).

Text:
1) {lrbt ltnt pn bʿl
2) wlʾdn lbʿl ḥmn
3) ʾš ndr} bʿlpdʾ
4) bn bdʿštrt

Translation:
1) To the lady, to Tinnit Fane Bal
2) and to the lord to Bal Amun
3) which dedicated Balpado,
4) the son of Bodashtart.

Remarks:
The part of the text between { } is written in Punic script, the rest is Neo-Punic. This may be occasioned by a practice to have several votive stones available at the stonecutter's where the prospective buyer only had to have his name inserted. Inadvertently, the addition was not made in Punic, but in Neo-Punic script. There are some other texts where the use of Punic and Neo-Punic script in the same text is attested, cf. further the remark sub Hr. Maktar N 1.

Djebel Mansour (Gales)

Djebel Mansour N 1

Bibliography: LIDZBARSKI 1908: 187-190; FEVRIER 1949b: 90-91; ADAMS 2003: 226-227; *RÉS* 679; *KAI* 140.

Text:
1) bnʾ b[t] z [q]wʿr[ṭ]h bt npṭḥn
2) bʿl gʿl [ʾš]t qlr bn hmʿnt hknt
3) bʾ...tḥl.....yḥt/nk/bʾ/šʿs/šym
4) šʿṭr rgʿṭʾ brṭʾ hmʿnt nʿmp
5) [ʿmʾ w]ʾls/š bn qlr bn hmʿnt bʿlʾ
6) [gʿl] bʿnym rwpʾ wḥmlkt bʿ
7) [lʾ gʿl] wḥwʾ šʿnt ʿmšm w...

Latin parallel:
1) Qvarta Nyptanis [*filia* G]-
2) a[l]esis vxsor Celeris
3) Mantis (?) *filii* sacerdos magna
4) conditiv*m* s*va* pec*vnia* f*ecit* cv[ra]torib-
5) vs Satvrvm Rogato Brvti-
6) one Maniv [N]am[f]amone
7) Valente Celeris *filio* strv*ctoribus* [R]vf[o]
8) Imilcone vl ses vi[xit

Translation:
1) Built this temple Quarta, the daughter of Nyptan,
2) citizen of Gales, wife of Celer, the son of Amanat, the priestess
3) ...
4) Satur, Rogatus, Brutus, Amanat, Namph-
5) amo, Valens, the sons of Celer, the son of Amanat, citizens of
6) Gales. Builders were Rufus and Imilco, citiz-
7) ens of Gales, and she lived fifty years and ...

Remarks:
The name *Amanat* may be read *hmʿn/tn/t*, and the choice for the reading *hmʿnt* is based on the Latin text. In line 5 ADAMS 2003: 227, translates: 'son of Celer, sons of *hmnʿtʾ*, probably a slip of the pen. The spelling *bʿnym*

points to a pronunciation /*bānīm*/, rather than the expected /*bōnīm*/ > /*būnīm*/ (is this form actually preserved in *bunem*, in Wadi Umm el-Agerem LP1?). As ʿ in the rest of this text is used in its historically appropriate place (as in *bʿl* / *bʿlʾ*), indicating /*a*/ in Semitic words (*šʿnt*, *ʿmšm*) and in non-Semitic names (*[q]wʿr[t]h*, *šʿṭr rgʿṭʾ*, *nʿmp[ʿmʾ*, *gʿl*, *hmʿnt*), where the last two names are perhaps not quite certain, but at least nearly so, because of the Latin text *G]a[l]esis* and the possible reading *Mantis*, one wonders whether to suppose a nominal derivation from the root *bny* having the same meaning as the participle, e.g. according to the *qattāl* formation.

Djebel Massoudj

Djebel Massoudj 1

Bibliography: CHABOT 1943-45: 64-67; FÉVRIER 1954; SHIFMAN 1965: 122-124; GARBINI 1968: 13-17; SZNYCER 1977b: 178-181; *KAI* 141; TEIXIDOR 1964-1980: 100.

Illustrations: CHABOT 1943-1945 (photograph of cast); *KAI* Taf. x (drawing).

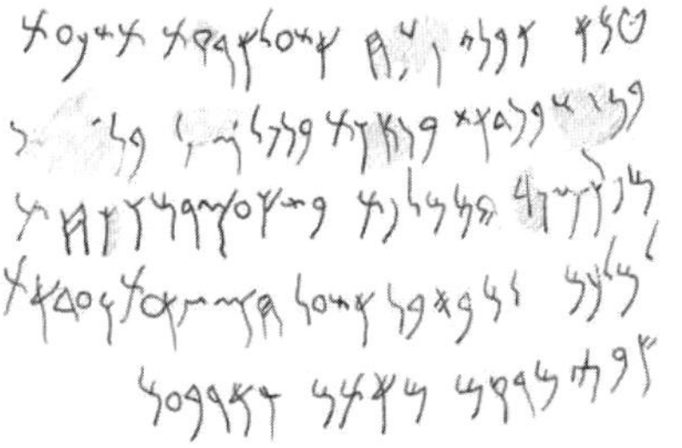

Text:
1) ṭnʾ t ʾbn z m̊š̊ḥ ʾš ʿl ʾrṣt tškʿt
2) bn..š bn dwš bmnḥt bnplsm bm...t
3) mkwsn hmmlkt bšt ʿsrm wʾḥt
4) lmlkm lmbʾbn ʾš ʿl hsywʿt wʿd ʾt
5) ʾbn z mrṣm mʾtm wʾrbʿm

Translation:
1) Erected this stone mšḥ who is set over the lands of Tushkat
2) son of ….son of Dush …
3) Makusan, the king, in the year twenty-one
4) of his kingship. From … and unto …
5) this stone 240 'distances'.

Remarks:
Why this text, written in a characteristic Punic ductus, has been added to the collection of Neo-Punic texts is not clear, as CHABOT 1943-1945 speaks of a Punic text. Nonetheless, it is of course a Late Punic text, and as such finds its place in this collection. The difficult word, read here tentatively as *mšḥ*, in line 1 is read *nbḥ* by SHIFMAN 1965, and explained as a personal name. The reading *mšḥ* is defended by GARBINI 1968, and accepted by TEIXIDOR, 1964-1980: 100. SZNYCER 1977b: 178, reads this word as *wlbḥ*, interpreting it as a Libyan name. Whatever the correct reading, from a semantic point of view it seems more attractive to suppose that following the object the subject is mentioned. A combination of *t ʾbn z* with a following noun, as supposed by GARBINI, seems less probable. In l. 4 SHIFMAN 1965 divides *lmb ʾbn*, to determine the exact distance <from> the stone, which is hardly probable from a syntactical point of view, cf. also GARBINI 1987: 38. GARBINI 1968: 14, points to the attestation of a *pagus Thuscae* in a Latin text from Mactar, also SZNYCER 1977 notes that *ʾrṣt tškʿt* is to be translated 'the territories of Tushkat', comparing *Thusca* - Τυσκα (cf. also VATTIONI 1994: 113). Thusca encompassed 50 villages, cf. APPIAN, *Libyca* 68 (… χώρας πεντήκοντα πόλεων ἣν Τύσκαν προσαγορεύουσιν). Note that in Hebrew *ʾrṣ* may be used in combination with a tribal name, cf. *ʾrṣ bnymn*, 'the territory of Benjamin', Jud. 21: 21. The explanation of the inscription as a Late Punic milestone, because of the expression in the last line, is ingeneous. However, the explanation of the words preceding the number of 'miles', remains difficult. The word *ʾbn* seems to occur twice, but *ʿd ʾt* is enigmatic, while *sywʿt* also remains uncertain.

Dougga

Dougga N 3

Bibliography: DUSSAUD 1914; CHABOT 1916: 128-129a; VATTIONI 1994: 118; GHAKI 1994: 37.

Illustrations: CHABOT 1916: 128.

Text:
1) bym n^{ɔ}m wbrk ṭn
2) ^{ɔ} ^{c}bn lg^{c}wd bn
3) b^{c}[n]wk bn kyw
4) ^{ɔ}mdyty

Translation:
1) On a pleasant and blessed day was
2) erected the stone for Gaud, the son of
3) Banuk, the son of Kiu
4) the Maditi.

Remarks:
The expression *bym n^{c}m wbrk* to indicate a day on which an important sacrifice was offered, is equivalent to the expression *diem bonvm et favstvm* in Latin texts, cf. FANTAR 1974: 12 n. 2. The expression is limited to Dougga, Teboursouk, Ksar Lemsa, Constantine and Ksiba Mraou as far as Neo-Punic texts are concerned. The Latin expression is found in Teboursouk, Cherchell, Mila and Ksar Toual Zouamel, while a Greek equivalent is attested in Dougga. FANTAR 1974: 47, describes the expression as a Libyco-Punic one, because of its geographical repartition. The name *b^{c}nwk*, spelled without *w* in the next text, is also attested in Hr. Maktar N 2, 4: *b^{c}n̊k*. For *kyw* VATTIONI 1994: 118 tentatively points to *Ceius, Ceiu* in *CIL* viii 6066, 7825 (or are these names renderings of Latin *Gaius*?). Note that the ethnicon *^{ɔ}mdyty* in this and the next text is spelled differently.

Dougga N 4

Bibliography: DUSSAUD 1914; CHABOT 1916: 128-129b; VATTIONI 1994: 119; GHAKI 1994: 37.

Text:
1) bym n^{ɔ}m wbrk
2) ṭn^{ɔ} ^{c}bn l^{c}m
3) ṣt bn g^{c}wd bn
4) b^{c}n̊k bn kyw
5) ^{ɔ}mdty

Translation:
1) On a pleasant and blessed day
2) was erected the stone for Am-
3) sit, the son of Gaud, the son of
4) Banuk, the son of Kiu
5) the Maditi.

Remarks:
^{c}mṣt may be read *^{c}mst* according to VATTIONI 1994: 119. In case the first reading is correct, the name must be the feminine counterpart of *^{c}mṣ*, which would lead to the reading of *bt* instead of the first *bn* in line 3, thus VATTIONI 1994: 118.

Hr. Aouin

Hr. Aouin N 1

Bibliography: LIDZBARSKI 1902: 43-44; LANDAU 1903: 29; ADAMS 2003: 217; *RÉS* 79.

Illustrations: BERGER & CAGNAT 1899, next to : 53 (photograph).

Text:
1) [hmzbḥ s]t ytn qynṭ^{ɔ} m^{c}rqy prṭ[mq^{ɔ}]
2) rp^{ɔ} št špṭm ^{c}bdmlqrt w^{ɔ}dnb[^{c}l]

Greek parallel:
Κουινκτος Μαρκιο[ς Πρωτο]μαχος Ηρακλειδο[υ ιατρος]

Latin parallel:
*Q*uint*vs* Marci[vs] Protomacvs [medicvs] facta L*vcivs* . M*arcivs* . cos . m[ense

Translation:
1) This altar gave Quintus Marcius Protomacus
2) the doctor, in the year of the suffetes Abdmelqart and Adonibal.

Remarks:
LANDAU 1903 restores: 1) *[hmzbḥ z]t ytn*

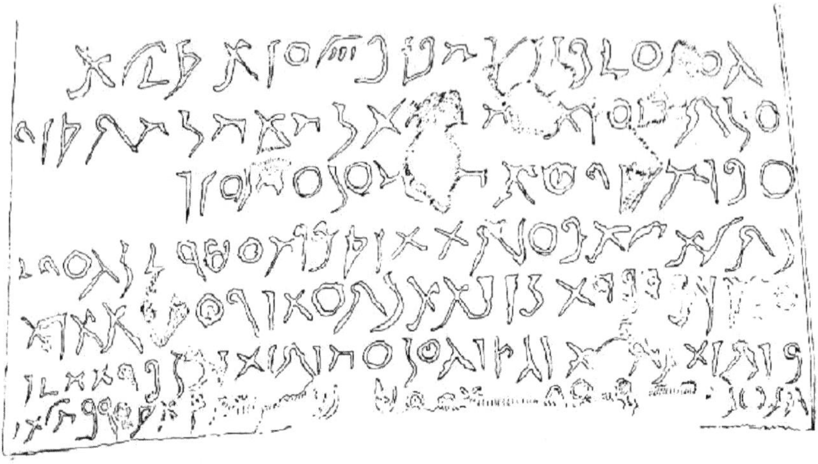

Hr. Brirht N 1

qynṭʾ mʿrqy prṭ 2) *[mkʾ h]rpʾ št špṭm ʿbdmlqrt wʾdnb[ʿl].* Cf. also the remark sub Lepcis Magna N 4.

Hr. Brirht

Hr. Brirht N 1

Bibliography: DERENBOURG 1876; LIDZBARSKI 1898: 435, 3 C2; ADAMS 2003: 225-226; *NP* 123; *NSI* 53; *KAI* 142; Latin text: *CIL* viii 793.

Illustrations: LIDZBARSKI 1898, Taf. xix 1 (drawing).

Text:

1) gʿ[d]ʿy bn plkš bn pḥlʿn ʾqylʾ
2) ʿwh šʿnʾ[t] šy[š]m wšʾš wšhqnd
3) ʿ bt šqndʿ ʾš[t]m ʿwʿ šʿnt vacat
4) phlʾ lʾbʿthm mnqbt/n šʿṭry wgʿdy
5) ʿ[..]kbʿbdmwnn/tʾʾphʿmtrʿ[..]ʾʾtm
6) bthnm phlʾ ngṣtg ʿwʿ šnht mnpwbdmšyk
7) h[.]ʿ[......]ʿd[...] šʿṭr pb[..]w[...]ʾqʿ/dr bšlm[.]

Latin parallel:

1) Dis Manib*vs* sacr*vm*
2) Gadaevs Felicis fil*ivs*
3) pivs vix*it* annis lxvi hic
4) sit*vs* est Secvnda Secvndi
5) fil*ia* v*ixit* a*nnis* [...] Satvrio et Gadaevs
6) patri piissimo posvervunt.

Translation:

1) Gadaeus, the son of Felix, the son of Palan Aquila
2) lived sixty six years and Secund-
3) a, the daughter of Secunda, his wife, lived years ...
4) Made for their parents the grave Saturius and Gadaeus
5) ...
6) they made (?) ... he/she lived years ...
7) ... ... Satur ...

Remarks:
The reading *ʾš[t]m* in line 3 seems much more probable than *ʾš[t]ʾ*, as e.g. with RÖLLIG, *KAI* a.l., ADAMS 2003: 225. The same holds true for the reading *lʾbʿthm* instead of *lʾbʿnhm*. The word *qbr*, 'grave', preceded by *mt*, has been proposed for the word(s) following *lʾbʿthm*, however, the reading of the last letter of this word as *r* seems highly speculative when compared to the certain specimen in the name *šʿṭry*, directly following. DERENBOURG 1876: 178 n. 2 proposes the reading *mnṣbt*, which would be an attractive solution as far as the meaning is concerned, but the *q* seems to be undeniable in the extant drawing. The lines 5 to 7 remain without any reasonable explanation. RÖLLIG reads *ʾqbr bšlm* at the end of line 7, cf. also ADAMS 2003:225. What the

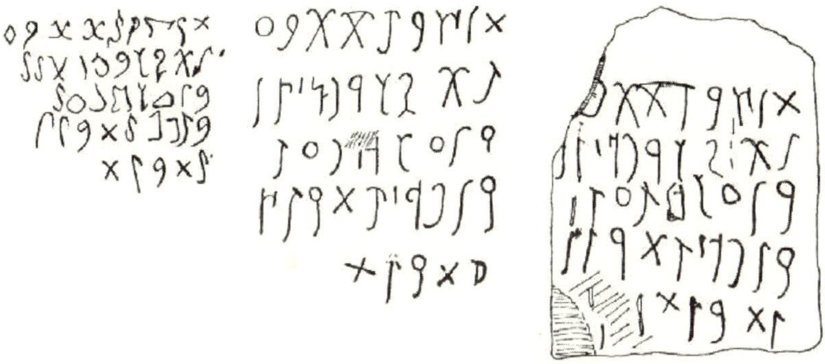

Hr. Djerou N 1

relation of 'the grave in peace' should be to the preceding text remains uncertain. We cannot propose a better reading, although unconvinced of the proposed solution.

Hr. Djerou

Hr. Djerou N 1

Bibliography: DUSSAUD 1921: cclix-cclx; CHABOT 1932-1933: 448; LEVI DELLA VIDA 1964a: 61; JONGELING 1984: 10-12; *NP* 6.

Illustrations: TEMPLE 1835, (lithograph) 182; GESENIUS 1837, tab. 27, lxvi; DUSSAUD 1921:cclx; CHABOT 1932-1933: 448; JONGELING 1984: 10,11 (drawing).

Text:
1) mnṣbt m^{ɔ} b^{c}
2) n^{ɔ} ywrḥtn
3) bn ^{c}wṭp^{c}tn
3) bn ^{c}wṭp^{c}tn
4) bn ḥsm btṣ
5) tm btm

Translation:
1) Stele which bui-
2) lt Yuratan,
3) the son of Autifatan,
4) the son of *ḥsm*, on his own
5) costs completely.

Remarks:
For the editorial history of this text, that was published three times as a separate text cf. JONGELING 1984: 10f. The reading seems without reasonable doubt; for line 3, cf. JONGELING 1984. The combination of the verbal root *bny* and the object *mnṣbt* also in Ksour Abd el-Melek N 1 and Metameur N 1. In lines 4-5, LEVI DELLA VIDA 1963: 79f., id. 1964a: 61, is the first to point to the use of *m*^{ɔ} as a marker of relativity (cf. also AMADASI 1980: 34, like LEVI DELLA VIDA quoting two editions of Hr. Djerou N 1 as relating to different texts). Note that this use of the relative pronoun is also attested in Latino-Punic texts. LEVI DELLA VIDA also established the reading *btṣtm btm*, now generally accepted, against e.g. CHABOT 1932-1933: 448, who supposed a personal name *ḥsmrtn*. DUSSAUD 1921 reads the name *ḥsm*. He, however, proposes for the signs following the reading *bn ṣqmbtm*. The name ^{c}*wṭp*^{c}*tn* was read by DUSSAUD 1921, as ^{c}*w..*^{c}*t*, CHABOT 1932-1933: 448, gave ^{c}*wṭs*^{c}*tn*. The existence of *Altifatan*, mentioned by CORIPPUS, is in favour of the reading ^{c}*wṭp*^{c}*tn*.

Hr. Maktar

Hr. Maktar N 1

Bibliography: CHABOT, *Punica* xii 2; MENDLESON 2003: 37; *NP* 35; *CIL* viii 1008.

Illustrations: SCHRÖDER 1869, Taf. xvi 11 (drawing); MENDLESON 2003 *NP*u4 (photograph).

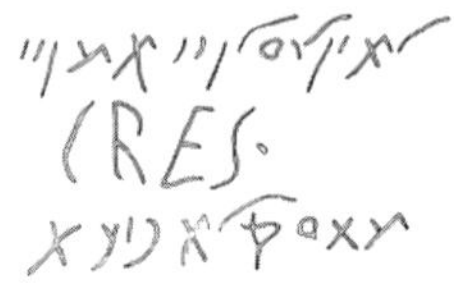

Text:

1) l^{ɔ}dn lb^{c}l ndr ^{ɔ}š ndr
2) Cres*cens*
3) šm^{c} ql^{ɔ} brk^{ɔ}

Translation:

1) To the lord to Bal, votive offering which dedicated
2) Crescens
3) he heard his voice, blessed him.

Remarks:

The use of Neo-Punic script for most of the text and Latin script for the name of the dedicant shows that this type of stele could be bought without a name that could be filled in later (cf. also Carthage N 5). There is at least one other example of a Punic text in which the name of the dedicant is mentioned in a different script, viz. *CIS* i 191, where the dedicant, Ευκλεα, is rendered in Greek script.

Hr. Maktar N 39

Bibliography: CHABOT, *Punica* iv A 1; FÉVRIER 1971; JONGELING 1986: 249-250; SZNYCER 1998; JONGELING 1999: 82; MENDLESON 2003: 40; *Numidica* i; *NP* 7.

Illustrations: BISI 1976, taf. 1,1; SZNYCER 1998: 48 (photograph), id., 54 (drawing); MENDLESON 2003 *NP*u21 (photograph).

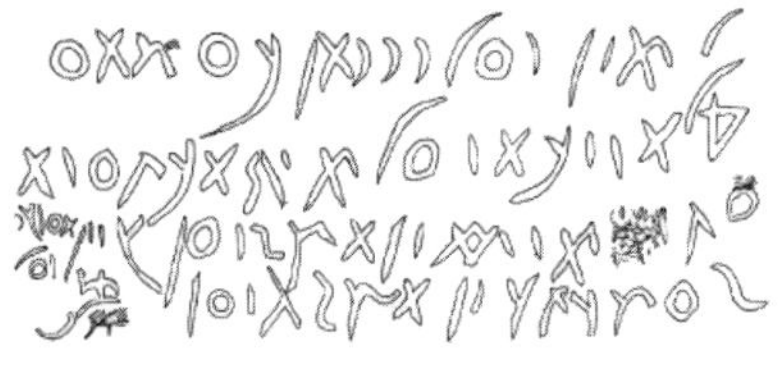

Text:

1) l^{ɔ}dn b^{c}l ḥmn k^{c} šm^{c}
2) qlm brkm b^{c}l^{ɔ} hmkt^{c}rm
3) ^{c}t r ^{ɔ}ršm bn msyr^{c}n w
4) y^{c}sktn bn msygr^{c}n
5) rb m^{c}rwz
6) ^{ɔ} bn b^{c}l
7) šlk

Translation:

1) To the lord Bal Amun, because he heard
2) their voice, blessed them, the citizens of Maktar,
3) in the time of the officials Arisham, the son of Masiran and
4) Iasuktan, the son of Masigaran,
5) the president Maruz-
6) o, the son of Bal-
7) shillek.

Remarks:

The fifth to seventh lines consist of a group of small signs in the lower left corner of the text. The first two signs are of the small type indicating *b, d* or *r.* The reading *rb* follows from the comparable phrase in e.g. Maktar N 11. Note that *r* in this context is explained as an abbreviation of a abstract derivation of the root *rbb.* FÉVRIER 1958-1959, 30-31, (cf. id. 1971, id. 1966, 98) read *bt,* which is ingeneous, but unnecessary.

Hr. Maktar N 76

Bibliography: FÉVRIER & FANTAR 1965: 49-59; VAN DEN BRANDEN 1977: 55-65; KRAHMALKOV 1975; TEIXIDOR 1964-1980: 17-18.

Text:

i

1) [ ]ḥšt bn yhb^{c}t ^{ɔ}š ^{c}l knṣwl^{c}t
2) [ ] tyl^{ɔ} hykrt r^{c}qym by^{c}tn š^{c}bt
3) [wm]ṭbt ^{c}lm̊ yst mšlt š^{c}b̊ ṣ ql^{c}rn̊t

ii

4) np^{c}l bkwlbm ns^{ɔ}m by^{c}tn šb^{c}t
5) hykrm̊ mqd^{c}š^{ɔ} np^{ɔ}l km̊ p^{ɔ}lt m^{c}ṣrt
6) hy ^{c}l h[m]^{c}qm bkl b^{c}t lknṣwl^{c}t

iii

7) bkl ^{ɔc}n ^{ɔ}š lyd^{ɔ} ^{c}lnm t ^{c}ṭrt
8) w^{c}lky hmzr^{ɔ} ^{ɔ}š y^{c}tn^{ɔ} t ^{ɔ}šb^{c}t
9) l^{c}nt[ ]^{ɔ}m[ ]š^{c}qlt

iv

10) dr^{ɔ} kn^{ɔ} šlm w^{ɔ}š ln̊m zr^{c} ẘ šp^{c}t
11) w^{ɔ}n^{ɔ} šm^{ɔ}tm ^{ɔ}š y^{c}tn^{ɔ} t ^{ɔ}šb^{c}t
12) [mz]r^{ɔ} ^{ɔ}š ^{c}gr^{ɔ} bml^{c}[kt]
13) [ ]bn ^{ɔ}ršm

v

14) s^{ɔ}wr^{ɔ} bn ^{c}ršqs

15) sw^{c}w^{ɔ} bn brkb^{c}l
16) [ ] bn m^{c}smk^{c}t
vi
17) mtnb^{c}l bn lq[y]
18) ^{ɔ}ykn^{c} bn [
19) p^{c}w[st^{ɔ}
vii
20)qwd̊ r^{c}t^{ɔ} bn g^{c}y
21) [ ]^{c}l[ ]y^{ɔ} bn mtnb^{c}l
viii
22) b̊ ẙ k s̊ ^{ɔ}[ ]l bn g^{c}ẙ
23) lqy bn m^{c}grs^{c}n
24) ypt^{c}n bn ^{c}bdmlqrt
25) [ ]bn mtnb^{c}l
ix
26) ^{ɔ}ykn^{c} bn ḥm̊ lk̊ t
27) g^{ɔ}ml^{ɔ} bn r^{ɔ}sttẙt̊ $^{ɔ̊}$
28) p^{c}wst^{ɔ} bn [
29) slkny bn tynb̊
x
30) m^{c}ksm^{ɔ} bn brkb^{c}l
31) p$^{ɔ̊}$r̊t̊n^{c}t^{ɔ} bn m^{c}ksm^{ɔ}
32) $^{ɔ̊}$wtn^{ɔ} bn r^{ɔ}m^{c}n^{c}
xi
33) b^{c}l[

Translation:

1)]*ḥšt* the son of Yebat, who is in charge of the consulate,
2) …. by giving abundantly
3) ….
4) it was made with elevated …, by giving abundantly,
5) he gave generously … sanctuary … as the work …
6) … the place in everything … for the consulate
7) … … which is next to the gods …
8) and because the assembly who gave the abundance,
9) ….
10) …. progeny and clan,
11) and here follow their names, who gave abundantly
12) the assembly who …. in the work.
13) … the son of Arishim,
14) Severus the son of Arsaces (?)
15) Suavus the son of Barikbal
16) … the son of Masmakat
17) Mutunbal the son of Lucius
18) Aykna the son of …
19) Faustus …
20) Quadratus the son of Gaius
21) … the son of Mutunbal
22) …. the son of Gaius
23) Lucius the son of Magarsan
24) Yeptan the son of Abdmelqart
25) … the son of Mutunbal
26) Aykna the son of Imilco
27) Gemellus the son of Restitutus
28) Faustus the son of …
29) Salkani the son of Taynab (?)
30) Maximus the son of Barikbal
31) Fortunatus the son of Maximus
32) Avitannus (?) the son if Romana
33) …

Remarks:

The use of the Latin word 'consulate' in this text rather points to a clumsy attempt to pose as Roman than an adaption of a Roman style government. FÉVRIER & FANTAR 1965: 50, 57, translates *hykrt r^{c}qym* as 'he established the foundations', explaining *hykrt* as a yiph. of *krt*, which then would mean 'to build by cutting', while *r^{c}qym* is compared with Hebrew *rāqīa^{c}* used here with the meaning 'foundation.' The whole proposal seems highly speculative. In case the next words mean 'by giving in abundance', which seems more attractive, one must suppose that the inf. cstr. of *ytn* in Phoenico-Punic is formed in a way quite different from the Hebrew formation. The supposition in *DNWSI* s.v. *ytn*$_2$ that this word is a nominal derivation of the root *ytn*, meaning 'presentation' is a rather easy way out of the problem. *šb^{c}t* is translated 'contribution' by FÉVRIER-FANTAR 1965: 51, and related, with reservations, to the root *šp^{c}*, 'to flow abundantly', while a relation to the root *śb^{c}* seems more attractive. In the next line, FÉVRIER-FANTAR 1965: 51, propose to read *wm]ṭbt*, explained as the fem. form of *mṭbḥ*, altar. In case the reading *mṭbt* is correct, there is no reason why this word should not be derived from the root *ṭwb*. For the next words, the proposals of FÉVRIER-FANTAR 1965: 51, do not help much, but we do not have anything useful to add. For *klwbm* FÉVRIER-FANTAR 1965: 52, think of a relation with Hebrew *klwb*, 'basket', or Latin *columna*. Because of the following *ns^{ɔ}m* one would rather opt for the second solution. The spelling with *-b-* pro *-m-* is easily explained as hypercorrect use of *b* as in *šb^{c}* pro *šm^{c}*. In the next line, line 5, FÉVRIER-FANTAR 1965: 52, propose to read *hykrt* instead of the extant *hykrm̊*. We would rather take *hykrm* as a yiph. of the root *krm*. The root occurs in Hr. Maktar N 64 (^{ɔ}*ykrm*^{ɔ} *t hmnḥt*), where it is translated as 'they offered generously the offering.' The next words may mean 'his fallen sanctuary', but the wording seems to be awkward. *mqd*^{c}*š*^{ɔ} may also be explained as a pl. cstr., of course, but this leaves us with a word *np*^{ɔ}*l* of difficult interpretation. *p*^{ɔ}*lt* is perhaps best explained, with FÉVRIER-FANTAR 1965: 52, as a derivation from the root *p*^{c}*l*, however, whether *m*^{c}*ṣrt* really should be translated 'enclosure wall' remains doubtful. We note that Hebrew *māṣōr* means 'siege--enclosure, siege', and *məṣūrā* 'siege-works, rampart', which does seem somewhat out of place in the context of a building insciption relating to a temple. Also the use of the vowel letter for */a/* following the first consonant poses a problem. One is inclined to suppose the word to be a derivation from the root *mṣr* or *ṣry*, to explain the syllable */maṣ-/*, rather than from the root *ṣwr*. Both roots, however, do not yield a meaning that might have been used in this context. In the next line, 6, *hy* ^{c}*l* may be explained as two words, as FÉVRIER-FANTAR 1965: 52, do, but it is also possible that *hy*^{c}*l* is meant, which could be a yiphil of the root ^{c}*ly*. *b*^{c}*t* is compared by FÉVRIER-FANTAR 1965: 52, with *b*^{c}*t* in *KAI* 64, meaning 'tariff', however, because of the highly uncertain context it is also possible to explain the word as the prep. *b* followed by the noun ^{c}*t* 'time.' ^{c}*ṭrt* is translated 'cornice' by FÉVRIER-FANTAR 1965: 53, which is, of course, possible. Line 8 starts with *w*^{c}*lky* which may be divided in the copula *w* followed by the preposition ^{c}*l* which is then followed by the conjunction *ky*. This combination of preposition and conjunction is attested a few times in Hebrew (Dt. 31: 17, Jud. 3: 12, Jer. 4: 28, Mal. 2: 14, Ps. 139: 14), always meaning 'because.' Note, however, that the conjunction 'because', corresponding to Hebrew *kī*, is normally represented as */ka/*, */ko/* or */kə/*, see JONGELING 1986. The following word is probably a variant form of the well-known *mzrḥ*, here showing the pronunciation of the word */mizrō/*. Of line 9 not much is left. The next column lets us recognize some more words, but the translation given by FÉVRIER-FANTAR 1965: 54: 'they have named their family, which they have, and which is theirs (as) progeny, and (as) clan', for line 10 seems farfetched. Both *šlm* and ^{ɔ}*š lnm* might be explained as the nota relationis followed by the preposition *l* + suffix 3 pl.masc., however, the two following each other only connected by *w* is not to be expected. *šlm* is therefore better related to the root *šlm*, 'to be complete.' The last word in this line, *šp*^{c}*t*, is connected to the root *špḥ* from which Hebrew *mišpāḥā* is derived. The parallel to *zr*^{c} at least gives some plausability to this solution, note, however, also the existence of Hebrew *šif*^{c}*ā*, 'multitude [of men]' (ii Reg. 9: 17). The names in the following part of the text are mainly without problems. It is interesting to see a person named *lqy bn m*^{c}*grs*^{c}*n*, mentioned in line 23, who most probably is a relation, possibly the son, of *m*^{c}*grs*^{c}*n bn lqy* mentioned in Hr. Maktar N 57.

Hr. Maktar N 77

Bibliography: FÉVRIER & FANTAR 1965: 48; GARBINI 1986: 50; JONGELING 1999: 83.

Illustration: PICARD 1954: vol ii, pl. cxxii, Cb 1031 (photograph).

Text:
1) l^{ɔ}dn b^{c}l ḥmn k^{c} šm^{c}
2) qlm brkm b^{c}l^{ɔ} hmkt^{c}rm
3) ^{c}t r ^{c}ykn^{c} bn ^{ɔ}drb^{c}l w
4) brk bn s^{c}ldy^{ɔ} rb ^{c}ykn^{c}
5) k^{c} šm^{c} qlm brkm št
6) [

Translation:
1) To the lord Bal Amun, because he heard
2) their voice, blessed them, the citizens of Maktar
3) in the time of the officials Aykna, the son of Adirbal and
4) Barik, the son of Saldio, the president Aykna
5) because he heard their voice, blessed them, the year …

Remarks:
For the formula in the first four lines, cf. Hr. Maktar N 39. The fifth line seems a mistaken repetition of lines 1 and 2, or is part of another text. In case *št* should be explained as the

word for 'year', it then represents another way of dating than the one used in line 3.

Hr. Maktar N 112

Bibliography: VATTIONI 1995, 110-111; JONGELING 1999: 83.

Illustrations: FANTAR 1993, vol. ii, 403 (photograph).

Text:
1) l^{ɔ}dn b^{c}l ḥmn k^{c} šm^{c} qlm
2) brkm b^{c}l^{ɔ} hmkt^{c}rym ^{c}t r
3) yr^{c}t^{c}n bn mtnb^{c}l wbrkb^{c}l bn
4) b^{c}lšlk rb m^{c}syr bn
5) p^{c}šks^{c}t

Translation:
1) To the lord Bal Amun, because he listened to their voice,
2) blessed them, the citizens of Maktar, in the time of the officials
3) Iuratan, the son of Mutunbal and Barikbal, the son of
4) Balshillek, the president Masir, the son of
5) Pashkasat.

Remarks:
VATTIONI 1995 reads the name in line 3 as *šb^{c}t^{c}n*, but the reading *yr^{c}t^{c}n* cannot be doubted, cf. the other spellings in which this name appears: *ywr^{c}t^{c}n, y^{c}rḥtn.* In line 5, he reads a name *p^{c}šk^{c}k^{c}t*, however, the reading *p^{c}šks^{c}t*, for which cf. JONGELING 1999: 83 n. 11, seems more probable.

Hr. Meded

Hr. Meded N 21

Bibliography: GHAKI 1985: 174-175; FANTAR 1986: 26, 28, 1; VATTIONI 1994: 125, 21.

Illustration: FANTAR 1986, pl. vii, 2 (photograph).

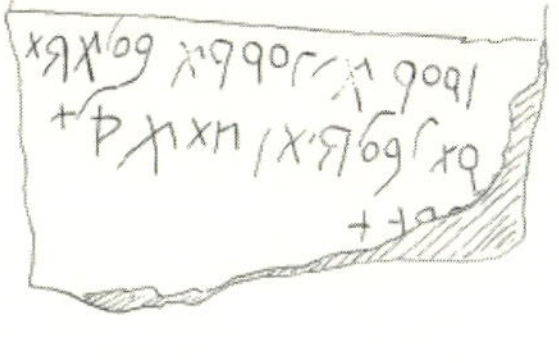

Text:
1) nd^{c}r ^{ɔ}š n^{c}dr^{ɔ} b^{c}l^{ɔ} hm
2) dm lb^{c}l ḥmn šm^{ɔ} qlm
3) brkm

Translation:
1) Votive offering which dedicated the citizens of Mi-
2) didi to Bal Amun, he heard their voice
3) blessed them.

Remarks:
There seems to be no room for the second *d*, expected in the Punic version of the name of Mididi, elsewhere attested as *hmddm.*

Hr. Medeine (Althiburus)

Hr. Medeine N 1

Bibliography: CLERMONT-GANNEAU 1900; FÉVRIER 1960: 170; VAN DEN BRANDEN 1973; *NSI* 55; *NP* 124; *KAI* 159.

Illustrations: LIDZBARSKI 1898, Taf. xvii (drawing).

Text:
1) l^{ɔ}dn b^{c}l ḥmn b^{ɔ}ltbrš ndr ^{ɔ}š ndr^{ɔ} ^{c}bdmlqrt knš bn kns^{ɔc}n [
2) m^{c}ryš bn tbrsn wšṭmn bn yksltn wmshb^{ɔ} bn lyl^{c}y wggm bn šsy^{c}t w
3) m^{ɔ}gm^{c} bn tbrsn wy^{c}smzgr bn sbg w^{ɔ}dnb^{c}l bn yll wgzr bn knzrmn wm^{c}ryš
4) bn lbw^{ɔ} wz^{c}lgm bn šṭw^{c}n wy^{c}st^{ɔ}n bn mshb^{ɔ} wḥbrnm hmzrḥ w
5) nsmrn bn^{ɔ}t w^{ɔ}yspn ^{c}lt mqdšm byrḥ krr št bll hzbḥ bn [ ] gṭ^{c}n b
6) špṭm mshb^{ɔ} bn yzrm w^{c}zrb^{c}l bn brk ws[d]ksln bn z^{c}zbl wmbyw hṣp^{ɔ} š
7) ^{c}l kmr ny^{c}ṭmn wkhn lb^{c}l ḥmn wrwsn bn ^{ɔ}rš k^{ɔ} šm^{c} qlm brkm
8) ^{ɔ}š h^{c}l^{ɔ} [k]^{ɔ} ^{c}lt ^{ɔ}w m[n]ḥt bmqdš
9) ^{ɔ}š [^{c}bd]mlk [šm] ndr^{ɔ}

Translation:
1) To the lord Bal Amun in Althiburus, a votive offering which vowed Abdmelqart *knš*, the son of Kansoan [and
2) Marish, the son of Tabarsan, and Shatman, the son of Yakaslatan and Massebo, the son of Lilay, and Gagam, the son of Shasiyat and

3) Mogama, the son of Tabarsan, and Yasmezgar, the son of Sibag, en Adonibal, the son of Yallul, and *gzr*, the son of *knzrmn*, and Marish,
4) the son of *lbwʾ*, and Zalgam, the son of *šṭwʿn*, and Yaston, the son of Massebo, and their colleagues of the assembly,
5) Nasmaran … over the sanctuaries, in the month Karar of the year of Bll, the sacrificer, the son of …
6) the suffetes Mashabo, the son of Yazram, and Azrubal, the son of Barik, and *Sdksln*, the son of *Zʿbl*, and *Mbyw*, the seer, who was
7) over the priests of Neitman, and priest for Bal Amun was Urusan, the son of Ariš, because he heard their voice and blessed them
8) the one who offers a holocaust here, or a *minḥa*-offering in the sanctuary
9) which … his vow.

Remarks:
Note that the last two lines are in another hand and probably a later addition to the text. *knš* in line 1 has been explained as a (cog)nomen, which seems not impossible as the name *knš* is attested in Punic 14 times (*CIS* i 417, 2070, 2549, 2652, 2700, 3963, 4281, 4354, 4521, 4556, 4561, 4745, 4881, 5098) and the name element occurs also in derivatives *knšʾ* (*CIS* i 2668, 5591), *knšy* (*CIS* i 5885, *Punica* xiii, 7), *knšyt* (*CIS* i 5823), *knšm* (*CIS* i 2247, 2555, 3876, 4145, 4503, 4522, 5019, 5272), and cf. also *kynš* (*CIS* i 4745). Note that *knšy* is also attested in Phoenician, cf. NAVEH 1966: 27-28. RÖLLIG, *KAI* 159 a.l., notes all possible explanations: relation with the personal names just mentioned, the possible reading *knz*, which can be explained as a personal name of Berber origin, cf. KNZ (*RIL* 125, 361 (?)), or (less likely) the supposition that *knš* might be an unknown title, as brought forward by e.g. CLERMONT-GANNEAU 1900. In line 2 *šṭmn* is perhaps to be compared to *šṭwʿn* in line 4. In line 3, COOKE 1903, sub 55, reads *wyʿṣmzgr*. In line 4, the reading *wḥbrnm hmzrḥ* was proposed by CLERMONT-GANNEAU. The first part of line 5 being of uncertain interpretation, COOKE 1903: 146, has supposed that *ʾyspn* might be a verbal form, yif. of the root *spn*. The explanation as a personal name seems more probable, however. In line 7 the personal name *wrwsn* has been read *wrwṣn* by several authors, cf. e.g. RÖLLIG, sub *KAI* 159. We follow COOKE 1903, sub *NSI* 59, because of the frequency of the ending */-san/* in Berber personal names. FÉVRIER 1960: 170, reads line 8-9: *8) ʾš hʿlʾ kʾ ʿltʾ wmnḥt bmqdš 9) ʾš ʿd mlk šm ndbʾ*, translating: 'They (the members of the *mizraḥ*), who have offered here (or: thus) his (i.e. the god's) holocaust and a *minḥā* in the sanctuary (and) who have offered spontaneously there a *molek* offering.' FÉVRIER 1955b: 53, notes that *mlk* here probably indicates an ordinary sacrifice. VAN DEN BRANDEN 1973, reads lines 8-9: 8) *ʾš ʿlʾ kʾ ʿlt ʾw mnḥt bmqdš* 9) *ʾš pʿ[l] mlk šm ndrʾ*, translating: 'and someone who has offered a holocaust in the sanctuary or an oblation, such a one has made the offering imposed by his vow.' In case *mlk* in line 9 indicates a molk-offering, it is more likely that three types of offerings are mentioned, *ʿlʾ*, *mnḥt* and *mlk*, as there is no indication that *mlk* may be used as a hyponym for any type of offering, and its meaning seems rather to be restricted to a human sacrifice or its substitute. The form *hʿlʾ* poses a problem. Both FÉVRIER and VAN DEN BRANDEN explained the form as a causative formation in the perfect. However, in Phoenician and Punic one expects a yiphil rather than a hiphil as in Hebrew.

Hr. Sidi Khalifat (Pheradi Maius)

Hr. Sidi Khalifat N 1

Bibliography: FÉVRIER 1959-1960: 64-66; HOFTIJZER 1963: 95-96; *Numidica* vi; *NP* 12.

Illustrations: SCHRÖDER 1869, Taf. xvii 1 (drawing).

Text:
1) ṭ^{c}n^{c} ^{ɔ}bn z ltpr
2) ^{c}t bt ^{c}wṭh ^{ɔ}ṣd
3) t š yst^{c}t^{c}n bn ms
4) ly^{c}n ^{c}št prmh
5) ^{c}w^{c} š^{c}nt [

Translation:
1) This stone was erected for Tafr-
2) at, the daughter of Aute, the freedwom-
3) an of Iastatan, the son of Mas-
4) lian, the wife of Primus
5) she lived years ….

Remarks:
ṣdt is probably the fem. counterpart of *ṣ(y)dn* attested in Sousse N 13, Ksiba Mraou N 2, Guelma N 8. *ṣdn* also occurs regularly in the expression *^{ɔ}š ṣdn* meaning 'freedman.' As this second construction is used both for males and females, it probably is a combination of the marker of relativity and the geographical name Sidon, 'the one belonging to Sidon', describing someone as a member of the group that formally traced their ancestry to one of the towns in the motherland Phoenicia.

Sousse

Sousse N 1

Bibliography: BERGER 1908; CHABOT, *Punica* xxii; *RÉS* 937.

Illustrations: BERGER 1908, pl. xliv (photograph).

Text:
1) ^{c}ṣm^{ɔ} ḥtmlqrt
2) bt grmlkt bn b^{c}lp/šls/k
3) bn ^{c}bd^{ɔ}š[mn] k̊ ^{ɔ}ḫ̊ ^{e}ṭm̊

Translation:
1) The bones of Otmelqart,
2) the daughter Germilkat the son of Balshillek,
3) the son of Abdeshmun ….

Remarks:
Most of the texts from Sousse were found written with ink on funerary urns. Forms of the word *^{c}ṣm* are mainly restricted to such texts. *k̊ ^{ɔ}ḫ̊ ^{e}ṭm̊* remains without explanation.

Teboursouk

Teboursouk N 5

Bibliography: FANTAR 1974: 403; GARBINI 1978: 7; GARBINI 1986: 56-57; AMADASI 2002: 116.

Illustrations: FANTAR 1974, pl. viii 18 (photograph).

Text:
1) bym nm wbrk ^{ɔ}š ṭ
2) yn^{ɔ} mtnt b/pd w^{c}my bn
3) kyn^{ɔ} š^{c}m^{ɔ} qlm tkn
4) lm ^{c}d mkprm

Translation:
1) On a pleasant and blessed day, on which has
2) erected as a gift *b/pdw^{c}my* son of
3) Kino, he heard his voice; may it be
4) for him as his expiation.

Remarks:
A problem is formed by *b/pdw^{c}my* in line 2. FANTAR explains the group of signs as two personal names: *b/pd* and *^{c}my*, partly because he sees a plur. suffix in the *-m* following *ql*. At the same time, in a note, he points to the use of *-m* as a sg. suffix. For the interpretation of the last line, cf. AMADASI 2002.

Tunisia OU

Tunisia OU N 2

Bibliography: HOFTIJZER 1963: 93f.; JONGELING 1984: 12; *NP* 9.

Illustrations: GESENIUS 1837, tab. 23, lix (drawing); HOFTIJZER 1963a, pl. xxix, 2 (photograph).

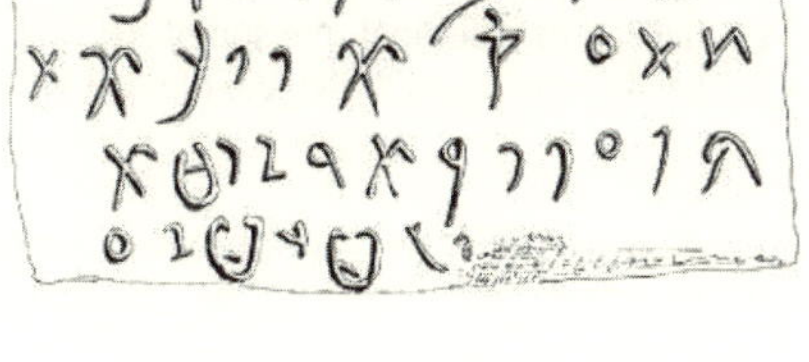

Text:

1) l^{ɔ}dn b^{c}l ḥmn k^{c}
2) šm^{c} ql^{ɔ} brk^{ɔ} m
3) h n^{c}dr r^{ɔ}dybṭ^{ɔ}
4) wṭẙ ṭy^{c}

Translation:

1) To the lord Bal Amun, because
2) he heard his voice, blessed him, wh-
3) at has dedicated Redemtus
4) and Titia.

Remarks:

The third sign in line 4 has been read as *k* by HOFTIJZER 1963, and although the upper part of *k* might look like this sign, the downward stroke is completely missing. We rather think that the sign may be an ill-formed *y*. LIDZBARSKI 1898 gives as his reading *ṭrṭy^{c}*, word of unknown meaning, but which might be *Tertia*, the wife of *Redemtus*. The signs in the lines 2 and 3, read *mht^{ɔ}nt*, 'gift' by HOFTIJZER 1963, are better transcribed *mh n^{c}dr*, to be explained as *mh*, relative pronoun, cf. the remark sub Hr. Djerou N1, and a form of the root *ndr*, probably 3 sg. m. perf. qal., since line 4 seems to have been added, as an afterthought (and in a different hand?), in the lower border of the text region.

Tunisia OU N 7

Bibliography: CHABOT, *Punica* xvii, 3; MENDLESON 2003: 37; *NP* 112.

Illustrations: MENDLESON 2003, NPu2 (photograph).

Text:

1) l^{ɔ}dn lb^{c}l ndr ^{ɔ}š ndr
2) g^{c}y y^{ɔ}ly ^{ɔ}rš
3) bn ^{ɔ}dnb^{c}l bn ^{ɔ}drb^{c}l
4) kh šm^{c} ql^{ɔ} brk^{ɔ}

Translation:

1) To the lord to Bal votive offering, which dedicated
2) Gaius Iulius Arish,
3) the son of Adonibal, the son of Adirbal,
4) because he heard his voice, blessed him.

Remarks:

Note that the dedicant was probably named *^{ɔ}rš bn ^{ɔ}dnb^{c}l bn ^{ɔ}drb^{c}l* in the traditional Punic way, but that he took on two Latin names to give the impression of the Roman *tria nomina*.

Tunisia OU N 13

Bibliography: CHABOT, *Punica* xvii, 9; MENDLESON 2003: 38.

Illustrations: MENDLESON 2003, NPu7 (photograph).

Text:

1) l^{ɔ}dn lb^{c}l ḥmn ndr š ypk
2) bt tz^{c}bš šm^{c}
3) ql^{ɔ} br̊k^{ɔ}

Translation:

1) To the lord Bal Amun, vow of Ifak,
2) the daughter of Tazabash, he heard
3) her voice, blessed her.

Remarks:

Until now *šypk* has been taken to be a personal name preceded by a verbal form. However, it seems more attractive to suppose *ndr* is the noun 'vow', followed by the nota relationis. *ypk* remains as a name of unknown origin, but probably a member of the large group of Berber names starting with *y-*. CHABOT, sub *Punica* xvii, 9, reads *brk^{ɔ}* in line 3, although MENDLESON 2003: 38, reads *b[r]k^{ɔ}*, yet on the photograph a small rest of *r* may still be discerned.

ALGERIA

Ain el-Kebch

Ain el-Kebch N 1

Bibliography: CHABOT, *Punica* xxv, 4; MARCY 1936: 86-90; ÁLVAREZ DELGADO 1964: 214-219; *RIL* 451.

Illustration: MARCY 1936, pl. 5; *RIL* sub no 451 (drawing).

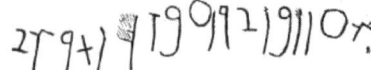

Text:
1) z̊ ᶜnn bn yrnᶜbt h̊ nmrsy

Libyan text:
1) ZNN RÇH
2) W IRNBT
3) NMRSH
4) MSWH

Translation:
1) Zanan, son of Yarnabat, the Namarsite.

Remarks:
ÁLVAREZ DELGADO 1964: 217 explains the name *zᶜnn* as a participle of the Semitic root *šnn*, which is highly improbable, even though MARCY 1936 reads the first sign of the name as *š* and CHABOT, *Punica* a.l., accepts this reading as a possibility. The Libyan text, however, seems to settle the problem. In the reading of RÇH in the Libyan text we follow Chabot, RIL a.l., although his drawing clearly shows RNH.

Arseu

Arseu N 2

Bibliography: JONGELING 1984: 162; *NP* 79.

Illustration: JUDAS 1860-1861, pl. 10, xxi (drawing); cf. DELLA MARMORA 1854: 186 (drawing of the complete stone).

Text:
1) ndr ᵓš nd[r] gṭm yšmᵓᵓ qlᵓ

Translation:
1) Votive offering, which *gṭm* vowed, may he hear his voice.

Remarks:
Note the spelling *yšmᵓᵓ* for */yišmō/*. One *ᵓ* is best explained as an incorrect historical spelling of the root *šmᵓ* instead of *šmᶜ*, while the other indicates the pronunciation of the ending. The *y* may also be the last sign of the name of the dedicant, of course, but names ending in *-y* are not frequent. Instead of *t*, the reading *pw* is also possible.

Cherchel

Cherchel N 1

Bibliography: LIDZBARSKI 1898: 438, 3 Dd1; FEVRIER 1952a; *NSI* 56; *NP* 130.

Illustration: EUTING 1876; LIDZBARSKI 1898, Taf. xix 2 (drawing).

Text:
1) skr drᵓ lᵓšt nᶜmt mhrt ṭnᵓ t hmnṣbt b/d/ršbᶜt
2) ᶜbdᵓšmn bn ᶜzrbᶜl lᵓmm ltᶜwnt ᵓḥr ᵓš pᶜl ṣywᶜn
3) lhḥym hᵓš šlᵓ ᶜzrbᶜl hyld/b/r šd/b/rhd/b/rbᶜl bᶜn šqln
4) ᵓmᵓ lšb/d/rt šnt ḥmšm d/b/rᵓyḥšd/b/rd/b/r lṭhrt nktbt
5) wnšmrᵓ d/b/rᵓtmyqnᵓ wᵓydrᵓ lymb/d/rᵓ mᶜšd/b/rt
6) kmšlm [ ] ᶜlᵓ hnškbt bt šmnm št

Translation:
1) As a memorial of her family for a pleasant and quick woman has erected the … stele
2) Abdeshmun, the son of Azrubal for his mother, for Tawnat, after made the tomb monument
3) for the 'living', her husband Azrubal, the … Shaqlan
4) His mother, to serve fifty years …. prescribed purity
5) …
6) … who passed away at the age of eighty years.

Remarks:
mhrt was read as *mhbt*, a pual participle of the root *ᵓhb* by FÉVRIER 1952a, less acceptable, because one expects the qal passive participle when the meaning "loved' is needed. *b/d/ršbᶜt* in line 1 is most probably an adjective explaining the preceding *mnṣbt*. One might compare Arabic *rasaba* 'to sink.' The traditional explanation as 'Rash, the daughter of …' seems less probable, as one expects a man to be the one who erected an important monument like this. FÉVRIER 1952a proposed to read *bšbᶜt*, 'with sumptuosity', which is

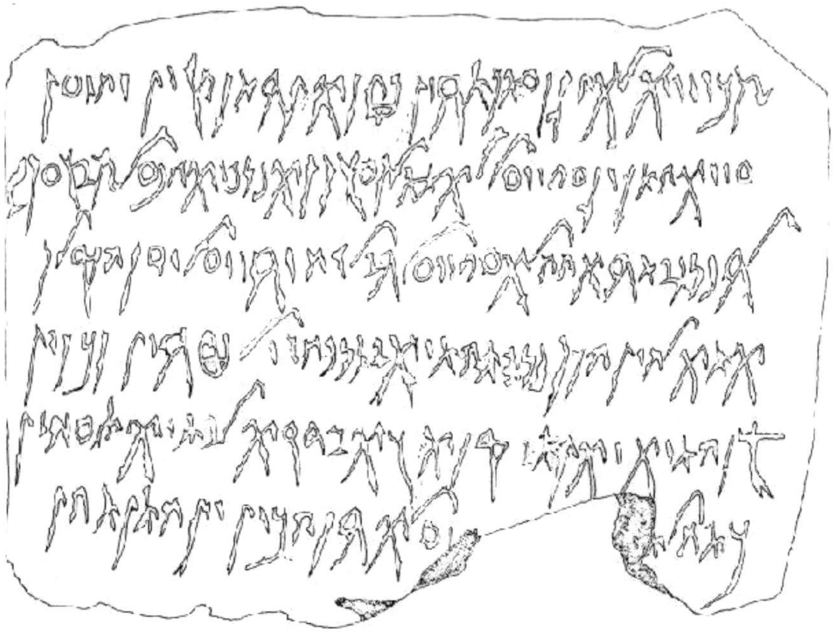

Cherchel N 1

doubtful. *lhḥym* brings to mind the designation of the cemetery as *byt ḥym* in Hebrew, or does it rather mean 'while still alive.' We read the last word in line 2 as *ṣywʿn,* to be compared to Hebrew *ṣywʿn,* as already notedby COOKE *NSI* a.l. *bʿn,* the word preceding *šqln* in line 3 is probably not to be explained as a deviating spelling of *bn,* cf. *bn* in line 2. Could it be a form of the root *bny*: 'Shaqlan built (it)'? In line 4 *lšb/d/rt* may be interpreted as *lšrt,* 'to serve,' but this remains uncertain. In the same line, the last two words, *ṭhrt nktbt,* may very well be translated, with FÉVRIER 1952a, as 'the prescribed purity', but the explanation of the preceding signs *d/b/rʾyḥšd/ b/rd/b/r l* as *bʾyḥzr dl,* the prep. *b,* followed by *ʾyḥzr,* yiphil inf. of *ḥzr,* 'to take care', and the preposition *dl* seems less attractive. The first word of line 5 may very well be read *wnšmrʾ.* FÉVRIER 1952a translates 'she took care.' *qnʾ* he translates as 'the creator', which leaves him with an unexplained word, *b/d/rʾtmy,* in between. Whether this is correctly explained as the preposition *b,* followed by the inf. yiph.of *tmʾ,* 'to pray', 'to invoke', is doubtful. The same holds true for his reading and explanation of the following *wʾydr ʾlym* as *w* followed by the inf. piel of *ʾdr,* 'to magnify.' The translation of *ʾlym* with 'god' is, of course, possible. However, the division of words being unclear, it remains highly uncertain. The reading of the next word as *bʾmʿšrt,* 'in happiness', or 'in justice', is also uncertain, and the explanation of this word as the prep. *b* followed by the well-known *mʿšrt,* which does not take into account the ʾ at the beginning, is also very doubtful. In line 6, the last few words probably contain the nifal of *škb,* which in Hebrew means 'to lie down', 'to fall', and, according to the context, may be used here in the sense of 'to pass away.'

Cherchel N 2

Bibliography: LIDZBARSKI 1898: 439, 3 Dd2; COOKE 1903: 148-150; DUSSAUD 1924: cxlvi; FÉVRIER 1951: 138-150; VAN DEN BRANDEN

1974: 143-145; GARBINI 1974b: 33; ROSCHINSKY 1979; GARBINI 1986: 67; *NSI* 57; *KAI* 161.

Illustrations: LIDZBARSKI 1898, Taf. xvi 4; *KAI* Taf. xxviii (photograph).

Text:

1) myqdš qnᵓm ḥy ḥym mkwsn mlk [m]šlyym
2) hmyll myšr ᵓrṣt rbt mmlkᵓt ḥšb nᶜm
3) lᵓ ṭnᵓ t hmᵓš st bmbw ᵓḥdr dl ᵓqbrᵓ yᶜzm
4) bn yzggsn bn bgᵓt bn msnsn myqm ᵓlm
5) skr k̊ bd ᶜl gm ᵓdr tmᵓ ᵓdrᵓ kmᵓ t bnm
6) w t ᵓkhnym ᵓš ᶜl mrm klᵓ nᶜsp lᵓ lmḥ[ ]
7) tbnm ᶜlm ᶜkbrt [ ] blhbᶜt zᵓ[
8) wšᶜwtm bd bᶜl [ ]lb̊ n̊ [ ]l̊ m̊ ᵓ̊ hšmᵓ̊ [
9) rbᵓ smᵓ bkl ḥwt bnᵓ bmṭᶜ ᵓ[
10) rṣᵓt hmḥṣrt šlᵓ t bnm rb [
11) pᶜl ᵓrš bn ᶜbdᵓ b[n

Translation:

1) Shrine of the most living person, Makusan, the king of the Massylians,
2) the lamented one, who did justice to many countries, benevolent king;
3) erected for him this statue in the entrance of the chamber with the tomb Yazam
4) the son of Yuzgagsan the son of Bogut the son of Masinissan, the one who makes the god stand;
5) an honourable memorial with enormous majesty, enormous perfection, ... the builders
6) and the priests that were over the
7) ... 10)
11) made (it) Arish, the son of Abdo, the son of ...

Remarks:

myll in line 2 has been variously explained, as a part. of the pu. of *yll*, the lamented one, cf. COOKE 1903: 149, FÉVRIER 1951: 142, less probable seems the derivation from the root *hll*. FÉVRIER ibid., RÖLLIG, sub *KAI* 161, combine *rbt* with the following *mmlkt*, 'lord of kings', but the sg. cstr. m. of *rb* is *rb*, not *rbt*, while the plural, also masculine, may be *rbt*, as in *KAI* 101, line 2, *rbt mᵓt*, compared to *rb mᵓt* ibid. line 3. Therefore the combination with the preceding *ᵓrṣt* is more probable, as is done already by e.g. BERGER 1888: 40. *ḥšb nᶜm* as a title gives the impression of being a translation from some Latin (or Greek) phrase. The expression *myqm ᵓlm* has been debated by many authorities, cf. the discussion in *DNWSI*, sub *qwm*$_1$ (pp. 1002-1003). *gm* in line 5 is explained by FÉVRIER 1951: 143-144, 148, as a derivation from the root *gmm* and meaning 'totality', 'majesty.' The interpretation is accepted e.g. RÖLLIG, sub *KAI* 161, but with some reserve. The last word of this line is read *ᵓtrnm* by FÉVRIER, ibid.: 143-144, and explained as the pl. of *trn*, preceded by the article, compared to Hebrew *toren*, 'mast, pole.' RÖLLIG, sub *KAI* 161, accepts this reading and tentatively translates with FÉVRIER: 'shaft of a column.' However, the fact that in the next line the word *khnym*, whatever its meaning, is preceded by the preposition, *t*, makes it most probable that the *t* in *ᵓtrnm* should be explained in the same way. This may be done by supposing that the *ᵓ* is the last sign of the preceding word, *kmᵓ*, which may be for */kəmō/*. This leaves us with a word that may be read as *rnm*, but the reading *bnm* is equally possible. The meaning of the word group, therefore, is best interpreted as 'the builders and the priests.' The same reading was adopted by LIDZBARSKI 1898: 439, without explanation, and by ROSCHINSKY 1979: 112, 115, but he combines *tbnm*, 'building', which seems less probable. The same word perhaps also at the beginning of line 7 and in line 10. The lines 7 to 10 remain without acceptable interpretation.

Constantine

Constantine N 7

Bibliography: CHABOT, *Punica* xviii/i 20; SCHRÖDER 1869: 268; *NP* 97.

Illustration: SCHRÖDER 1869, Taf. xvi 5 (drawing).

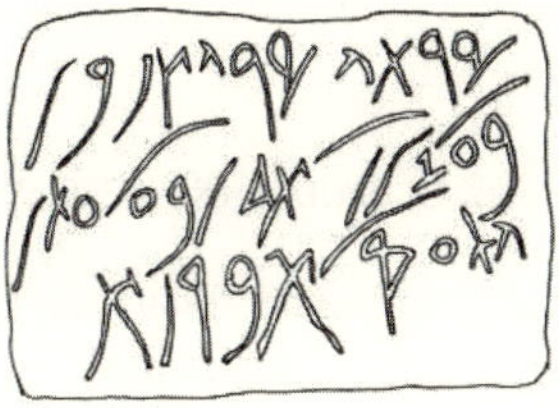

Text:
1) ndr ᵓš ndr šṣp bn
2) bᶜlytn lᵓdn bᶜl ᶜmn
3) šmᶜ qlᵓ brkᵓ

Translation:
1) Votive offering which dedicated Šaṣap, the son of
2) Balyaton to the lord to Bal Amun, he hea[r]d
3) his voice, blessed him.

Constantine N 10

Bibliography: SCHRÖDER 1869: 268; CHABOT, *Punica* xviii/i 28; *NP* 95.

Illustration: SCHRÖDER 1869, Taf. xvi 2 (drawing).

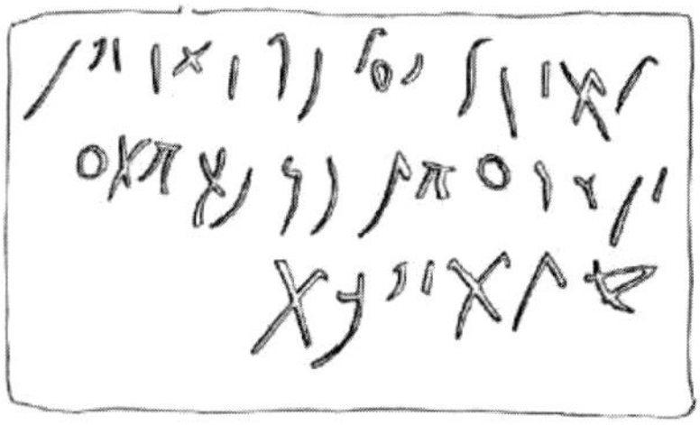

Text:
1) lᵓdn lbᶜl ḥmn brk
2) bn bdᶜštrt kᵓ šmᶜ
3) qlᵓ brkᵓ

Translation:
1) To the lord, to Bal Amun, Barik,
2) the son of Bodaštart, because he heard
3) his voice, blessed him.

Remarks:
The reading of *brk* at the end of the first line is confirmed by the *k* as written in *kᵓ* in line 2.

Constantine N 23

Bibliography: SCHRÖDER 1869: 269; *NP* 102.

Illustration: SCHRÖDER 1869, Taf. xvi 3 (drawing).

Text:
1) ḥn ḥn
2) ndr ᵓš ndr ḥnbᶜl
3) bn ᵓdnbl lᵓdn lbᶜl šmᶜ qlᵓ

Translation:
1) Grace, grace
2) Votive offering which dedicated Annobal,
3) the son of Adonibal to the lord to Bal, he heard his voice.

Remarks:
The words *ḥn ḥn* are written in the upper section of the stele where frequently images of a religious nature are to be found.

Constantine N 28

Bibliography: LIDZBARSKI 1898, 434 d 12; CHABOT, *Punica* xviii/ii 7; *RÉS* 1565; *SPC* 91.

Illustration: LIDZBARSKI 1898, Taf. xv 14 (drawing); *SPC* 91 (photograph).

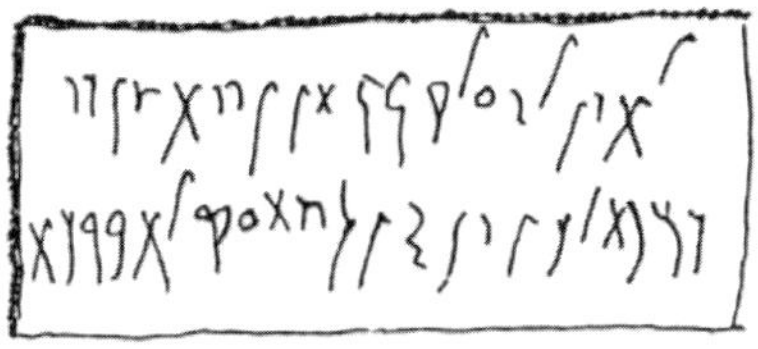

Text:
1) lᵓdn lbᶜl ḥmn ndr ᵓš ndr
2) ḥmlkt bn ytn šmᶜ qlᵓ brkᵓ

Translation:
1) To the lord to Bal Amun, votive offering which dedicated
2) Imilco, the son of Yaton, he heard his voice, blessed him.

Constantine N 42

Bibliography: CHABOT, *Punica* xviii/ii 82; *SPC* 44.

Illustration: SPC 44 (photograph).
Text:
1) lᵓdn lbᶜl ḥmn wltn[t]
2) pᶜn bᶜl ᵓš ndr ᵓd̊ rbᶜl bn
3) ᶜbdmlqrt bn ᶜqptn
4) k šmᶜ qlᵓ brkᵓ

Translation:
1) To the lord to Bal Amun and to Tinnit
2) Fane Bal, which dedicated Adirbal, the son of
3) Abdmelqart, the son of Aqfatan,
4) because he headr his voice, blessed him.

Constantine N 50

Bibliography: FÉVRIER 1953a: 161-171; VAN DEN BRANDEN 1972: 195-200 (cf. GARBINI 1974: 32); FERRON-AUBET 1974: 153 n. 198; JONGELING 1989: 127-134; *KAI* 162.

Illustrations: FEVRIER 1953a, pl. i; *KAI*, Taf. xxix, 162 (photograph).

Text:
1) lgdᵓ ᵓdn rzn bᶜl ḥmn pl ᶜbdkšr bl
2) b̊ ᶜt tᶜmt bṣmḥ t[ ]sft b̊ šᵓr̊ m
3) lᵓlm nᶜmm ẘ lmḥb̊ tᵓ lqd̊ št
4) ᵓp ᵓtᵓ ᵓtplt ᶜb̊ r̊ tm nn lᵓ b̊ tr̊ b̊ t
5) š qlt thlqnᵓt b̊ nm b̊ tt ᵓš
6) lkn lᵓ tᶜmt ᵓd̊ r̊ t

Translation:
1) To Gado, the lord, prince of Bal Amun, made (it) Abdkasher, citizen of
2) Bat Tamet …
3) to the pleasant gods, and to … for the holiness
4) …
5) …
6) to be for him a mighty …

Remarks:
GARBINI 1974 rejects the translations of VAN DEN BRANDEN 1972 and FERRON-AUBET 19-74 as untenable. In case the reading and translation of the first line are more or less correct, it is noteworthy that the ᶜ in *bᶜl* (*ḥmn*) is historically correct, while in *pl* and *bl* it is left out, in accordance with the contemporary pronunciation, no doubt. Possibly there was a greater need to use the historical spelling in the name of the god Bal Amun than in other words. The rest of the inscription also deviates from the customary formulae and until now has defied any credible interpretation.

Constantine N 54

Bibliography: FEVRIER 1955-1956: 155; *EH* 21.

Illustration: EH pl. vi D (photograph).

Text:
1) lbᶜl [w]ltnt pᶜnᵓ bᶜl wd̊ hrnm̊
2) ndr ᵓlᵉ š/ᵓ/m bn klbᵓ bšt šrm wšlm
3) tbrkyᵓ m̊ ṣyᵓ ᶜl t̊ t̊ ᶜ wm̊ bdnm

Translation:
1) To Bal and to Tinnit Fane Bal and *dhrnm*
2) vow of Olash, the son of Kalbo, in the year of *šrm* and Shallum
3) may you bless him …

Remarks:
dhrnm is probably not the name of a deity, however, the interpretation of FÉVRIER 1955-1956: 155: *dhrnm* = *dr*, 'family' + suff. 3 pl., 'their family' standing for 'their offspring' is also not easily accepted. Because *dhrnm* is not preceded by the preposition *l*, the word does not seem to be on the same level as *lbᶜl [w]ltnt*. In Constantine N 55 an unexplained *dᶜlhrm* occurs, which is probably realetd to *dhrnm*. The name *ᵓlᵉš/ᵓ/m*, if read as *ᵓlᵉš*, might be related to *ᵓlšᵓ* (*CIS* 3546). For *ᵓlšᵓ* and related names, see BENZ 1972: 379, who remarks upon the name element *ᶜlš*, noting that it is unexplained and compares it to the well-known *Elissa*. *tbrkyᵓ* is best explained as a impf. pl. rather than a sg. One may envisage a development /*tabrukūhū*/ > /*tabrukūyū*/, cf. *PPG* §129. If indeed *bšt šrm wšlm* is meant to indicate a date, one may compare several coins from Constantine which are inscribed with two names in Neo-Punic script, as is correctly remarked by BERTHIER & CHARLIER, *EH* a.l.

Guelma

Guelma N 1

Bibliography: CHABOT, *Punica* xi, 1; JONGELING 2003: 123; *NP* 22.

Illustration: LIDZBARSKI 1898, Taf. xviii 7 (drawing).

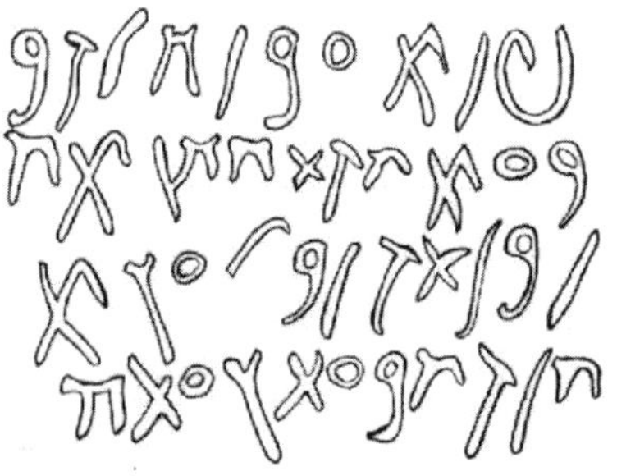

Text:
1) ṭn^{ɔ} ^{c}bn z ltb
2) b^{c} ^{ɔ}štm š zẘ^{ɔ}s
3) n bn mtnbl ^{c}w^{ɔ}
4) šnt šb^{c}m w^{c}mš

Translation:
1) This stone was erected for Tabi-
2) ba, wife of Zuos-
3) an, son of Mutunbal, she lived
4) 75 years

Remarks:
Note the construction with a proleptic suffix in line 2: *^{ɔ}štm š* + PN. *zw^{ɔ}sn* is a Libyan name of the type ending in */-san/*, also attested elsewhere. The reading *šb^{c}m* in line 3 is based upon the drawing published by JUDAS and reprinted e.g. by LIDZBARSKI. CHABOT, in *Punica*, read *s*, which according to the drawing is also possible of course, but less probable.

Guelma N 3

Bibliography: CHABOT, *Punica* iii, xi, 3; JONGELING 2003: 123-124; *NP* 24; *NSI* 58; *KAI* 169.

Illustration: LIDZBARSKI 1898, Taf. xviii 6 (drawing).

Text:
1) ^{c}bn z ṭ^{c}n^{c} lš
2) blt bt m^{c}ll ^{c}w
3) ^{c} š^{c}nt ^{ɔ}s
4) rm w^{c}mš ^{ɔ}
5) štm šypt^{c}n bn
6) kndy^{c}l

Translation:
1) This stone was ereceted for Shi-
2) bbult, daughter of Malal, she live-
3) d years twen-
4) ty and five, wi-
5) fe of Ieptan, son of
6) Kinidial

Remarks:
CHABOT in *Punica* iii (1916) reads in lines 4-5: *^{ɔ}št mšykt^{c}n*, 'wife of Mašiktan', cf. the earlier reading by SCHRÖDER 1869: *^{ɔ}št mšykt^{c}ḥ*. *Ieptan* is a well-known name and the construction with a proleptic suffix is also attested in Guelma N 1 (*^{ɔ}štm šzẘ^{ɔ}sn*). COOKE in *NSI* 58 still retains the older reading *^{ɔ}šrm* instead of *^{ɔ}srm*, CHABOT, in *Punica* iii, is, however, quite clear when he remarks that the reading *^{ɔ}šrm* is impossible. The name *šblt* is also attested in Punic (*CIS* 5948) and explained as Semitic by e.g. HALFF 1963-1964: 144, RÖLLIG, sub *KAI* 92, BENZ 1972: 413, translating it as 'ear (of corn)'. The frequent attestation of *Spicula* (also meaning 'ear (of corn)') as a personal name in Latin inscriptions from North Africa favours this explanation. The reading of the last name is certain, although the drawing shows *b* instead of *k*.

Guelma N 4

Bibliography: CHABOT, *Punica* xi, 4; JONGELING 2003: 124; *NP* 25.

Illustration: SCHRÖDER 1869, Taf. xvii 2 (drawing).

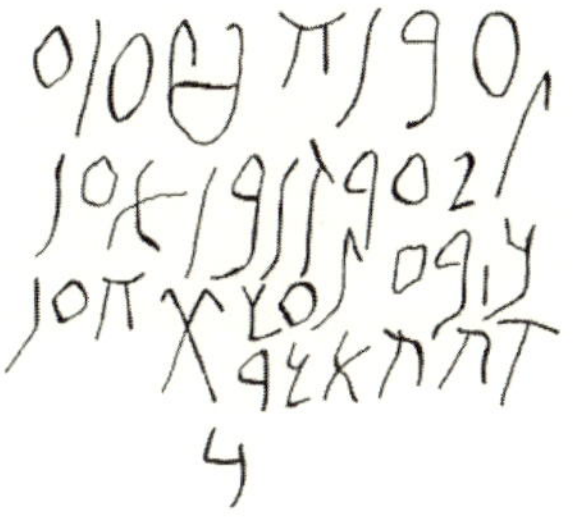

Text:
1) ^{c}bn z ṭ^{c}n^{c}
2) ly^{c}rtn bn m^{c}n
3) kl̊ ^{c}t ^{c}w$^{\circ}$ š^{c}n
4) t ššm wd

Translation:
1) This stone was erected
2) for Yartan, son of Man-
3) kalat, he lived year-
4) s sixty and one

Remarks:
LEVY, SCHRÖDER and LIDZBARSKI transcribed *m^{c}nkb^{c}l*, which is unacceptable, according to CHABOT, who reads *m^{c}nkl̊^{c}t*, or, eventually, *m^{c}nkr̊^{c}n*. LEVY and SCHRÖDER explained *wd* in the last line as *w* followed by *d* to express the number 'four', an ingeneous but unnecessary explanation.

Guelma N 9

Bibliography: CHABOT, *Punica* xi, 9; JONGELING 2003: 126; *NP* 32; *KAI* 168.

Illustration: SCHRÖDER 1869, Taf. xvii 12 (drawing).

Text:
1) g^{c}y yl m
2) nwl$^{\circ}$ ṭn
3) ^{c} l$^{\circ}$ ^{c}bn
4) n^{c}š^{c}y$^{\circ}$
5) brkt bt
6) rg^{c}ṭ$^{\circ}$

Translation:
1) Gaius Julius Ma-
2) nulus. Erect-
3) ed for him the stone
4) presented it
5) Berict, daughter of
6) Rogatus

Remarks:
SCHRÖDER 1869: 270 n. 3, translates *^{c}bn n^{c}š^{c}y$^{\circ}$* as 'den angelobten Stein.' We do not follow CHABOT's reading, *Punica* xi 9, and read *n^{c}š^{c}y$^{\circ}$* instead of *n^{c}s^{c}y$^{\circ}$*. Forms of *nš$^{\circ}$* are attested elsewhere in these texts and we don't have to search for a family relation in this word. However, should our translation be correct, one must assume that the 3rd person perf. fem. had lost its concluding *t* even when a suffix followed. When *yl* is correctly explained as an indication of the Latin name *Iulius*, it is an abnormal spelling, as one would expect *yly*, which is not attested, or *ywly*, which is attested several times in Neo-Punic texts, or even *ywl$^{\circ}$y*, attested once. One might suppose that *yl* is an abbreviation of the name Iulius, as it is attested in Latin inscriptions, but this would be the only example of a loan of this type in Phoenico-Punic (cf. however Rome N 1). For the name *Berict*, cf. also the remark sub Sirte LP12.

Guelma N 19

Bibliography: CHABOT, *Punica* xi, 19; AMADASI 2002: 117; JONGELING 2003: 130; *NP* 18.

Illustration: SCHRÖDER 1869, Taf. xv 5; LIDZBARSKI 1898, Taf. xvi 8 (drawing).

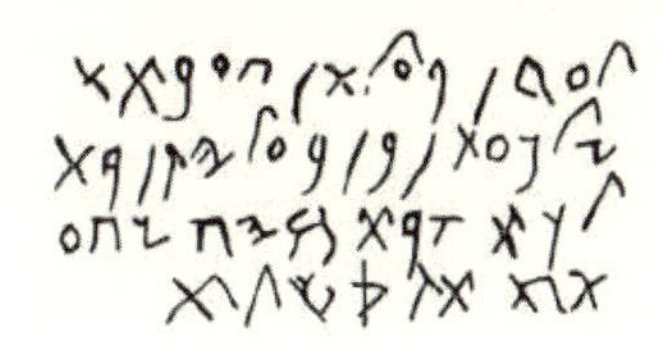

Text:
1) l^{c}dn b^{c}l mn z^{c}b^{ɔ} m
2) ylk^{c}tn bn b^{c}lytn bm
3) lk ^{ɔ}šrm hyš wš^{c}
4) m^{ɔ} ^{ɔ}t qwl^{ɔ}

Translation:
1) For the lord Bal Amun, sacrificed M-
2) ilkaton, son of Baliton, as a hzrm m-
3) olk-offering of a male, and he hear-
4) d his voice

Remarks:
The expression *bmlk hšrm ^{ɔ}š* occurs several times in the inscriptions from Guelma, and also elsewhere. Although the spelling differs, it is difficult to explain the last element *^{ɔ}š* or *^{ɔ}št* other than as 'man' or 'woman', while the meaning of *mlk* almost certainly indicate some type of sacrifice, which means that steles with texts containing these words were erected to commemorate a human sacrifice. The second word in this expression *^{ɔ}šrm / hzrm* remains without convincing explanation.

Guelma N 22

Bibliography: CHABOT, *Punica* xi, 22; ROSCHINSKI 1988: 618; AMADASI 2002: 117; JONGELING 2003: 131; *NP* 21; *KAI* 167.

Illustrations: LIDZBARSKI 1898, Taf. xviii 2 (drawing).

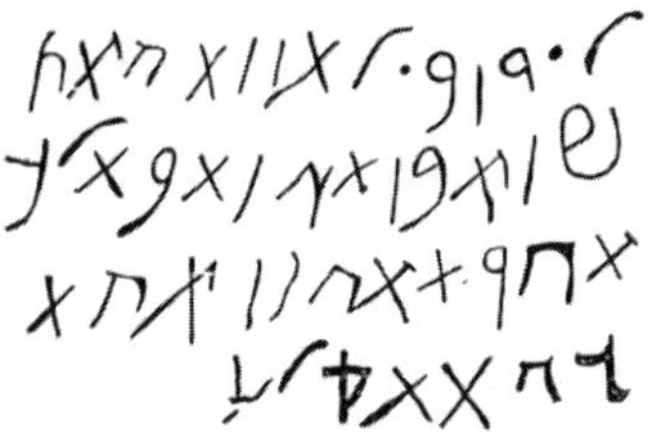

Text:
1) l^{c}dn b^{c}l mn n^{ɔ}š^{ɔ} pn
2) ṭn^{ɔ} bn mg̊nm bmlk
3) ^{ɔ}šrm ^{ɔ}št n^{ɔ}š^{ɔ}
4) wšm^{ɔ} ql^{ɔ}

Translation:
1) For the lord Bal Amun presented Fon-
2) tanus son of Magonim as a *hšrm* molk-offering,
3) of a female, he presented it
4) and he heard his voice

Remarks:
According to the drawing presented a.o. by LIDZBARSKI 1898, the reading *ql^{ɔ}* is possible, and this is the reading accepted by AMADASI 2002. Other editions gave the less probable *qly*.

Hr. Bou Atfan

Hr. Bou Atfan N 2

Bibliography: CHABOT, *Punica* x, 2.

Text:
1) ^{ɔ}bn ^{ɔ}š ṭ^{c}n^{ɔ}
2) lbdmlqrt bn
3) lbn ḥ̆ ym ḥw^{ɔ}
4) šb^{c}m wḥmš

Translation:
1) Stone that was erected
2) for Bodmelqart, the son of
3) Laban, his life he lived
4) seventy five.

Remarks:
CHABOT, sub *Punica* x 2, notes that the expression *ḥym ḥw^{ɔ}* is unexpected, while the absence of *šn(^{c})t* is also problematic. One wonders whether the stonemason wrote *ḥw^{ɔ} ḥw^{ɔ}* instead of *ḥw^{ɔ} šnt*, thus writing the correct number of characters and not bothering to correct the text. On the practice to count the number of characters in a text as a control procedure, cf. e.g. JONGELING 1996a. However, *ḥym* may easily be explained as the pl. of *ḥy*, 'life', as in Hebrew, or it may be the pl. cstr. followed by the suff. 3 sg. m.

Kef Bezioun

Kef Bezioun N 1

Bibliography: CHABOT, *Punica* vi, 1; FÉVRIER 1958-1959: 25-29; HORN-RÜGER 1979: 578; *KAI* 171.

Illustrations: HORN-RÜGER: 579, Taf. 106, 1 (photograph).

Text:
1) ṭn^{ɔ} ^{c}bn z ls^{ɔ}lwl
2) bt brkb^{c}l ^{ɔ}štm šb^{c}l
3) yn bn l^{c}by^{ɔ} ḥw^{ɔ} šnt
4) šb^{c}m hnkt n^{c}bn^{c}

Translation:
1) This stone was erected for Solul,
2) the daughter of Barikbal, the wife of Bal-
3) in, the son of Labio; she lived years
4) seventy; she was buried here.

Remarks:
The name *l^{c}by^{ɔ}* has been explained as a rendition of a Latin name (e.g. RÖLLIG in *KAI*, sub 171, *Labeo* (cf. *CIL* viii 7040); JONGELING 1984: 179: *Labbaeus* (cf. *CIL* viii 532)). The editor of Kef Bezioun N 1 in HORN-RÜGER 1979: 578, supposes a relation with *lby*, which he explains as Semitic, meaning 'lion', cf. however BENZ 1972: 337-338, who supposes *lby* to be an ethnic name 'Libyan. ' If correct, one might suppose two different names, as the ethnicon *Libyan* most probably had a palatal vowel in the first syllable and *l^{c}by^{ɔ}* in this text is vocalized with */a/* in this syllable. Both RÖLLIG, *KAI* a.l. and sub 136, and the editor in HORN-RÜGER 1979: 578, suppose the meaning 'dead body' for the enigmatic *hnkt* which however, is better explained as an adverb 'here', cf. HARTMANN and HOFTIJZER 1971. The verb *^{c}bn*, not attested outside Punic as far as we know, must, according to the context, mean something like 'to inter.' It is used parallel to forms of the verb *qbr* in expressions like *hnkt ^{c}bnt tḥt ^{ɔ}bn st qbrt*, 'here she was interred under this stone, she was buried.'

Kef Bezioun N 2

Bibliography: CHABOT, *Punica* vi, 2; FÉVRIER 1958-1959: 25-29.

Text:
1) ṭn^{ɔ} ^{c}bn z
2) lm^{c}qryn^{ɔ}
3) bn b^{c}lyn ^{c}w^{ɔ} š
4) ^{c}nt ^{c}srm wšb^{c} hnkt
5) n^{c}bn

Translation:
1) This stone was erected
2) for Macrinus,
3) the son of Balin, he lived ye-
4) ars twenty-seven; here
5) he was buried.

Remarks:
Macrinus may have been the son of *Balin* and his wife *Solul*, mentioned in Kef Bezioun N 1; for the name, cf. the remark sub Holt N 1.

Ksiba Mraou

Ksiba Mraou N 1

Bibliography: CHABOT, *Punica* xiv, 1.

Text:
1) ^{c}bn ^{ɔ}š ṭn^{ɔ} lšblt ^{ɔ}št gwm
2) z^{c}l ḥw^{ɔ} šnt ^{ɔ}rb^{c}m ṭy
3) n^{ɔ} l^{ɔ} gwmz^{c}l h^{ɔ}š šl^{ɔ}

Translation:
1) Stone that was erected for Shibbult, the wife of Gum-
2) zal, she lived forty years; ere-
3) cted it for her Gumzal her husband.

Remarks:
For the name *šblt*, cf. the remark sub Guelma N 3.

Ksiba Mraou N 3

Bibliography: CHABOT, *Punica* xiv, 3.

Text:
1) ^{ɔ}bn ^{ɔ}š ṭ^{c}n^{c} lsys^{ɔ}y
2) bt qwynṭ^{ɔ} ^{c}šwy ^{c}w^{c}
3) š^{c}nwt šmnm wḥmš
4) ^{ɔ}n b^{ɔ}mqm s̊t n^{c}s̊p^{ɔ} ^{c}ṣ
5) my^{c} bḥrṣ [ ]y^{ɔ}

Translation:
1) Stone that was erected for Sisoi,
2) the daughter of Quintus …, she lived
3) eighty-five years;
4) behold (?) to (?) this place were gathered her b-
5) ones in the earth (?)

Remarks:
The second part of this text is peculiar, but the

words *mqm*, *nʿs̊pʾ*, and *ʿṣmyʿ* seem to be without much doubt, the first and third ones also recognized as such by CHABOT, sub *Punica* xiv 3. The letters *ʾn* at the beginning of line 4, CHABOT, ibid., explained as the deictic *hn*, which is possible although uncertain. For *bḥrṣ* we suggest the translation 'in the earth.' As we do not have an illustration of this text at our disposal, it is difficult to decide whether eventually a reading *bhʿrṣ* is conceivable.

Qalat Abi s-Siba

Qalat Abi s-Siba N 1

Bibliography: CHABOT, *Punica* xvi, 1; FÉVRIER 1954a; LEVI DELLA VIDA 1965: 59-62; TEIXIDOR 1964-1980: 16; VAN DEN BRANDEN 1974: 145-146; JONGELING 1996a: 74-77; ADAMS 2003: 213-215; *CIL* viii 17467; *KAI* 165.

Illustration: CHABOT, sub *Punica* xvi, 1 (drawing).

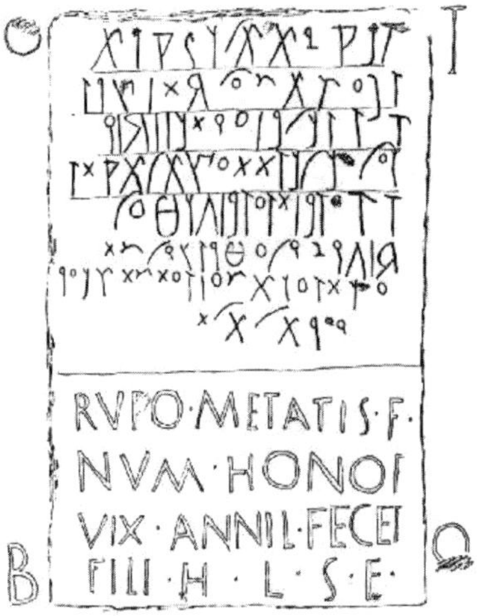

Text:
1) sbq yʾ ʾlk ẙ qrʾ
2) t pʿs ʾš ʿl hmnṣbt
3) st tkl bn ʿdm kn nḥr
4) wʿlk lktm mʿṣʾ lʾqmt
5) tsdt bn mtʿt bn gwṭʿl
6) hngry dl ʿṭrt wdl šm
7) tʿṣmt ʿwʾ šʿnt ʿmšm skʿr
8) drʾ lʾlm

Latin parallel:
1) Rvfo . Metatis . f*ilio*
2) Nvm*idae* . honor*ato*
3) vix*it* . anni*s* l . fecer*vnt*
4) fili . h*oc* . l*oco* . s*epvltvs* . e*st*
5) o*ssa* t*ibi* b*ene* q*viescant*
(line five is actually these four letters in the respective corners of the text-field)

Translation:
1) Stay still, passer by, and read
2) the text which is on this stel-
3) e, man trusts when he is young
4) and he goes his way, but finds opposition.
5) Tasdat, the son of Metat, the son of Gautal
6) the Nagarite, owner of a crown and owner of a name
7) of heroism, he lived fifty years; a monument of
8) his family for ever.

Remarks:
In the first line CHABOT, *Punica* a.l., read *s̊bqyʾ*, noting that the inclination of the downsroke of the first letter is comparable to the one of the *s* in line 2. This reading, which seems most preferable, also with LEVI DELLA VIDA 1965. FÉVRIER 1954a, followed by VAN DEN BRANDEN 1974, read *tbqy*. CHABOT does not give an explanation of this first word in line 1. LEVI DELLA VIDA 1965 divides otherwise and reads *sbq*, imperative of an otherwise unknown verb that means something like 'to stop', 'to stand still.' FÉVRIER, combining *ʾʾlk,* supposes this to be for the article followed by a participle of the root *hlk*, 'passer by' (cf. below the Latin parallels *viator* and *preteriens*). LEVI DELLA VIDA 1965 combines *yʾ*, a vocative particle like Arabic *yā,* not attested elsewhere in Phoenico-Punic, leaving *hlk,* which he explained as FÉVRIER did. Whether this *hlk* should be explained as a qal participle of *hlk* to go, or as a noun derived from the same root, comparable with later Hebrew *hélek*, cannot be decided. The next sign, interpreted by CHABOT as a divider, by FÉVRIER as a *w*, is again taken to be a divider by LEVI DELLA VIDA. The comparison with other *w*-signs in the text makes FÉVRIER's

reading less probable. As texts normally do not contain elaborate word dividers, the sign most probably is a character from the alphabet. In our opinion, it is rather a very unusual *y* than anything else. If correct, *yqrᵓ* must be a jussive form of the root *qrᵓ*, 'to read.' This type of funerary inscription, which, as it were, speaks to people passing by and asks them to read the text on the stone, are well known in the Roman world, cf. texts stating: *Resta viator et lege* ... (*ILS* 2783), *te rogo, preteriens, cum legis ut dicas* ... (*ILS* 8131; cf. further LEVI DELLA VIDA 1965: 65, JONGELING 1996a: 75-76). Note that in this text an expression that is clearly of Roman origin is translated into Punic, while the Latin counterpart of the text is much shorter and goes without it. The second line does not present any problems. FÉVRIER discusses the meaning of *pᶜs*, normally meaning 'tablet.' He supposes a shift in meaning from 'tablet' via 'inscribed tablet' to 'inscription', which seems not improbable. Note that Latin *tabula* may indicate a 'tablet,' but also an 'official document,' while, of course, the *tabula ansata*, the 'tablet with handles' indicates a special type of inscribed text. The third and fourth lines are difficult and have found different interpretations. CHABOT does not offer a translation, FÉVRIER divides *t kl bn ᶜd mkn nḥr wᶜl kl ktmm ᶜṣᵓl ᵓqmt*. *t kl bn* consisting of the object marker, the noun *kl*, 'all', and *bn*, the preposition *b* combined with the suff. of the 3rd person sg., referring to the tablet. *nḥr* FÉVRIER derives, tentatively, from the *ḥwr*, 'to be white', *nḥr* together with *mkn* meaning 'blank space.' The following words FÉVRIER translates 'and on the *ktmm* beside the tumulus.' For *ktmm*, he proposes tentatively the translation 'stone with inscription', which he relates with Hebrew *miktām*, of uncertain meaning, traditionally explained as 'something written' but now translated otherwise. *ᶜṣᵓl* is supposed to be a variant spelling of Hebrew *ᵓṣl*, 'side,' and used as a preposition 'next to.' However, both vowel indicators, *ᶜ* and *ᵓ* remain unexplained in such an interpretation, as in Phoenician and Punic, the double closed syllable at the end of a word is not rendered with an epenthetic vowel, while at the beginning of the word a vowel */i/* would be expected. FÉVRIER's remark: 'one notes that the Neo-Punic spelling seems to indicate a pronunciation */aṣél/*,' describes the problem, but does nothing to resolve it. *ᵓqmt* he divides in *ᵓ*, the article, followed by *qmt*, which he relates to Hebrew *qōmā*, 'height.' VAN DEN BRANDEN 1974 in the main follows FÉVRIER's interpretation. *mkn* he explains as 'pedestal', and *nḥr* he relates to Accadian and Ugaritic *nẖr*, 'dolphin.' Because of this interpretation VAN DEN BRANDEN supposes that the socle of the monument was decorated with the image of a dolphin. Although the animal is well-known in Punic iconography, it seems a less attractive solution. *ktm* he derives from the *ktm*, 'to cover', the noun meaning 'cover, plaque.' As with FÉVRIER's interpretation, we must suppose the former existence of more tablets with inscriptions, of which nothing remains and which seems rather uncommon pratice. RÖLLIG, *KAI* a.l., does offer some of FÉVRIER's proposals in his comment, but accepts in fact only his explanation of *ᶜṣᵓl*. LEVI DELLA VIDA 1965 connects *t kl* with the preceding verb *qrᵓ*. The following words LEVI DELLA VIDA translates: 'when a man is (still) young', *bn ᶜdm* being equivalent to Hebrew *bn ᵓdm* and *nḥr* with Hebrew *nᶜr*. The next line LEVI DELLA VIDA divides in the following way: *wᶜl kl ktm mᶜṣᵓ lᵓ qmt*, 'and over all the Ketam he finds for himself preeminence.' He compares Ketam with the tribal name *Katāma*, well attested in Arabic sources. We are inclined to follow mainly LEVI DELLA VIDA, but to read *tkl* in line 3 as one word, comparable to Accadian and Aramaic (Syriac) *tkl*, 'to trust.' *kn* is a perfect form of *kwn*. The following *wᶜlk lktm*, for which we propose 'and he goes his way', *ᶜlk* being a perfect qal of *hlk* and *lktm* the infinitive of the same root with suffix of the 3rd pers. sg. For *lᵓqmt* we have proposed, with some hesitance, a nominal derivation of *lqm*, for which one may compare the Arabic root of this form, that can be translated with 'to hinder.' The following lines are easier, but here too the author of the text gives his praises to the deceased in flowery language, *dl ᶜṭrt wdl šm tᶜṣmt* is only attested in this text. ADAMS 2003, 214-215, notes that the Latin counterpart of this phrase consists only of the word *honorato*. He concludes that the author of the text was fluent in both languages and that he did not try to translate literally, but used expressions appropriate in the languages he used. Note that the name of the deceased in the Latin text, *Rufus*, differs from the one he bears in the Punic text, *tsdt.* As the name used in the Punic text, is of Berber origin, we assume that for those who made this tomb monument, the Punic culture together with the indigenous one formed more or less a unity in comparison to the culture of higher standing, the Roman one (cf. on this point ADAMS 2003, 215-216).

Qalat Abi s-Siba N 2

Bibliography: CHABOT, *Punica* xvi, 2.

Text:
1) ṭnyᵓ lᵓ bᶜnm
2) ᶜwᵓ šnt ššm w
3) ᶜmš ḥ̊ nᶜkt skr
4) [dr]ᵓ lᵓ ẘlm

Translation:
1) Erected it for him his son.
2) He lived sixty years and
3) five, here is the memorial of
4) his family for ever.

Remarks:
CHABOT *Punica* a.l. notes that *ḥ* in line 3 may also be read as *h* + *n*, that, however the reading *ḥ̊ nᶜkt* is more probable, as it is probably a variant of the enigmatic *hnkt* found elsewhere (cf. the discussion sub Hr. Maktar N 32). We agree with HOFTIJZER 1961: 347-348, that the context in which *hnkt* normally occurs is quite different from this text. He also remarks that *[dr]ᵓ* at the beginning of line 4 is impossible. We are inclined to suppose that it should be there somehow. The reading *[šm]ᵓ* might have been a good conjecture, were it not for the occurrence of *sk]r drᵓ lᵓwlm* in Hr. Gen Rieime N 1, *skᶜr drᵓ lᵓlm* in Qalat Abi s-Siba N 1, *]drᵓ lᵓwlm* in Ain Youssef N 1 and also *skr drᵓ lᵓšt nᶜmt* in Cherchel N 1. For the last word, he notes 'the appearances are in favour of the reading *l[ᵓw]lm*,' which strengthens our previous remarks. CHABOT supposes *ṭnyᵓ* to be a plural form. We wonder whether it cannot be a singular followed by a suffix, in which case *bᶜnm* is also a singular, of course.

Tirekbine

Tirekbine N 1

Bibliography: CHABOT, 1943-1954: 463-464.

Text:
1) lᵓ[dn] lbᶜl wltnyt pᶜn
2) ᵓ bᶜl ndr ᵓynᶜḥ
3) l[ᵓdn] lbᶜl wltnyt pnᵓ bᶜ[l]
4) ḥ̊ [ ] šmᵓ qlᵓ

Translation:
1) To the lord to Bal and to Tinnit Fan-
2) e Bal vowed Aynah
3) to the lord to Bal and to Tinnit Fane Bal
4) because he heard his voice.

Remarks:
The name in line 2 may be *ynᶜḥ*, in which case the preceding verb is *ndrᵓ* and the name a feminine one. The dedicatory formula to the gods Bal and Tinnit, lines 1-2a is completely repeated in line 3, which shows that incorrect texts could probably easily be sold to people unable to read. Note the interesting difference in the spelling, *pᶜnᵓ* in line 1-2, and *pnᵓ* in line 3. Both spellings are attested frequently, but this text shows that a scribe could use both spellings indifferently. The first sign of the last line, read by CHABOT as *ḥ*, is difficult to explain. Only autopsy of the original will enable us to decide whether we should perhaps read *kᶜ*.

MOROCCO

Melilla

Melilla N 1

Bibliography: IAM 18.

Illustrations: IAM : 105 (drawing).

Text:
1) bdᶜštrt

Translation:
1) Bodashtart.

MALTA

Malta

Malta N 5

Bibliography: GARBINI 1965: 58; *ICO* Malta Np 6.

Text:
1) špṭ

Translation:
1) Shafot

PANTELLERIA

Pantelleria

Pantelleria N 1

Bibliography: CIS i, p. 181.

Illustrations: LEVY 1870: 13 (drawing).

Text:
1) mnṣbt
2) wqbr
3) b^{c}lyḥ
4) y bn ^{c}bd
5) mlqrt

Translation:
1) Stele
2) and grave of
3) Balyah-
4) i, the son of Abd-
5) melqart.

Remarks:
According to *CIS* i, p. 181, this inscription is a spurious one that cannot have been found on Pantellaria. The wording of the text is indeed unusual, *mṣbt w qbr* is not attested elsewhere. However, as the name *b^{c}lyḥy*, also not attested elsewhere, is of a probable construction, we are inclined to suppose that the text is genuine (*yḥy* as a second element in a personal name is attested in the uncertain *mryḥy* and in *kmšyḥy*). The form of the letters, very easily drawn, may also raise suspicion, but we do not know whether the drawing published by LENORMANT was made by him after the orignal of his informant, or whether it is a reproduction of the original drawing. For the time being we are inclined to accept the name *b^{c}lyḥy* as a genuine name in the corpus of Neo-Punic inscriptions.

SICILY

Palermo

Palermo N 1

Bibliography: AMADASI 1990a: 91; *ICO* Sicilia Np 1; *CIS* 134.

Illustrations: ICO, tav. xxii; (photograph).

Text:
1)]$^{\supset}$ḥy y$^{\supset}$ql bn yt$^{\supset}$ wbny

Translation:
1) his brother, *y$^{\supset}$ql*, the son of *yt$^{\supset}$* and his son.

Remarks:
A funerary inscription on a limestone slab. The word division and translation is the one proposed by AMADASI 1990a: 91. Earlier studies supposed a personal name *$^{\supset}$ḥyy$^{\supset}$ql.*

ITALY

Pompei

Pompei N 1

Bibliography:
GARBINI 1977; A.M. BISI INGRASSIA 1977: 152, 2; GARBINI 1978: 1, 2; GARBINI 1986: 19.

Illustrations: A.M. BISI INGRASSIA 1977: tav. lxix, 45 (drawing).

Text:
1)]dgm/$^{\supset}$

Remarks:
BISI INGRASSIA 1977 proposes to read *mgr* (a common noun related to the well-known *magalia*). However, there seems to be no reason to suppose that the text should be read from left to right.

Rome

Rome N 1

Bibliography: *CIL* xv 4898; A.M. BISI INGRASSIA 1977: 152, 1; GARBINI 1978: 1, 1; MAZZA 1983; GARBINI 1987: 19.

Illustrations: A.M. BISI INGRASSIA 1977: tav. lxix, 45; MAZZA 1983: 61 (drawing).

Text:
1) q^{c}yql^{c}yn$^{\supset}$

Translation:
1) Caecilianus.

Remarks:
BISI 1977: 152, reads *qdy ql* ^{c}*yn*$^{\supset}$ translating: 'Quday the voice, his eye', which is improbable. MAZZA 1983, accepted by GARBINI 1986, reads. *q*^{c}*yq l*^{c}*t*$^{\supset}$, for *Caec. Laetus*. One wonders whether the perfectly normal Latin abbreviation *Caec.* is to be expected in a Neo-Punic inscription, although the adopted reading and interpretation, proposed by GARBINI 1978: 1, presupposes that the Punic rendition of this Latin name is something like /*qayqəlayne*/.

SARDINIA

S. Antioco

S. Antioco N 3

Bibliography: LEVI DELLA VIDA 1964: 310; ADAMS 2003: 212-213; AT 100; *NSI* 60; *CIS* 149; *ICO* Sardegna Np 5; AMADASI 1990a: 47, 80-81; *KAI* 172.

Illustrations: DILLMANN 1881: 429; LIDZBARSKI 1898, Taf. xviii 1 (drawing); *CIS* i tav. xliii; *ICO* tav. liii; AMADASI 1990a, fig. 13 (photograph).

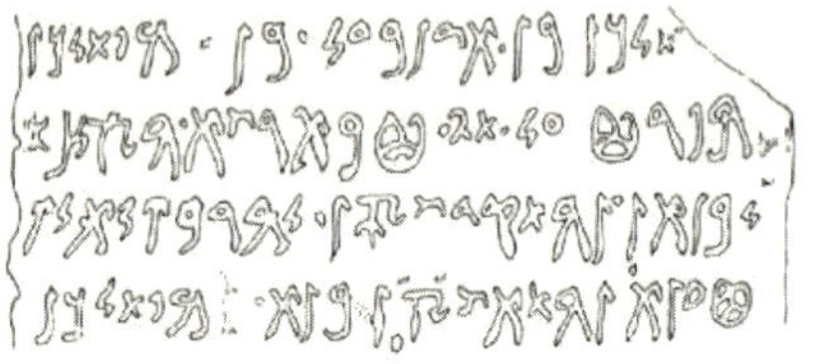

Text:
1) [lḥ]mlkt bn $^{\supset}$dnb^{c}l bn ḥmlkt
2) hprṭ ^{c}l myṭb$^{\supset}$ rš$^{\supset}$ hslkẙ
3) lbn$^{\supset}$t t hmqdš st lhrbt l$^{\supset}$lt
4) ṭyn$^{\supset}$ t hm$^{\supset}$š st bn$^{\supset}$ ḥmlkt

Latin parallel:
1) Himilconi Idnibalis [
2) qvei hanc aedem ex s(enatvs) c(onsvlto)
3) coeravit Himilco f*ilivs* statvam [

Translation:
1) For Himilco, the son of Idnibal, the son of Himilco,
2) who … with the approbation of the senate of Sulcis
3) to build this sanctuary for the lady, the goddess,
4) his son Himilco erected this statue.

Remarks:
It seems most attractive to divide *myṭb*$^{\supset}$ *rš*$^{\supset}$ and to explain both words as pl. cstr., cf. e.g. FRIEDRICH-RÖLLIG 1970: 42, RÖLLIG sub *KAI* 172. In this case *rš*$^{\supset}$ is the pl. cstr. of *r*$^{\supset}$*š* 'head.' However, the division *myṭb* $^{\supset}$*rš*$^{\supset}$ is also possible, in which case $^{\supset}$*rš*$^{\supset}$ is best explained as a part. pl. cstr. derived from the root $^{\supset}$*rš*, 'the chosen ones', as an approximate rendition of Latin 'senatus', cf. LEVI DELLA VIDA 1964: 310, AMADASI, *ICO* Sardegna Np5, *PPG* §225b. Most commentators suppose that the goddess for whom the temple was built is not mentioned by name, but it is perhaps better to explain $^{\supset}$*lt* not as a common noun but as an epithet that has become a divine name, like, e.g., its masc. counterpart $^{\supset}$*l*, *El*.

Wales

Holt

Holt N 1

Bibliography: Guillaume 1940; Levi Della Vida 1940; Thacker-Wright 1955, Collingwood-Wright 1995, nr. 2502.4.

Illustration: Guillaume 1940; Thacker-Wright 1955 (photograph), Collingwood-Wright 1995: 4 (drawing).

Text:
1) mʿqrynʾ

Translation:
1) Macrinus

Remarks:
The only Neo-Punic inscription found north of the Alps, incised on a pottery sherd. The same name is also to be found in Bir Shmech LP1. The name element */maka/e/o/ur-/ being not infrequent in names from North Africa (cf. e.g. the Libyan names MKR, *RIL* 651, MKRN, *RIL* 650, MKRH, *RIL* 386, cf. also Jongeling 1994: xxvi and xxviii) it seems possible that a Latin name beginning seemingly with the same element was chosen with this Berber name element of unknown meaning in view. Bechaouch and Pflaum classify this name as a Berber one, but the occurrence of *Macer* and *Maccarus* in e.g. a list of Gallo-Roman pottery marks (Leglay 1962: 29-34) makes this explanation less probable. Note also that Pausanias names the hero that first came to Sardinia as *Sardus the son of Macer* (Pausanias x 17,2). Whether the name of the martyr *Macorus* (gen. *Macori*, cf. *ActaSanct.* ed. Bolland, ii, April: 480 & *MartAfrEccl* 365, 17 April) should be included here is difficult to say. On the deity *Macer,* cf. Lipiński 1995: 366-369.

Latino- and Greco Punic Texts

LIBYA

Bir ed –Dreder

The cemetery of Bir ed-Dreder has produced the largest single group of Latino-Punic texts yet. Of the numerous steles found, some twenty-one were inscribed, of which eleven are actually legible to some extent. The graves (for a reconstruction of one of the mausolea, cf. BARKER *et al.* 1996, fig. 5.36) seem to be those of native auxiliary troops in Roman service. The authors were able to examine the originals in December 2003, whereby we were able to confirm the accuracy of the drawings and photographs first published by GOODCHILD.

Bir ed-Dreder LP 1

Bibliography: BEGUINOT 1949: 15; *IRT* 886a; GOODCHILD 1954: 98; LEVI DELLA VIDA 1963: 80f.; VATTIONI 1966: 46f.; VATTIONI 1976: 545; COACCI POLSELLI 1979: 49; ELMAYER 1984: 93f.; *TRE*: 350-354; HÄBERL 2000: n.p.

Illustrations: *IRT* 886a (drawing); GOODCHILD 1954, figs. 9a, 9b (drawing and photograph); reprinted: ELMAYER 1984, a.l.; *TRE* a.l.; HÄBERL 2000, a.l.

Text:

1) flavi saich-
2) am bn ma-
3) carcvm
4) σonmo-
5) n tribyn-
6) vs bymy-
7) ft yrirab-
8) an machrvς v-
9) ꞩeb

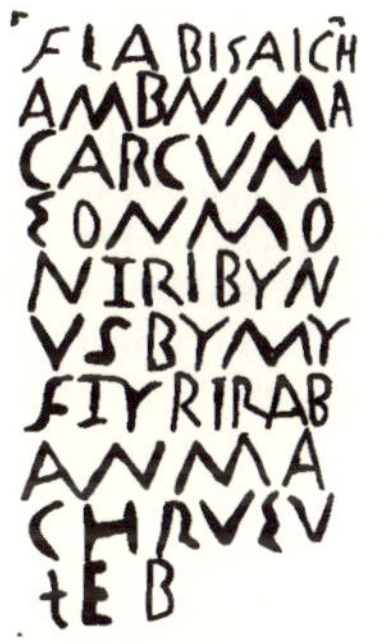

Translation:

1) Flavi[us] Saich-
2) am son of Ma-
3) carcum
4) [the] σonmon [the] tribun-
5) e at the be-
6) hest of Yrirab-
7) an, Machruς e-
8) rected [this stele]

Remarks:

The initial section of this inscription is quite clear. *Flavi* displays the usual ending for Latin names of the *–i* declination. *Saicham* is an otherwise unattested Libyco-Berber name. *bn* is written here without vowel indication (cf. the following text). *Macarcvm* (also spelt this way in an unpublished Latin text from Ghadames) is well attested in various forms *Macargvm* (*CRAI* 1979, 447), *Macvrgvm* (*AÉ* 1948, 114), *Magargvn* (CORIPPUS 5, 283), *Macargvs* (Bu Njem 68:6, 79: 4, 88: 5) and possibly *Macergvm* (*CIL* viii 20843); see in general JONGELING 1994: xviii, xxi and sub $m^{c}qr$ in the Neo-Punic glossary. In light of *[Fla]bivs M[aca]rcv[...]obm.n trib[...* and *Macarcvm tribvnvs σob[...*in Bir ed-Dreder LP 3, one might conclude that the title *tribunus* (here spelt with a *y* in an unaccented syllable, but with the Latin nominative ending, an unassimilated loan) applied to the father and not the son. In this case, the son, *Saicham*, might have inherited the imperial gentilicium of the second Flavian dynasty as a rank indicator from his father, who as a (nominally?) high-ranking officer received this name when he was enlisted into Roman military service (cf. MÓCSY 1964: 259), cf. ad LP 2. *σonmon* has remained without convincing explanation until now (possibly related to the *...]obm.n* and *σob[...*in LP 3?) and might be a title. *bymyft* until now has been the subject of various interpretations: e.g. LEVI DELLA VIDA (1963: 81) thought it a deformation of *manṣibt* which is unlikely; COACCI POLSELLI (1979: 49) saw *by-* as the preposition 'in' followed by a word she related to the *mpt* in *KAI* 30, which has been interpreted by some as some kind of official (cf. the discussion in *DNWSI* s.v.), related to Arabic *mufti* (<√*pty*IV), i.e. 'dignitary', which is somewhat far-fetched. COACCI POLSELLI's translation 'Flavius Saicham the son of Macarcum Σonmon, tribune, by means of the dignitary Yriraban Machruς has made (it)', is problematic as the name of the deceased is mentioned nowhere. The problem is how one interprets lines 6-9, especially the verb *vşeb*. If one interprets it as a yiph. 3 sg. m., one might translate *in the ... of Y., M. erected it*, although the form (also attested in an unclear context in Bir ed-Dreder LP 5) is unusual, one might rather expect *inşeb* (cf. Gasr Doga LP 1, or /*in*/>/*ũ*/?). On the other hand, one might see it as a yuph. 3 sg. m., i.e. *in the ... of Y. M. it was erected.* The former suggestion however is more likely in our opinion, as the persons named in the Dreder texts seem only to have one name except when they also bear an imperial praenomen. We tentatively propose here a prefixed *m*-nominal (participle?) derivation of the root *btt* 'to cut' (cf. Hebrew, Arabic) meaning 'decision, command' (cf. Arabic *batt*) with vowel reduction (and *b*>*f* cf. *mynşyft* ad Nawalia LP 1). *Yriraban* is a Libyco-Berber name also attested in Bir ed-Dreder LP 9 (vid. a.l.), whilst *Machruς byn Rogate* is attested as the possible erector of LP 5.

Bir ed-Dreder LP 2

Bibliogrphy: IRT 886b; GOODCHILD 1954: 99; VATTIONI 1976: 545; ELMAYER 1984: 95f.; *TRE*: 354-357; HÄBERL 2000: n.p.

Illustrations: GOODCHILD 1954, figs. 10a, 10b (drawing and photograph); reprinted: ELMAYER 1984, a.l.; *TRE*, a.l.; HÄBERL 2000, a.l.

Text:

1) ivlivs m-
2) asthalvl
3) byn chyr-
4) did ryb m
5) şir blam
6) ban saba
7) (…)aas̊ad
8) […] emis
9) […]lervch
10) […] dnim
11) (…)irtlyi
12) (…)its̊o
13) (…)mchyl
14) (…)erssv

Translation:

1) Iulius M-
2) asthalul
3) son of Chyr-
4) did [the] commander of the g-
5) uard…

Remarks:

The first ten lines of this text seem more or less identical to the first thirteen lines of LP 5 (which seems to have been *Masthalvl*'s brother's epitaph), yet unfortunately both are damaged on their left sides, hindering any possible reconstruction. The deceased seems to be *Ivlivs Masthalvl* the son of *Chyrdid.* The praenomen *Iulius* (here in the Latin spelling, and not the supposed colloquial Punic form **ivli*) is along with *Flavius* an important clue for dating these texts. The use of imperial gentilicia as rank indicators of seemingly high-placed military officials would appear to date these texts to the joint reign of Iulius Constans and Flavius Iulius Constantius (II), AD 340-350 (cf. BORHY 1989: 154). *Masthalvl*, a Libyco-Berber name, contains the frequent elements *mas(tha)-* and *–lvl*. *byn* and *ryb* are both *regentes* and hence have their stem vowel reduced to schwa (resp.: *bən* < **bin*, *rəb* < **rabb*, cf. KERR 2003: 138f. and note *ρυβαθων* in El-Hofra GP1). *Chyrdid* is a Libyco-Berber name (cf. KRDD *RIL* 418, 638 and 640). The last word we are able to identify with any certainty in this inscription is *mṣir* in lines 4f. (cf. LP 5: 5-7: *b]yn chy[rdid] ryb[...*), which we interpret as a nominal derivation from the root √*nṣr*, cf. Accadian *maṣṣartum*, Aramaic *maṭṭartā*. We render this construct collocation roughly as 'commander of the guard', and presume that it is the Punic equivalent of the Latin loan *tribunus* in other Dreder texts. It would seem that as in the preceding text, the son inherited his imperial praenomen from his father, cf. ad LP 4. Although the remaining lines of this text have been subject to various interpretations, the visible remains render all such mere speculation.

Bir ed-Dreder LP 4

Bibliography: *IRT* 886d; GOODCHILD 1954: 101; VATTIONI 1976, 546; VATTIONI 1993a: 465f.; *TRE*: 358; HÄBERL 2000: n.p.

Illustrations: GOODCHILD 1954, figs. 12a, 12b (drawing and photograph); reprinted: ELMAYER 1984, a.l.; *TRE*, a.l.; HÄBERL 2000, a.l.

Text:

1) maσicama
2) byn isachv
3) tribvnvs st̊ r

Translation:

1) Maσicama
2) son of Isachu[ar?]
3) [the] tribune ...

Remarks:

Maσicama, or possibly *Maσigama*, by all accounts a Libyco-Berber name, possibly with the prefixed element *mas-* (cf. JONGELING 1994: xiiif.). On *byn*, cf. our comments ad LP 2. The name *Isachu* has been amended by some with the ending *–ar*, due to the occurrence of such names (cf. *Isicvarlvl* in the following text, *Isigvari* in LP 14 and *Isicvar* *IRT* 902), which although possible is not necessary (cf. *Isagvas* CORIPPUS 5, 218, and possibly ISKW *RIL* 799). The final three letters would seem to be an unidentified abbreviation.

On the title *tribvnvs* indicating a military rank of the Roman army, we note the following: in all of the partially comprehensible texts from Bir ed-Dreder, when a military rank, i.e. either *trbvnvs* or *ryb mṣir*, is given, it follows the name immediately (cf. apart from this text, LP 3, 13 and 14), namely *imperial praenomen-given name-rank* (the exception being this text, where the father was a tribune, but neither father nor son bears an imperial praenomen). In LP 1, 2 and 5, the title follows the name of the father, the son has no title (preserved) but the imperial gentilicium as a praenomen lacking in his father's name (cf. LP 1 *flavi saicham bn macarcvm ... tribynvs* with LP 3 *[fla]bius m[aca]rcu[m...] ... trib[...*, where both have the same praenomen, and LP 2 and 5 where the two brothers both have the praenomen *Ivlivs,* probably inherited from their father *Chyrdid*), hence our suggestion ad LP 1 and 2 that the son inherited the praenomen but not the military rank from his father. In LP 9 neither father nor son has an imperial praenomen and neither has any (identifiable) military rank.

Bir ed-Dreder LP 9

Bibliography: BEGUINOT 1949: 15; *IRT* 886h; GOODCHILD 1954: 105; VATTIONI 1976: 548; ELMAYER 1984: 98f.; *TRE*: 368-370; HÄBERL 2000: n.p.

Illustrations: GOODCHILD 1954, figs. 16a, 16b (drawing and photogaph); reprinted: ELMAYER 1984, a.l.; *TRE*, a.l.; HÄBERL 2000, a.l.

Text:
1) yriraban
2) byn isicvar-
3) lvl babar
4) eimse vl(?)h
5) ni

Translation:
1) Yriraban
2) [the] son of Isicuar-
3) lul …

Remarks:
It would seem that this is the epitaph of *Yriraban*, possibly the erector of LP 1. The name is Libyco-Berber, remiscent of *(s)iraban* and *Rirachan* in LP 6. On *Isicvarlvl*, it would seem to be the name *Iisicuar* (cf. the preceding text), appended with the common Libyco-Berber suffix *–lvl*. On *byn* cf. ad LP 2. This is the only legible Dreder text in which neither the bearer of a military rank nor his son have a Latin praenomen (cf. ad LP 4). The rest of the text remains enigmatic.

Bir ed-Dreder LP 14

Bibliography: *IRT* 886k; GOODCHILD 1954: 101; VATTIONI 1976: 548; ELMAYER 1984: 100; *TRE*: 370-371; HÄBERL 2000: n.p.

Illustrations: GOODCHILD 1954, figs. 12a, 12b (drawing and photograph); reprinted: ELMAYER 1984, a.l.; *TRE*, a.l.; HÄBERL 2000, a.l

Text:
1) flabivs isi-
2) gvari trybv-
3) nys byn iarnv-
4) han byc
5) tin ir

Translation:
1) Flavius Isi-
2) guari [the] tribu-
3) ne, son of Iarnu-
4) han …
5) …

Remarks:
Regarding the Libyco-Berber name *Isigvari*, cf. ad LP 4. The father *Iarnvhan* is somewhat unusual due to the *h*, which had already lost its consonantal value in Neo-Punic, nonetheless the initial element *iar-* is well attested (cf. JONGELING 1994: 62f and *RIL* II, xviii). The rest of this text is written in a somewhat less careful fashion, and still defies plausible interpretation.

Bir Shmech

Bir Shmech LP 1

Bibliography: *AÉ* 50(1950) 205 (=*RMDAT* 1949: 22); GOODCHILD 1950a: 137f.; *IRT* 889; FÉVRIER 1953b: 467-471; FRIEDRICH 1957: 297f.; LEVI DELLA VIDA 1963: 86f.; LEVI DELLA VIDA 1964b: 311; SZNYCER 19-63-1966: 101; VATTIONI 1966: 45f.; LEVI DELLA VIDA 1967b: 263; *KAI* 179; KRAHMALKOV 1973: 61-64; GARBINI 1974: 10; VATTIONI 1976: 550f.; COACCI POLSELLI 19-78: 237f.; ELMAYER 1983: 90f.; ELMAYER 1984: 149-51; ELMAYER 1985: 82f.; *TRE*: 379-382.

Illustrations: GOODCHILD 1950a, pl. 16a (photograph); *IRT* a.l. (drawing); reprinted: ELMAYER 1983, a.l.; ELMAYER 1984, a.l.; ELMAYER 1985, a.l.; *TRE*, a.l. (drawing).

Text:
1) flabi dasama vybinim
2) macrine felv centeinari bal ars
3) σymarnar sabare σ
4) avn

Translation:
1) Flavius Dasamau and his son
2) Macrinus made (this) *centenarium*, (the) architect
3) who [made it was] Sabarrus …
4) …

Remarks:
The interpretation of the first three lines of this text has generally been unanimous since FÉVRIER, who equated *bal ars* with Punic *bᶜl ḥrš* (*KAI*[5] 72b: 4, 81: 9, 302: 11, 303: 3, cf. HOFTIJZER-JONGELING *DNWSI* sub *ḥrš* 5) in the meaning 'artisan, craftsman.' *Dasama* is an otherwise unattested Libyco-Berber PN (though compare possibly with DSMS *RIL* 102), his praenomen indicating either that he himself or his father had some high-ranking allegiance with Rome (cf. ad Bir ed-Dreder LP 1). *Macrinus* (here in the usual Punic spelling) is a Latin PN also attested in Neo-Punic texts (*mᶜqrynᵓ* Kef Bezioun N2, Holt N1). The spelling of *binim* 'his son' displays a reduced vowel, coloured by vowel harmony, in the first syllable (i.e. the *i* is not historical, cf. *libinim* Gasr Doga LP 1). *centeinari* (the orthography is somewhat unusual, the *ei* would seem to indicate /ī/) is a Latin term peculiar to Africa to designate a 'fortified farm' guarding the frontier, which was borrowed by Punic as a technical loan (cf. ad Gasr el-Azaiz LP 1).

The remaining two lines of the inscription have not met with any unanimous interpretation and are admittedly difficult. However the reading proposed by LEVI DELLA VIDA, reading *σvmar* and interpreting it as a ptc. qal 3 sg. m. is unlikely, and although *PPG* still mentions this interpretation as their sole specimen for equating *σ* with /š/ (§§45b, 48e), it is not mentioned in their discussion of the participle (§§139f.). A comparison of the *y* in *vy* in line one and the grapheme following the first *σ* in line three, makes it clear that *y* must be read, *σy* then being the marker of relativity. There is an unpublished inscription from Wadi Chanafes (LP 1) that displays a similar collocation:

1) mynȿyfth yth mv felv fydens
2) vysevere labvnom amsva-
3) ia byn masvna by ·∗ↀDCC
4) vybal ars ys fel regine ys iasobb/ rygnno

'Stele, the one which made Fydens / and Severus for their father Amsua-/ia the son of Masuna for 1700 [folles?] / and the architect who made <it> was Reginus who …' Of interest here is first half of the fourth line. Should *Sabarrus* (a Libyco-Berber name, cf. *Sabarro CIL* viii 1639 and *Saburra* mentioned several times by Caesar, cf. JONGELING 1994: 122) be the name of the architect, then in the preceding letters on would logically expect a verb referring to his building activity (cf. *fel* in the inscription Wadi Chanafes LP 1). Nonetheless, line three is written awkwardly, possibly to avoid inscribing the heads of the two victories and the letter forms are atypical compared with the rest of the inscription. What we have read as *marnar* might also be read *maban a r* (i.e. the fourth letter being a ligature for *an*). We can give no convincing explanation for all of these letters. The final section too remains puzzling, although it would seem the final letter of line three, the *σ*, might be the marker of relativity (cf. the Wadi Chanafes text, which however is unclear too) with following complete loss of vowel as in *labunom* Wadi Umm el-Agerem LP 1 (< */ləᵓabūnōm/), *lobvthem* Gasr el-Azaiz LP 1 (< */ləᵓōbūtēm/).

Breviglieri

Breviglieri LP 1

Bibliography: GOODCHILD 1949: 33; GOODCHILD 1950: 229; GOODCHILD 1951: 74; *IRT* 877; LEVI DELLA VIDA 1963: 87; VATTIONI 1976: 543; ELMAYER 1983: 87f.; GARBINI 1986: 75; ADAMS 2003: 232; *TRE*: 344-347; *KAI*[5] 304.

Illustrations: GOODCHILD 1951, pl. 13, 1 (photograph); *IRT*, 877 (drawing); re-printed: ELMAYER 1983, a.l.; *TRE*, a.l. (drawing).

Text:
1) centenari
2) mv felthi a-
3) na marci ce-
4) cili bymv-
5) pal fesem a
6) pero y nban
7) em bvcv bvo
8) ms ayo nema

Translation:
1) Centenarium
2) which I A-
3) na Marcius Cæ
4) cili(us) ([from 2] made] …
5)-8) …

Remarks:
In December of 2003, the authors were able to examine this inscription in Tripoli and confirm the reading of *IRT*. Only the first three lines of this text can be read with any certainty. Its chief interest is that as a dedicatory building inscription, it attests to another fortified farm or *centenarivm* (cf. ad Bir Shmech LP 1, Gasr el-Azaiz LP 1) defending the Roman frontier and seemingly commanded by a Punic-speaking *centenarivs*.

The letter sequence *thiana* has in the past been read as an otherwise unattested name *Thi/lana* (which would then lead to a person bearing three names, the Roman *tria nomina* being otherwise unattested in these texts). VATTIONI 1976 first proposed reading *felthi ana* 'and I built', reading the first word as a verb qal 1 sg. c. followed by the personal pronoun 1 sg. c. Indeed the boastful use of a verb of building together with the personal proun is not unusual (cf. IKings 8: 13 *bānô bānîṯî bēṯ-zəb̲ūl lāḵ* 'and I have built thee a *lofty* temple' as well as the repeated use of *ᵓnk bnty* in the Mesha Inscription (*KAI* 181), and note also *…ista omnia perfecta sunt a me* … (*IRTS* 19). VATTIONI however did not explain how *ana* could be the personal pronoun 1 sg. c. In Phoenico-Punic this is usually spelt *ᵓnk* or *ᵓnky* (cf. *PPG* §§110f., note esp. the spellings *anec* and *anech* from the *Poenulus*; there is no evidence that Phoenico-Punic had a variant form like Hebrew *ᵓănī* and even if a short form existed, one would expect **ani* and not *ana*, as attested in Arabic). Might *ana* be the given name (an abbreviation of *(H)anno*)?

The rest of the text is very difficult, and no convincing explanation has been proposed as of yet. Several of the letter forms are quite odd, e.g. what has been rendered with a *p* above (the first letter of lines 5 and 6), looks like a ligature for *p+l* (cf. ad Lepcis Magna LP 1). The presence of *p* in this text would be surprising alongside *f* (lines 2 and 5), cf. *PPG* §37 3a (p.22).

Gasr el-Azaiz

Gasr el-Azaiz LP 1

Bibliography: DE MATHUISIEULX 1904: 30; *CIL* viii 22664; *IRT* 893; LEVI DELLA VIDA 1963: 9; VATTIONI 1976: 552; ELMAYER 1983: 81; BROGAN 1976-77[1983]: 108f.; VATTIONI 1993b: 452-454; *TRE*: 385-389; KERR 2005.

Illustrations: [DE MATHUISIEULX 1904: pl. xx1 1; *CIL* viii 22664; *IRT*, 893; ELMAYER 1983, a.l.;] BROGAN 1976-77[1983], pl. xlii, xlii a (photograph); *TRE*, a.l. (photograph); KERR 2005 (photograph).

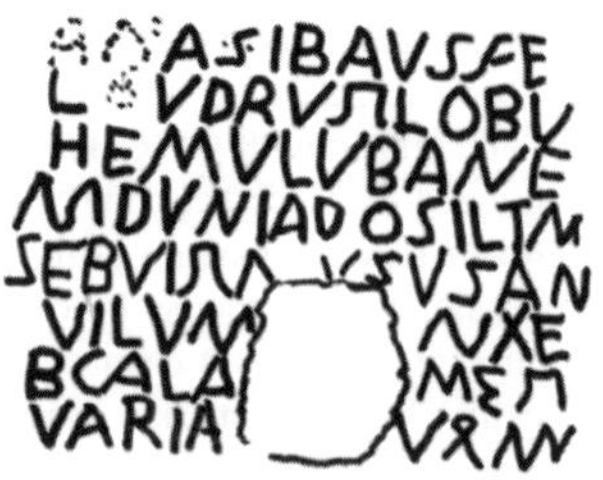

Text :

1) anaꞩ̊iba ys fe
2) l vdrv*na* lobv
3) [t]hem vlybane
4) m dvniad osilim
5) sebvi*na*n vsysan
6) vilvn NA*NA*A ixe
7) b calaMDAS mσ*na*
8) varia MICAvran

Translation:

1) The *centenarium* which ma-
2) de Udruna for his
3) parents and for his son-
4) s Duniad, Osilim,
5) Sebuinan and Sysan
6) and Ilun ?? erec-
7) ted Calamdas ?
8) ?, Micauran

Remarks:

This dedicatory building inscription was found above the enterance of a fortified farm by DE MATHUISIEULX, who published a very poor photograph (that according to *IRT* was heavily touched up). *CIL* and *IRT* both published a drawing made from that photograph. It is hard to make much sense out of either. In the early 1970's, Lady BROGAN rediscovered the site with the text still *in situ*, and published several excellent photographs. A comparison of the older images with the newer ones shows that we are indeed dealing with one and the same text. Unfortunately, in the intervening seventy odd years, the inscription was shot, severely damaging the last four lines. In any case, all of the studies preceding BROGAN's publication are obsolete. The text is interesting as it displays cursive Latin ligatures, which the lapicide probably neglected to convert into uncial characters when copying the text from his (presumably) cursive *Vorlage*. In our transcription, upper case letters indicate letters missing in BROGAN's photograph, but tentatively taken from the older images; cursive letters indicate our interpretation of ligatures.

KRAHMALKOV (2000: 334 sub *nṣb*$_{\text{II}}$ and 2001: 127 sub *qatīl* et passim) read *a nasib ays fel Svdrv* ..., 'Sudru made <this> stele …' which is unlikely since the text was not found on a stele (vide supra). In KERR 2005 we proposed the reading rendered above. The interpretation we suggested was that *naꞩiba* is the Punic equivalent of the North African Latin term *centenarivm*, that is a fortified farm on the Roman frontier in North Africa, and is based on interpreting Biblical Hebrew *nəṣīḇ* as a 'military commander' (and not a 'body of troops' as has been proposed), the equivalent of a *centenarivs*, the former being commanded by the latter. Whereas Latin could use the neuter case, Punic only had the feminine case at its disposal (cf. *maṣṣaḇ* 'a garrison of troops' vs. *maṣṣāḇāh* 'garrison, outpost'). Archaeologically speaking, Gasr el-Aziz is comparable to structures designated as a *centenarium* in Latin and Latino-Punic inscriptions (Bir Shmech LP 1 and Breviglieri LP 1).

The name of the *centenarius* (or **naṣib*) who built the place was Udruna (the latter symbol is ⊓ which can be a ligature for *n*+*a*), a Libyco-Berber name similar to *Uttruna* (*CIL* viii 20624). He built it 'for his parents and for his sons.' The spelling of both *lobvthem* and *vlybanem* with non-reduced vowels might be surprising, for the former re. *lybyth{h}a* Ghirza LP 1, *lybythem* Zliten LP 1 (yet note the singular suff. 3 pl. m. *labvnom* Wadi Umm el-Agerem LP 1 and Wadi Chanafes LP 1 apud Bir Shmech LP 1), whilst for the latter this is the first example of the plural noun with the suffix 3 sg. m. (the other plural form is the regens *byne*, Wadi Umm el-Agerem LP 2) the singular example from Gasr Doga LP 1 reads *libinim* (cf. *binim* Bir Shmech LP 1), possibly reminiscent of Hebrew *bənō* vs. *bānāw*.

The remainder of the text is difficult to interpret due to the recent damage and one must revert to the the older images for what they are worth. These lines seem to contain names (possibly the children of Udruna), some of which have can be compared with Latin texts from North Africa. *Dvniad* is otherwise unattested, but possibly related to names such as *Tvnada* (*ILAf* 192) and *Tanadvm* (acc., CORIPPUS 7, 605). *Osilim* is odd and otherwise unattested, but may contain the Semitic element *–ilim* (cf. ad Gasr Doga LP 1), possibly with the initial element *ᶜz* 'strength' (cf. *ᶜzbᶜl* etc., BENZ 1972: 165f.). *Sebvinan* (?) is peculiar and seems unparalleled (though on Libyco-Berber names ending in *–an* cf. JONGELING 1994: xiv f.). *Sysan* is similar to *Syꞩan* in Wadi Umm el-Agerem LP 1. *Ilun* would appear to also be attested in *BAC* 1932-

1933: 120, *Iluni* (dat.). *Calamdas* (?) seems similar to *Calam* (*CIL* viii 10834) and *Calamena* (acc., CORIPPUS 8, 467), and the Libyan name KLMH (*RIL* 642). With regard to *Varia*, we note that *vari-* is a common initial element in Libyco-Berber names (cf. JONGELING, *op. cit.* 146f.). *Micauran* (?) might be compared with *Micara* (*CIL* viii 21773), *Micurenus* (*CIL* viii 233380), Libyco-Berber MKRN, cf. ad Holt N 1.

The interpretation does have a somewhat funerary ring (cf. e.g. Zliten LP 1). In our previously mentioned study, we compared this text with several Latin dedicatory building inscriptions having funerary overtones (e.g the *praedivm Sammacis*, *AÉ* 1901 150, described as a *praesidivm aeternae*) and concluded that this was because the builders of such fortified farms (or *gsur*), the nascient new native elite emerging under Roman hegemony, attempted to immortalize themselves and the dynasties they founded.

Gasr Doga

Gasr Doga LP 1

Bibliography: GOODCHILD 1951: 45, 74; *IRT* 873; LEVI DELLA VIDA 1963: 79f.; VATTIONI 1976: 542; SEGERT 1976: 265; COACCI POLSELLI 1978: 236f.; *TRE*: 341-342.

Illustrations: IRT, 873 (drawing).

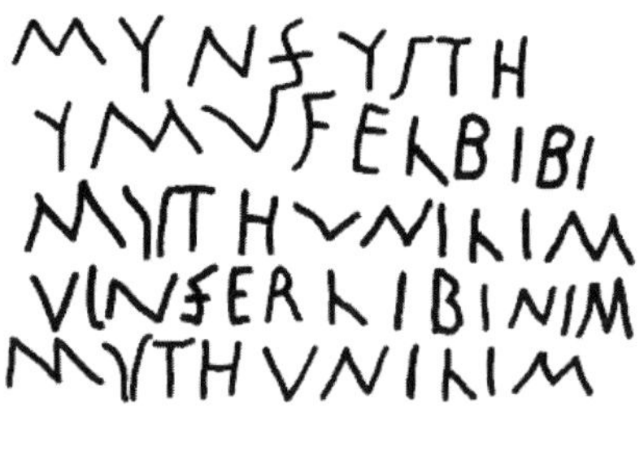

Text:
1) mynꞩyf[!]th
2) ymv fel bibi
3) mythvnilim
4) v-inꞩeb! libinim
5) mythvnilim

Translation:
1) Memorial
2) which made Bibi
3) Mythunilim,
4) and erected for his son
5) Mythunilim.

Remarks:
The authors were able to examine this inscription in Tripoli in December 2003 and confirm the reading given by *IRT*. This is one of the few Latino-Punic texts which is more or less understandable in its entirety, although several issues regarding spelling remain. Although the drawing seems to read *mynꞩysth* (on this word, cf. ad Nawalia LP 1), the supposed *s* has more the shape of an *f* in which the bar has been omitted (cf. the *f* in *fel* on line 2). In the past, the following *y* has been seen as the feminine demonstrative pronoun (e.g. *PPG* §110, cf. Hebrew *hīʾ*), although one would rather expect **ī* or the like, and additionally, as there is enough room on line one for this letter, its presence on the following line strongly suggests a connection with *mv*. A spelling *ymv* is indeed unusual, but is now also attested in Nawalia LP 1 (cf. a.l.) in the same collocation. It might be explained by prosody, i.e. to break up the consonant cluster (scil. */mənṣəφθmv/*> */mənṣəφθəmv/*). Support for this conjecture might be gained from comparing similar phrases from other such inscriptions: *centenari mv fel* (Breviglieri LP 1), *a(m)-memoria mv fela, nasif mv fela* (Ghirza LP1), where the word preceding *mv* ends either with a vowel or a single consonant. In the case of Nawalia LP1, the numeral *xxx* precedes *ymv*. A plural form of the root *šlš* would be expected (cf. *šlšm* Al-Qusbat N1 and note too Guelma N 27, Hr. Maktar N 68), i.e. ending in *–im*. The epenthetic short vowel would thus also have been inserted here to keep the two *m*'s, resp. ending and beginning a word, distinct (or a schwa-like vowel was heard to indicate a hiatus between the two words).

The name of the deceased, *Bibi*, is attested elsewhere (cf. *Bibai IRT* 729, *Biba CRAI* 1945: 196, and Neo-Punic *bb*^{c} Dougga N 5) and is in all likelihood of Libyco-Berber origin, cf. BB (*RIL* 708). The father's name, *Mythvnilim* ('gift of the gods'), is of course Semitic, with vowel reduction in the first syllable (cf. with vowel assimilation in Latin texts, e.g. *Mvthvnilim CIL* i 755, *Mvtthvnilim CIL* viii 23904 and using a central vowel (or indicating an indistinct vowel?) in *Methvnilim CIL* viii 12322 (probably for /*məθunilīm*/), cf. *Mythvmbal* ad Nawalia LP 1). We read the verb *inṣeb*, although the final letter is an *R*, one might assume that the illiterate lapicide probably miscopied his *Vorlage*. In *libinim* all unaccented syllables are reduced and changed to *i* by vowel harmony (cf. *binim*, Bir Shmeh LP1).

Ghirza

Ghirza LP 1

Bibliography: *CIL* viii 19971(=10991=iii 744); *IRT* 901; VATTIONI 1966: 49-50; LEVI DELLA VIDA 1967b: 265; GRATWICK 1971: 42; VATTIONI 1976: 552; COACCI POLSELLI 1979: 39f.; KRAHMALKOV 1979b: 26f.; ELMAYER 1984: 101f.; BROGAN-REYNOLDS 1984: 262-263; GARBINI 1986: 78f.; VATTIONI 1993c: 457f.; *TRE*: 391-392; KERR 2003: 148; ADAMS 2003: 232f.

Illustrations: *CIL* iii 744 (drawing); BROGAN-REYNOLDS 1984 a.l. (drawing).

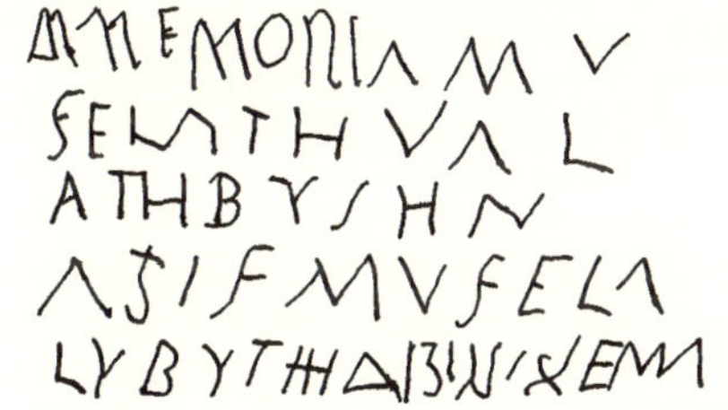

Text:
1) a[m]memoria mv
2) fela thval-
3) ath byth[!] n-
4) asif mv fela
5) lybythha binixema

Translation:
1) The memorial which
2) made Thual-
3) ath, the daughter of N-
4) asif, which she made
5) for her parents …

Remarks:
An inscription first recorded by travellers in the nineteenth century, subsequently taken by authorities to Istanbul, where it has not been seen since. Unfortunately *IRT* did not include DETHIER's drawing (as did *CIL* iii and BROGAN-REYNOLDS), and there is some discrepancy between it and *IRT*'s transcription. The first word *memoria* is preceded by what seems to be an *A*, or a ligature *A+M* (vs. *IRT M*), which would seem to be the Punic article, i.e. 'the memorial' (cf. e.g. St. Augustine *memoria martyrum*, 'a monument to the … martyrs', *De civitate dei* xxii 8.8 and not infrequent in Latin inscriptions). The usual Punic word for such structures is *mynṣyft* (cf. ad Nawalia LP 1), here the use of a Latin loan might have been influenced by the word's use in two Latin texts from Ghirza (*IRT* 898, 900) to denote the monumental 'temple-tombs' (resp. North B and North C, cf. BROGAN-SMITH 1984: 134-150, 151-159) found at Ghirza (unfortunately the original location of the present text was not recorded). The verb *fela* is qal 3 sg. f., which corresponds to the grammatical subject, *Thvalath byth Nasif*. The Libyco-Berber name *thvalath* is somewhat odd, as it appears in the pattern of feminine nouns in modern Berber (e.g. *t*-√-*t*), usually attested for place-names of the period (e.g. Thagaste, Theveste), cf. JONGELING 1984: 82-84. *byth*, here meaning 'daughter', shows the same phonetic realization as its masculine counterpart *byn* (cf. ad Bir ed-Dreder LP2). *Nasif* would seem to be a Libyco-Berber name attested elsewhere (cf. ad Wadi Umm el-Agerem LP2, and note *Ivlivs Nasif* in Bir ed-Dreder LP6), and might be related to *M. Nasif*, the co-erector of tomb North A (BROGAN-SMITH *op. cit.* 122-133, cf. the Latin inscription *IRT* 899). The repetition of *mv fel* in line 4 does seem somewhat redundant. With regard to line 5, it is unfortunate that most interprators have not availed themselves of DÉTHIER's drawing, long available in *CIL* iii. *lybthha* in line 5 (the second *h* might have been a failed attempt to render a ligature *h+a*) has several interpretations. *bytha* (following earlier commentators) might mean 'her daughter' or 'her house' (in the sense of family). Nonetheless, it would seem

more probable in our opinion to interpret the collocation *lybytha* as the clitic prefix *l-* + pl. of *ᵓb* + suff. 3 sg. f. meaning 'for her parents' (cf. *lybythem* in Zliten LP 1), corresponding to Latin *parentibvs* (cf. *IRT* 899/*IRTS* p. 140 also from Ghirza). We are unable to provide any convincing explanation for the rest of the text (n.b. transcribed by *IRT* as *bilinema*).

Lepcis Magna

Lepcis Magna LP 1

Bibliography: BARTOCCINI 1926: 30,; LEVI DELLA VIDA 1927: 18f.; LEVI DELLA VIDA 1929: 186f.; FRIEDRICH 1957: 296; LEVI DELLA VIDA 1963: 70 n16, 73; VATTIONI 1966: 41; *KAI* 178; GORDON 1968: 287; GRATWICK 1971: 43; VATTIONI 1976: 537; SEGERT 1976: 265; KRAHMALKOV 1994b: 72; *TRE*: 325-327.

Illustrations: BARTOCCINI 1926, fig. 33; *KAI* 178 (drawing).

Text:
1) felioth iadem lyro-
2) gate ymma-
3) nnai

Translation:
1) Hand-craftsmanship by/of Ro-
2) gatus, a skilled
3) craftsman

Remarks:
This epigraph was seemingly the first Latino-Punic text discovered, and may too be the oldest (yet cf. ad Zliten LP 1). The same text was found stamped on seven or eight bricks in the unfinished imperial baths, which give a *terminus ante quem* of AD 127. Interestingly enough, word dividers are used.

The first word is usually taken as a derivation of the root *pᶜl*. This is quite plausible, although the *i* is somewhat unusual, yet it might belong to the Semitic nominal suffix –*iya*, possibly a derivation such as Arabic *fāᶜilīya*. The next word is the rectum of the construct phrase and interpreted as a derivation from *yad* 'hand.' The exact morphology is unclear and there are at least three possibilities: i) dual (cf. Hebrew *yādayīm*), ii) a plural (cf. Hebrew) or iii) a du. or pl. with a suffix 3 sg. m. We are inclined to take it as a dual with a proleptic suffix. The following letter group is usually read as *σyrogate* although the first letter looks more like an *l* + (a backward) *p* (cf. Breviglieri LP 1 and note *IRT* 829). Whatever the letter, one does expect some kind of analytical genitive construction similar to Modern Hebrew *bēṯō šel* PN 'the house of PN', which is also frequent in Neo-Punic. *Rogatus* is a Latin cognomen considered specifically African (cf. MARICHAL 1992: 65).

The remaining letters *ymmannai* are usually seen as a derivation from the root *ᵓmn* (cf. Hebrew *ᵓāmmān*, Accadian *ummānu* 'artisan') although the final *–ai* is somewhat odd. One might take the initial *ym-* as the article (<*a* +gemination, cf. ad Ghirza LP 1) and followed by a root *mnC*$_3$, indicating a profession (cf. JONGELING 1994: 151).

Lepcis Magna LP 3

Bibliography: IRT 827; LEVI DELLA VIDA 1963: 84f.; VATTIONI 1966: 47f.; SZNYCER 1963-1966: 100; KRAHMALKOV 1972: 72; VATTIONI 1976: 539; SEGERT 1976: 266; *TRE*: 332-333.

Illustrations: IRT, 827; *TRE*, a.l. (drawing).

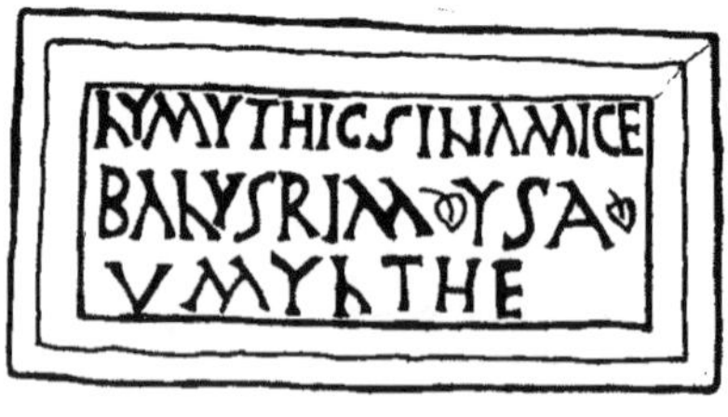

Text :
1) lymythicsin amice
2) bal ysrim ysa(b?)
3) vmylthe

Translation:
1) For Mythicsin, 'amigo',
2) the *viginturion*, erect(ed)?
3) it (?) Mylthe

Remarks:
This text was found with a male bust and certainly belonged to a funerary monument, although its find-spot is unrecorded. The initial *ly-* is obviously the preposition, followed by the name of the deceased. LEVI DELLA VIDA (followed e.g. by SEGERT) took *myth* to mean 'dead, deceased', which however would be stating the obvious (cf. also ad Hr. Gen Rieime N 1). We would rather take *mythicsin* as a PN, cf. *Mətūšāʾēl* Gn 4:18, *Mətūšālaḥ* Gn 5: 21 (re. e.g. Accadian *mutu*, Geʿez *mət*, Ugaritic *mt* 'husband, man'). *Icsin* is admittedly otherwise unattested as a name-element, and is in all likelihood Libyco-Berber. *Amicus* 'friend' (here in its Punic form) is common as a name in Latin (cf. from Africa *CIL* viii 162, 236, 4853, 6464 et passim). In line two, *bal ysrim* has generated some discussion. LEVI DELLA VIDA took *ysrim* 'twenty' to be part of a 'years lived' formula, seemingly taking *bal* pro *byn*, cf. ad Zliten LP 1. KRAHMALKOV (1972; unfortunately this inscription seems to be missing from *idem* 2000, 2001) followed this line in more detail and wondered whether the collocation *bal* + number 'may have been peculiar to the dialect of Tripolitania.' This would appear unlikely. The best solution in our opinion was first proposed by VATTIONI 1966, namely 'commander of 20 (scil. men).' We note that the construct phrase *noun* (e.g. *rb*, *bʿl) + numeral* is widely attested in Semitic to denote officials. The spelling *ysrim* has vowel reduction in the unaccented syllable (cf. also *esrim xx* in Lepcis Magna LP 2/*IRT* 826, where *esrim* probably stands for /*əsrīm*/). *Ysa* has remained without any convincing explanation. We suggest with due hesitation to connect it with the following *v* and interpret it as a derivation of the root *nṣb* (cf. ad Bir ed-Dreder LP 1), possibly with an assimilated suffix 3 sg. m (*isabo* >*isau̯*, re. /*b*/ becoming a bilabial fricative (cf. e.g. *Flabivs* Bir ed-Dreder LP 14), also feature of Latin, e.g. *bixit* pro *vixit*, *cvvicvlo* pro *cvbicvlo*, *post ovitum* etc.). *Mylthe*, the name of the erector of the monument, might be related to *Milthvn*, cf. ad Wadi Umm el-Agerem LP 1 (derived from a Latin form *Milthvs*?).

Nawalia

Nawailia LP 1

Bibliography: ELMAYER 1998: 129-132; DI VITA-EVRARD 1998, 131.

Illustrations: ELMAYER 1998, pl. 14b. (photograph).

Text:
1) myns̸ẙ -
2) f̊th lym-
3) ythvmb-
4) al ave sanv-
5) th xxx ymv
6) fel lo ab-
7) v iv???

Translation:
1) Memor-
2) ial for M-
3) ythumb-
4) al *lived* yea-
5) rs 30, which
6) made for him his fath-
7) er Iu…

Remarks:
This inscription from the Tarhuna region of the Tripolitanian Gebel is the most recently discovered and published stele of the Latino-Punic corpus (and not included in *PPG* or KRAHMALKOV 2000 and 2001). The inscription itself is somewhat reminiscent to that of Gasr Doga LP 1 (*supra*) in several aspects, although it does display hitherto unattested formulations. The opening (*myn̈syft ly-*) is unique. Although *myn̈syft* is traditionally interpreted as 'stele' (cf. Hebrew *maṣṣēḇāh*), 'memorial' would be a more appropriate translation, at least within the corpus of Latino-Punic texts, when one notes that the funerary edifices designated such were not just steles, but rather mausolea (e.g. Gasr Doga, cf. the drawing in HAYNES 1965, fig. 22 and Wadi Umm el-Agerem, cf. BARKER *et al.* 1996, figg. 1.7, 1.8; there is no detailed information on the tombs at Nawalia). Ghirza LP 1 would seem to indicate that this term was the Punic equivalent of the Latin term *memoria* (cf. a.l.). As indeed many of the traditionally 'Punic' funerary structures were indeed steles (e.g. the 'obelisk tombs', often with Neo-Punic inscriptions), we suppose that there was a semantic development from 'stele' > 'funerary edifice' in general. With regards to the phonetic development of this word, we note the following: Phoenician showed a form similar to that of Hebrew, namely *mṣbt.* (e.g. *KAI* 34), whilst at some stage in Punic geminate dissimilation took place (cf. *PPG* §58c esp. n25), cf. *mnṣbt* cf. e.g. *KAI* 78: 4); the systematic rendition of historical *b* with the Latin grapheme *f* in this word is probably due to the following voiceless dental fricative /θ/ (cf. also *myft* in Bir ed-Dreder LP 1). In both syllables, vowel reduction has occurred (/*mənṣəfθ*/), including the final one, which was in all likelihood accented. We assume that this is due to the final double consonance, which is enough to produce a long syllable, hence the vowel is reduced (in Latin linguistics this is known as the law of Ten Brink, cf. KERR 2003: 146f.).

Mythumbal, 'gift of Bal', is a well attested Semitic personal name (cf. JONGELING 1994: 102-104 and Neo-Punic *mtnbᶜl*) with vowel reduction in the initial syllable and assimilation of the nasal to the following labial.
With regard to the following collocation, *ave sanvth xxx ymv fel* ..., the components are familiar, although it is quite unusual when taken together. *Ave sanuth* (note the ligature *a+n*) is a calque of the Latin *vixit annos*, though one would rather expect *avo* ('he lived', i.e. qal 3 sg. m., cf. ad Sirte). The form itself looks like the Latin imperative sg. 'fare well' (possibly a Punic loan; in SUETONIUS, *Claudius* 21, the emperor's response to the naval combatant's *Ave* [i.e. farewell], *Imperator, morituri te salutant*, 'Avete vos!' might have been interpreted with the Punic meaning, cf. the commentaries) often used as a farewell to the dead (=*vale*) in Latin epitaphs (e.g. *CIL* viii 4570: *Have Tertia / d(is) M(anibus) s(acrum) / Sittia Tertia / vixit annis / LIIII Caesen/nia Paulina et / Caesennia Fest/a filiae piissi/mae fecerunt / vale*). If it were Punic however, we might expect a form **avi*; nonetheless, it would be odd here, as the verb has the meaning 'to live' in Punic and is employed in that meaning in the *avo sanvth* formula. It might be best to suppose a stonecutter's mistake for *avo* (or was Latin *ave* mistakenly intended?). The position of this collocation too is somewhat odd. The text itself seems to be a conflation of the Punic *myn̈syft mv fel* formula with one familiar from Latin epitaphs, e.g. *AÉ* 1912, 177: *Q(uinto) Papio Q(uinti) f(ilio) Saturnino / Iuliano centurioni / leg(ionis) II Part(hicae) vix(it) ann(os) LX / Papia Victoria soror / piissima fratri suo / fecit*, i.e. with *lymythumbal ave sanuth xxx* inserted between *myn̈syft* and *ymv*. *ymv*, i.e. *mv* spelt with an epenthetic vowel, is probably due to the preceding numeral ending with an *-m* (i.e. *šlšm*, cf. ad Gasr Doga LP 1).

After *fel lo* (cf. Mod. Hebrew *pāᶜal lō*), we would expect the name of the dedicator. The *ab* at the end of line six indicates that this is *Mythvmbal*'s father. Line 7 is difficult as the stone was reused as a trough by cutting a basin into it, by which this line was somewhat damaged. ELMAYER's reading *ymv fel ab viva* ... 'which (his) father Viva made ...' is not possible as although the fourth letter might be a *b, d* or *g*, it cannot be an *a*; additionally, one would expect a suffix 3 sg. m. after *ab*. This was correctly recognized by DI VITA-EVRARD, who ingeniously suggested reading *abviv Dioxe (?)*, i.e. taking *–viv* as the suffix (cf. *PPG* §234, p. 154f.), which however is usually used for the genitive, although of course in late Punic this is not strictly adhered to (cf. Hr. Guergour N 3 line 4: *ṯynʾ lʾ ʿbẘyʿ* 'erected it for him his father'). Despite the plausibility of this solution, the suffix does seem kind of 'heavy' for Latino-Punic and one might read *abv ivbd/ gi/l...*, 'his father Iv...' i.e. a Lybico-Berber name beginning with *iv-* (cf. JONGELING 1994: 70f.). Admittedly the suffix *–v* instead of the usual *–o* is odd.

Sirte

In the catacombes of Sirte, many short Christian funerary texts were found in Latin, Greek and Punic. All of the latter are presented here for the sake of completeness. These Punic texts are the only direct proof we have for Punic-speaking Christianity, often referred to by Church fathers such as St. Augustine. Of interest is the fact that the in the Latin texts, the names are usually in the vocative with nominative function (cf. ADAMS 2003: 513f., additional African examples in ADAMIK 1987); this is a strong indication that Punic indeed borrowed words and names from Latin in the vocative (pace e.g. AMADASI 1995).

Sirte LP 1

Bibliography: BARTOCCINI 1928: 195; *IRT* 855; VATTIONI 1966: 52; *KAI* 180d; VATTIONI 1976: 539; GARBINI 1986: 74; *TRE*: 337.

Illustrations: BARTOCCINI 1928, pl. I, 8 (drawing).

Text:
1) avo aniboni
2) sanv V

Translation:
Anibonius lived 5 years

Remarks:
Avo is clear, in the following word, the *A* and the *N* are joined, rendering *Aniboni*(*us*). The name, usually spelt *Annibonius*, is a Latin adaptation of the Semitic name *ḫnbʿl* (i.e. *Annibal, Annobal*) in which the final element *–bal* has been reinterpreted to Latin *bonvs* (cf. JONGELING 1994: 9 with references). The second line is usually read *sanv* [..., i.e. the years lived missing. Looking at Bartoccini's drawing, one sees that the third sign looks more like a ligature for *N+V*, rendering *sanv v*, i.e. '5 years' (or less likely, one might interpret *san v* as an abbreviation).

Sirte LP 2

Bibliography: BARTOCCINI 1928: 192; *IRT* 855; FRIEDRICH 1957: 296; VATTIONI 1966: 52; *KAI* 180a; GRATWICK 1971: 43; VATTIONI 1976: 540; SEGERT 1976: 266; *TRE*: 337; ADAMS 2003: 235.

Illustrations: BARTOCCINI 1928, pl. I, 15 (drawing).

Text:
1) mercvri
2) avo sanv
3) vi

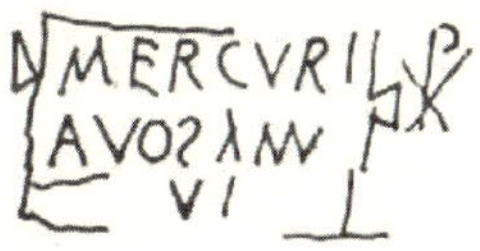

Translation:
Mercurius lived 6 years

Remarks:
The reading is quite clear. Note the different syntax vis-à-vis the preceding, namely SVO (vs. VSO) as customary in Latin texts, scil. PN *vixit annos*. Might this be due to Latin influence?

Sirte LP 3

Bibliography: BARTOCCINI 1928: 192; VATTIONI 1976, 540; *TRE*: 337.

Illustrations: BARTOCCINI 1928, pl. I, 16 (drawing).

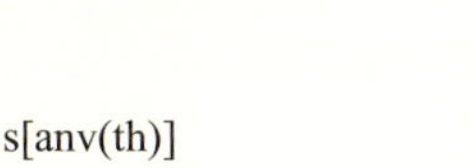

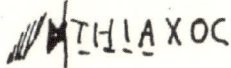

Text:
]-thi avo s[anv(th)]

Translation:
...]-thi lived ... y[ears]

Remarks:
Judging by the drawing, the line preserved ap-

pears to be line two of in total three lines; the remains can be read as quite satisfactorily as a SVO-type inscription. Although the sixth letter looks like an *X*, it would appear to be a *V* in which the lapicide carried the down stokes on too far. The final letter is obviously the upper portion of an *S* (cf. the preceding inscription, mirrored!).

Sirte LP 4

Bibliography: BARTOCCINI 1928 : 192; *IRT* 855; VATTIONI 1966 : 43; VATTIONI 1976: 540; *TRE*: 337.

Illustrations: BARTOCCINI 1928, pl. I, 26 (drawing).

Text:
1)pom[*peia*]
2) ava

Translation:
Pom<peia?> lived …

Remarks:
The personal name appears to be an abbreviation. There does not seem to be enough room for *sanuth* + the age of the deceased. Nonetheless VATTIONI (1976) proposed reading the first *a* of line two as being part of the PN, i.e. *pom*[pei]*a* and reading the remaining *va* as the customary Latin abbreviation for *vixit annos*, which is possible. If the text is Punic, then the deceased was a female (cf. ad LP 6).

Sirte LP 5

Bibliography: BARTOCCINI 1928, 193; *IRT* 855; VATTIONI 1966: 53; *KAI* 180e; VATTIONI 1976: 540; SEGERT 1976: 266; *TRE*: 337-338.

Illustrations: BARTOCCINI 1928, pl. II, 29 (drawing).

Text:
1) abdvsmvn av
2) sanvth λ

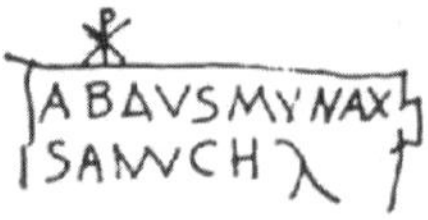

Translation:
Abdusmun liv[ed] 30 years

Remarks:
The Semitic PN should not be read *Abδusmyn* as done by e.g. RÖLLIG *KAI* a.l. and SEGERT 1976: 266, 305: the *D* is not necessarily a Greek letter form, it is more likely just an unsuccessful Latin D. The penultimate letter of the name is not a *Y*, but rather a badly joined *V*, cf. the *V* of the following word *av*. The name, *Abdvsmvn*, is of course Semitic ('servant of Eshmun', cf. Cherchel N 1) with vowel harmony in the medial syllable. There appears to be no room for the expected *-o* of that word. Previous interpreters read the following line as *sanv cii*, making *Abdusmun* a centenarian and leaving the (Greek) λ unexplained. We prefer reading *sanuth λ*, the *c* being a sloppy *t* (often the *t* can look like a *c* with a horizontal stoke on the top), the *h* is quite clear and cannot really be read as *ii*. The final character is Greek, and was probably considered more convenient than *xxx*.

Sirte LP 6

Bibliography: BARTOCCINI 1928: 193; VATTIONI 1976: 540; *TRE*: 338.

Illustrations: BARTOCCINI 1928, pl. II, 30 (drawing).

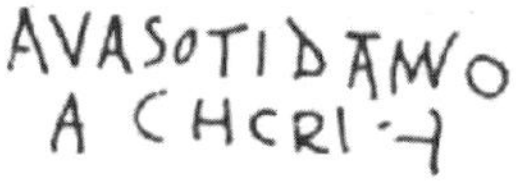

Text:
1) ava sotidat mio
2) [s]a[nv]th cri …

Translation:
Sotidat … lived … years …

Remarks:
This text is rather enigmatic. VATTIONI read *avasoti danno / achcri* without being able to offer a translation. The *anno* might be point to *[vixit] anno[s]*, making the text Latin. Nonetheless the initial *ava* seemingly points to a Punic text, cf. ad LP 5. The name, *Sotidat* is admittedly unusual and unattested (or read *ava s Otidat*? –the *s* then being an abbreviation for *sanv*[*th*], cf. ad LP 12). The second line seems rather reminiscent of *sanuth*: the *s* and the *n* missing, the the *c* as a *t*, cf. ad LP 5. The final letters might have been an attempt to render *Christus*.

Sirte LP 7

Bibliography: BARTOCCINI 1928: 193; VATTIONI 1976: 541; VATTIONI 1993a: 464f.; *TRE*, 338.

Illustrations: BARTOCCINI 1928, pl. II, 39 (drawing).

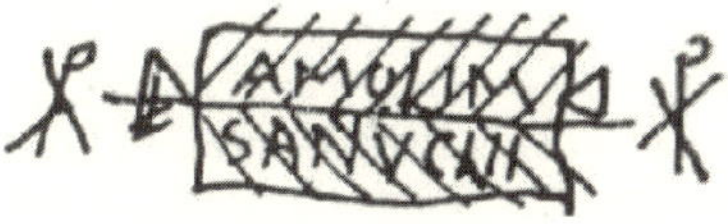

Text:
1) av$^{!}$o lim
2) sanvt lii

Translation:
Lim lived 52 years

Remarks:
The text seems to read *amolim* in the first line. The reading proferred here bases itself rather heavily on the *avo sanv*[*th*] formula, although *lim* as a personal name is most unusual, unless it is an abbreviation. BARTOCCINI 1928 (followed by VATTIONI 1993a) has suggested interpreting *amolim* as a rendition of the PN *Amothilim*, i.e. 'handmaiden of the gods.' This solution is attractive (on the loss of *–t* /*θ*/, cf. the spelling *sanv*; one might posit a development *amothilim* > *amoïlim* > *amôlim*) cf. the female names *Amobbal* (*CIL* viii 4408) and *Amubal* (*ILA* ii 3073) vs. *Amotbal* (*CIL* viii 16923, cf. GANDOLPHE 1999: 223), Neo-Punic $^{\supset}$*mtb*^{c}*l* (Lepcis Magna N 24). Should this interpretation be correct, we might then have an abbreviated formula, 'PN *x* years', the verb being implicit (if it wasn't just forgotten).

Sirte LP 8

Bibliography: BARTOCCINI 1928: 193; VATTIONI 1966: 53; *KAI* 180b; VATTIONI 1976: 541; *TRE*: 338.

Illustrations: BARTOCCINI 1928, pl. II 40 (drawing).

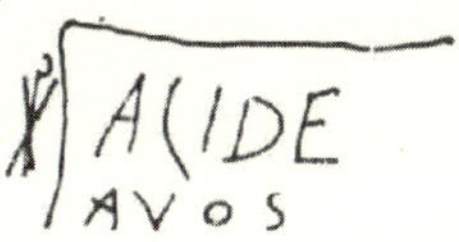

Text:
1) alide
2) avo s[anv(th)…]

Translation:
Alidus lived … y<ears>

Remarks:
The name *Alidus* is also attested in a Latin inscription from Africa Proconsularis (*CIL* viii 17204).

Sirte LP 9

Bibliography: BARTOCCINI 1928: 199; VATTIONI 1976: 541; *TRE*: 338.

Illustrations: BARTOCCINI 1928, pl. II 43 (drawing).

Text:
1)]sanv iii
2)]sa

Translation:
[… lived] 3 years … ye[ars]

Sirte LP 10

Bibliography: BARTOCCINI 1928: 193; FRIEDRICH 1957: 296 n2; VATTIONI 1966: 53; VATTIONI 1976: 541; *TRE*: 338.

Illustrations: BARTOCCINI 1928, pl. II, 46 (drawing).

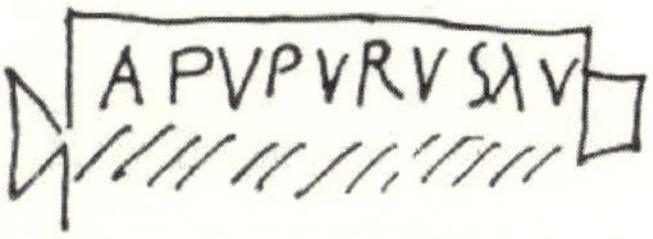

Text:
1) apvpvrvs av[o sanv(th)…]

Translation:
Apupurus liv[ed years …]

Remarks:
Might *Apvpvrvs* be related to $^{\supset}$*p*^{c}*pr*^{c} in H. Maktar N 78 (transcribed by JONGELING 1984: 151 as *Epapphra*, cf. VATTIONI a.l.)? One might also read *apvpvru s[anv(th)* ... cf. ad Wadi Uaeni LP 1.

Sirte LP 11

Bibliography: BARTOCCINI 1928: 193; FRIEDRICH 1957: 296; VATTIONI 1966: 42f.; *KAI* 180c; VATTIONI 1976: 541; *TRE*: 339.

Illustrations: BARTOCCINI 1928, pl. II 50 (drawing).

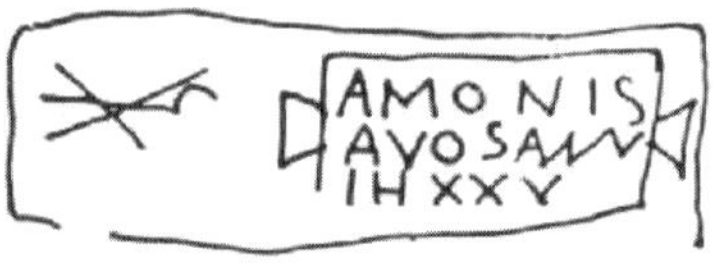

Text:
1) amonis
2) avo sanv
3) th xxv

Translation:
Amonis lived 25 years

Remarks:
Amonis is in all likelihood a name of Semitic origin with the theophoric element *ḥmn*. Although the name seems to be in the Latin genitive (cf. *Ammonis*, CORIPPUS 3: 81, 7: 519; nom. *Ammon*, *idem*. 2: 110 et passim), it is in all likelihood either a misspelling or a phonetic rendition (*-ivs*>*-îs*) of *Ammonivs*, *Hammonivs* (e.g. *CIL* viii 21333). The rendition of geminiation in Latino-Punic is not systematic (cf. *Aniboni* LP 1, *anaṣiba* Gasr el-Azaiz LP 1 vs. possibly *a(m)memoria* Ghirza LP 1).

Sirte LP 12

Bibliography: BARTOCCINI 1928: 193; VATTIONI 1976: 541; *TRE*: 339.

Illustrations: BARTOCCINI 1928, pl. II 51 (drawing).

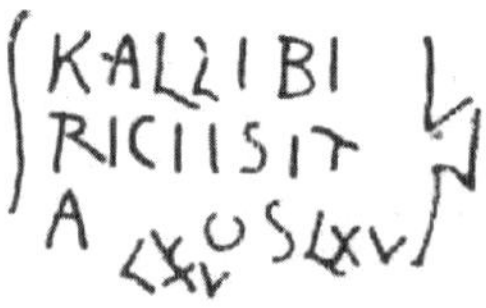

Text:
1) kalli bi-
2) rich$^{!}$ sit
3) avo s<anv> lxv
4) lxv

Translation:
Kalli Birich who lived 65 y[ears] 65

Remarks:
The name *Kalli* is otherwise unattested (possibly related to *Kallibi* in Latin 51 from Sirte?). *Birich* is of course a good Semitic name derived from the root *brk*. The vocalisation would point to a feminine name (vs. *Baric* and variants as masc., cf. JONGELING 1988: 223ff.), cf. e.g. *Octavia Birich* (*CIL* viii 27559) and *brkt* Lepcis Magna N 4, Guelma N 9. Naturally *avo* is qal 3 sg. m., which is incongruent. This spelling is probably comparable to spellings such as e.g. *wḥwʾ šʿnt ʿmšm* 'and she lived fifty years' for *Qvarta Nyptanis [filia]* (Neo-Punic *[q]wʿr[t]h bt nptḥn*) in Djebel Mansour N1 vs. e.g. *wšhqndʿ bt šqndʿ ʾš[t]m ʿwʿ šʿnt* [vacat] 'and Secunda the daughter of Secunda his wife lived years ...' in Hr. Brirht N 1. The use of the demonstrative *sith* with *avo sanv[th]* is unique in Punic, and seems to have been influenced by Latin PN *qui vixit annos ...* (e.g. *CIL* viii 1522). *S* would appear to be an abbreviation for *s[anv(th)]*. The repetition of the numeral (i.e. in Roman numerals, one might expect it to be written out in full once and repeated as a numeral, cf. e.g. *KAI* 14: 1, Lepcis Magna LP 2 and in Latin at Bu Njem 76-79) is odd.

Wadi Uaeni

Wadi Uaeni LP 1

Bibliography: OATES 1954: 115f.; LEVI DELLA VIDA 1965: 59f.; VATTIONI 1966: 43; GRATWICK 1971: 43; KRAHMALKOV 1973: 62f.; VATTIONI 1976: 542; GARBINI 1986: 80; KRAHMALKOV 1994a: 454f.; *TRE* 342-343; ADAMS 2003: 233.

Illustrations: OATES 1954, pl. 16b (photograph).

Text:
1) iv flav
2) sanv av lxvi
3) hoc fillyth
4) mia sanv av
5) xxxiii

Translation:
1) Iu(lius) Flav(ius)
2) lived 66 years;
3) this [was] the work of
4) Mia, [who] lived years
5) 33

Remarks:
The photograph is rather difficult to read, and the reading given above must be viewed as tentative. This text is interesting for several reasons. On the name of the deceased, *Iulius Flavius*, cf. ad Bir ed-Dreder LP 2. The funerary formula PN *sanv av* instead of the usual *avo* PN *sanv[th]* or PN *avo sanv[th]* is peculiar. *Av* would seem to be an abbreviation (in the first case for *avo*, in the second for *ava*, cf. e.g. ad Sirte LP 12). The first word of the third line is the Latin demonstrative pronoun (the *h* itself indicates a non-Punic word), or does it belong to an abbreviation? The presence of such a morphological element here in a Punic text is indeed rather unexpected, especially since the only borrowing from Latin in these texts are technical loans (e.g. *memoria, centenarium*) and some inscriptional formulae (e.g. *avo sanv[th]*). We concur with ADAMS 2003 that it was 'probably an *ad hoc*, momentary switch adopted by one particular writer for reasons which are obscure.'

The next word, *fillyth*, is unclear. A derivation from the root $p^{c}l$ would seem likely. As it would appear that the daughter of the deceased, *Mia* (who must have died shortly after her father), erected the monument. One might expect a verbal formation qal perfect 3 sg. f. (cf. Mod. Hebrew *pā^{c}ălāh*), although *fillyth* hardly looks as if it could be derived from such a form, especially in light of the two attestations of *fela* in Ghirza LP 1. One might rather expect a nominal formation cf. Hebrew *pə^{c}ullāh* (a fem. **qutull* formation?), possibly with vowel reduction in the second syllable and partial assimilation in the first, due to its being the regens of a construct state.

Wadi Umm el-Agerem

Wadi Umm el-Agerem LP 1

Bibliography: IRTS 24; LEVI DELLA VIDA 1963: 75f.; LEVI DELLA VIDA 1965: 60; VATTIONI 1966: 54f.; VATTIONI 1971: 184; KRAHMALKOV 1972: 70f.; VATTIONI 1976: 549; KRAHMALKOV 1979: 175-79; ELMAYER 1984: 102f.; *TRE*: 373-375.

Text:
1) masavchan vysyǥan
2) felv labvnom iyllvl
3) bvn.m.milth.n varis
4) vnom anobal br̊n/vem..
5) chon *chaross*

Translation:
1) Masauchan and Syǥan
2) made for their father Iyllul …

Remarks:
This text has only been published in transcription. The present authors were able to examine the text *in situ* in December 2003 and take several photographs. In the intervening half century, the mausoleum seems to have been restored. Whereas *IRTS* reports a 'block of coarse limestone lying beside a ruined mausoleum …', we found the inscription just under the cornice of a mausoleum, which had seemingly been restored in the meantime, we noticed that the stones had been cemented together.

The first two lines of the text are quite clear. The third and fourth lines are rather damaged. The fifth line is squeezed in between the fourth and the lower edge of the *tabula ansata*.

In the third line, one might expect the filiation of *Illvl* (cf. LP 2*: masavchan byn Iylvl*)

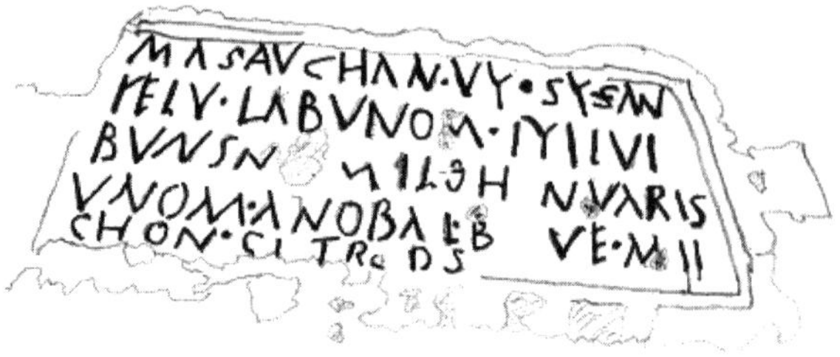

Wadi Umm el-Agerem LP1

and that which was built (i.e. the object of *felv*). The *bvn.m* might an attempt to render *byn*, followed by the father's name. The letter between *N* and *M* has a form reminiscent of ʃ, and the reading suggested by the *editio princeps*, *bvnem*, is unlikely. It would also seem doubtful that the ʃ and the *M* belong to a name, as *milth.n*, possibly the Libyco-Berber name *Milthun* (cf. *Karthago* 8 (1957): 78f.), follows. One might on the other hand see *bvn.m* as a nominal derivation of the root *bny* 'to build.' *Milth.n* might either be the father or connected with the following (lines 3-4), *varisvnom Anobal* 'and their architect(?)' (*aris* a *qatīl* formation from √*ḥrš*?, cf. ad Bir Shmech LP 1), *Annobal* seems also to be mentioned in LP 2 in some building capacity. The rest of the inscription does not make too much sense, possibly it has suffered damage since its initial discovery. In any case there is no room for the restoration *m[asav]chan*, first proposed by LEVI DELLA VIDA 1963: 76. Should *chaross* have been legible in the lower line, one might compare it with Arabic *karrasa* i) 'to lay a foundation (of a building)', ii) 'to consecrate, dedicate, inaugurate.'

Wadi Umm el-Agerem LP 2

Bibliography: *IRT* 906; *IRT*S 141f; LEVI DELLA VIDA 1963: 71-74; VATTIONI 1966: 50-52; KRAHMALKOV 1972: 70; VATTIONI 1976: 550; KRAHMALKOV 1976: 61; ELMAYER 1984: 103f.; *TRE*: 375-378.

Illustrations: *IRT*, 906 (incomplete copy); *IRT*S, pl. 33 (photograph); *TRE*, a.l. (incomplete copy).

Text:

1) thanvbda vbyne nasif felv mynꞩ
2) yf̊th [l]ymasavchan byn iylvl
3) bydinario yl ∗ↀↀΘ fy ly-
4) thychleth vybvny annobal
5) chylyv5v(?)bylndsi*ana* chvlam

Translation:

1) Thanubda and the sons of Nasif made <this> memo-
2) rial [fo]r Masauchan the son-of Iylul
3) paid in coin *amounting* to *denarii* 2100 of fo<lles> as
4) expense(s), and its builder(?) was Annobal
5) …

Remarks:
The present authors examined this inscription at the Wadi Umm el-Agerem in December 2003 and where able to check the readings provided by *IRTS* (note there is also a fair plaster copy at the museum in Beni Walid). The first four lines are quite clear, the fifth is written in the frame of the *tabula ansata* and is somewhat illegible.

Thanubda would seem to be a Libyco-Berber name, possibly related to *Thanubra* (*CIL* viii 22758). *Byne* is probably a regens pl. (cf. KRAHMALKOV 1972), cf. spellings such as *bnʾ mʿsnkʿw* 'the sons of Masankaw' (Breviglieri N 1). The spelling of the copula as *v-* here is noteworthy and might have been realized as /*u*/ before a labial (cf. Hebrew *BuMaP*), although this is not rendered systematically in Latino Punic (pace KERR 2003: 148f.; note the substandard pronunciation in Modern Hebrew e.g *və-bayīt*), cf. e.g. *vy-binim* and *vybal ars* ad Bir Shmech LP 1. *Nasif* is also attested in Ghirza LP 1. *Masavchan*, the son of *Iylvl* is in all likelihood the same person as in LP 1. It is a Libyco-Berber name paralleled elsewhere, cf. *mʿṣwkn* Wadi El-Amud N 1 (note the copy of this text at Beni

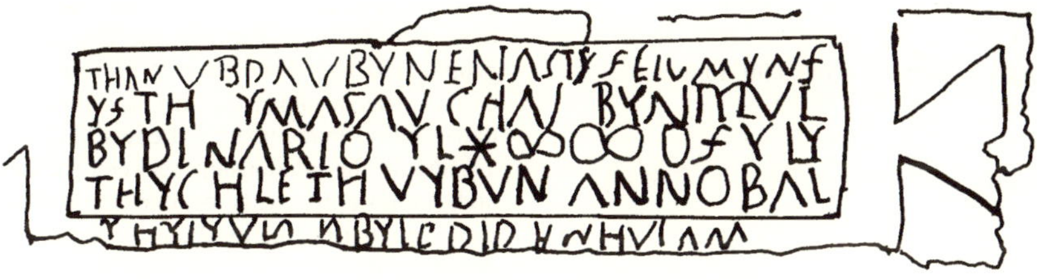

Wadi Umm el-Agerem LP2

Walid reads *maꞩavchan*), *masavca* (*CRAI* 1972: 334), *Masucani* (*CIL* viii 9613) and MSKN (*RIL* 349). VATTIONI 1966 suggested reading *vy-* 'and' before the latter name, which however is unlikely, as the inscription would then not mention the name of the deceased and lines 3f. would have no verbal government. With regard to *mynꞩyᶠth*, autopsy shows that the *f* is still discernable. In the past, the word was read as *mynꞩysth*, which was explained as the product of some odd phonetic development (e.g. LEVI DELLA VIDA 1963: 72f.). At present, the spelling with *f* is also attested in Nawalia LP 1 (supra), Libya OU LP 1 (*IRT* 828), Wadi Chanafes LP 1 (cf. ad Bir Shmech LP 1) and Wadi Ghalbun LP 1 (unpublished). *S* is only attested in two texts namely Gasr Doga LP 1 (cf. our comments, supra) and Bir Scedeua LP 1 (*IRT*S 20, only attested by a drawing). We hence presume that the word was spelt with *f*, and the two anomalous examples are due to a lapicide's error (or in the latter case, possibly copied as *s* by mistake).The collocation *bydinario yl* ∗*ⲰⲰΘ fy* indicates the cost of the mausoleum, and seems to be a clumsy attempt to calque the Latin *in nummo denarivm follis* (cf. *IRT* 898, 900 from nearby Ghirza). The Latin loan *denarius*, in a spelling familiar from vulgar Latin (cf. too $dn^{\text{c}}ry^{\text{ɔ}}$ in Lepcis Magna N 9/*KAI* 130), seems here to be used in the sense of 'in coin' (or is *by-* here a *b-pretii*, 'for money', cf. Cicero, *Liber secundus ad Atticum* 2.6). In the numeral, LEVI DELLA VIDA read *C*, but the sign is clearly round, hence probably a Θ (=C) was intended, which would correspond to the usage of Φ (=M). *Fy* would seem to be some kind of abbreviation for *folles*; the older readings -LEVI DELLA VIDA read it as ꞩ and saw it as the marker of relativity (a mistake, instead of σ), VATTIONI 1966 also reading ꞩ, took it for an abbreviation for *sestersii-* are untenable epigraphically speaking. Monitarily speaking too, *folles* would be more logical (i.e. a bag filled with coins and issued by the mint from the reign of Diocletian until Constantine M. reintroduced gold bullion; hereafter a *folles* was not worth much), as several Latin texts on similar mausolea use the term (e.g. the Ghirza texts mentioned). Should our suggestion be correct, the site can be dated to the first half of the fourth century AD.

Thychleth was explained by LEVI DELLA VIDA quite convincingly as a derivation from the root *kly*, cf. Hebrew *taḵlīṯ*. LEVI DELLA VIDA took to mean either 'addition' or 'completion', the latter meaning was adopted by VATTIONI 1976. The former's interpretation 'addition' is based on the supposition that this lexeme belongs to the following clause, which he read as *vy bvny Annobal [?] chylyv ⲰⲰ v ...* 'in addition the builder Annobal added 1000 denarii.' We would rather connect *thychleth* with the preceding, in the sense of 'expense', a meaning which the word seems to have elsewhere in Phoenico-Punic (cf. *DNWSI* 1214f. s.v.). *Lythychleth* /*lǝθǝχlḗθ*/ would then seem to be a gloss, cf. the Latin (*IRT* 898, 900) *discvssimvs ratiocinio ad ea erogatvm est svmtos mercedibvs in nummo* ∗ *follis singvlares nvmero qvadraginta qvinqve milia sescentos*... 'we calculated the expense exactly – there was paid in coin as wages 45,600 folles of denarii simplices …'

The rest of lines four and line five are quite enigmatic. *Annobal* would seem to be the same person as mentioned in LP 1, possibly the architect. Might *bvny* be a derivation from the root *bny* 'to build' (*bvna Annobal* 'her (scil. *mynꞩyfth*) was Annobal': *bvnannobal* >*bvnǝannobal*)? We can distill no sense from line five (which is utterly illegible in the copy). Note that the seventh letter, read by LEVI DELLA VIDA as ↀ, '1000', looks more like the numeral 5 rotated 90° to the left.

Zliten

Zliten LP 1

Bibliography: BARTOCCINI 1927: 232-36; BEGUINOT 1949: 15; LEVI DELLA VIDA 1963: 83f.; SZNYCER 1963-1966: 101-102; VATTIONI 1966: 39-41; VATTIONI 1976: 539; KRAHMALKOV 1976: 62f.; GARBINI 1976: 12; COACCI POLSELLI 1979: 40f.; *TRE*: 334-336.

Illustrations: BARTOCCINI 1927 a.l.; *TRE*, a.l. (drawing).

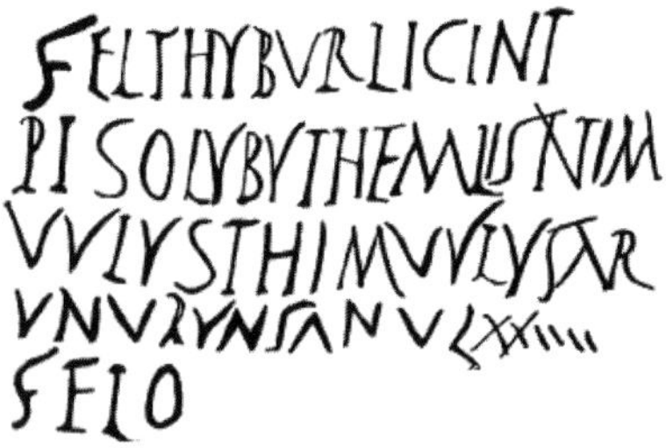

Text:
1) fel thy bvr licini
2) piso lybythem lisnim
3) vylysthim vylysar
4) vnv byn sanv lxxiiii
5) felo

Translation:
1) Licinius Piso made this grave
2) for his two parents
3) and for his wife and for Sar-
4) unu aged 74 years,
5) he made it.

Remarks:
This text was described as a graffito from a tomb by BARTOCCINI. It is said to go along with a Latin inscription (*IRT* 852), now built into a local mosque:

Dis / Manibvs / Sacrvm / Q(vinti) Licini / [Pi]sonis / Q(vintvs) Licinivs / Rvfvs fil(ivs) / patri carissi(mo) / ex voto / d(e) s(vo) f(ecit).

Both are said to date from the first century AD (see now DI VITA-ERVARD in *British Epigraphic Society Newsletter* 9 (2003): 8). If correct, this would make this text the oldest dated Latino-Punic text (vs. Lepcis Magna LP 1). Should the relationship between the Latin and Latino-Punic texts be correct, it would then seem that the Latino-Punic text was composed by/for Licinius Piso when he had the tomb built, whilst his son was responsible for the Latin text upon his father's demise.

In the Latino-Punic text, *Licini(us) Piso* is the subject of *fel*. The object is *bvr*, accompanied by the *nota accusativi*. With regard to the latter, the spelling *thy* (vs. *yth*) might be due to to the presence of the article. The word *bvr*, indicating that which was made, has been related to Hebrew *bōr* 'water pit, cistern' Arabic *buʾra* 'site; pit; abyss', and taken to mean a 'tomb.' One might compare this lexeme with *bʾr* attested in Wadi el-Amud N 1 (there does not seem to be any room for the proposed initial *q* and the vocalisation with ʾ is somewhat odd for *qbr*, (*/qabr/>/qbar/*?) 'grave'). Indeed both texts are quite similar in that they are not built for a single person, but rather for an entire family. Could *bvr* be a technical term for a 'family grave'?

Lybythem 'his parents' (cf. *ʾbtm* Lepcis Magna N 19) displays vowel reduction in the unaccented syllables (as in Ghirza LP 1, vs. e.g. Gasr el-Azaiz LP 1), as does *lisnim* (vowel harmony, cf. e.g. *libinim* Gasr Doga LP 1). The historical diphthong (cf. Hebrew *šənayīm*) in this lexeme has been contracted to a vowel rendered as */ī/*. The use of the plural of **ab* (e.g. Hebrew *ʾāḇ*) would seem to be an attempt to render Latin *parentes*. In line 3, *vylysthim*, again with vowel reduction (st. abs. **isth*?), is generally taken to mean 'and for his wife' which is very plausible (cf. *wlʾšty* Wadi el-Amud LP 1; *ʾštm* Guelma N1, N3, Kef Bezioun N 1, *ʿšt[ʾ]* El-Amruni N1). The following sections of the text have been more controversial. Our reading is based on the drawing. Although LEVI DELLA VIDA ingeniously suggested interpreting *vylysar* as 'and for the rest [of his family]' (cf. Hebrew *šəʾār*), it does not quite mesh with the remainder of the text. We suggest reading the PN *Sarvnv*[*s*], cf. names such as *Sarrune* (*CIL* viii 21596) or *Saron* (*idem.* 557), *Saronius* (*idem.* 24394); also fem. *Sarrona* (*idem.* 2187,

ILA i 1634). The next section of the fourth line would appear to contain the Semitic age collocation (cf. e.g. Hebrew *ben X šānāh*, Arabic *ibn X sana*, Ge^{c}ez *käwino wäldä X* ^{c}*amät*). We note here briefly that this formula is attested in Neo-Punic inscriptions (e.g. Ain Zakkar N1), although the ^{c}*w*^{ɔ} *šnt* formula, a calque of the Latin *vixit annos*, is much more frequent (Guelma N1 *et passim*, cf. the Neo-Punic glossary sub *ḥwy*). In Latino-Punic too *avo sanv[th]* is the rule, the present text being the exception. It would seem that the Semitic formula was gradually replaced by the Latinate one, the indication of the age of the deceased on an epitaph being foreign to Semitic in any case. In the final line, *felo* 'he made it', would seem to be an imitation of *de svo fecit*.

ALGERIA

El-Hofra

El-Hofra GP1

Bibliography: BERTHIER-CHARLIER 1955: 167f.; FRIEDRICH 1957: 282-90; *KAI* 175; GORDON 1968: 289; GRATWICK 1971: 41f.; VATTIONI 1976: 534.

Illustrations: BERTHIER-CHARLIER 1955, pl. xxviiia (photograph).

Text:

1) ΛΑΔΟΥΝ ΛΥΒΑΛ ΑΜΟΥΝ ΟΥ
2) ΛΥΡΥΒΑΘ!ΩΝ ΘΙΝΙΘ ΦΑΝΕ ΒΑΛ
3) ΥΣ ΝΑΔΩΡ ΣΩΣΙΠΑΤΡ!ΟΣ ΒΥΝ
4) ΖΩΠΥΡΟΣ ΣΑΜΩ ΚΟΥΛΩ ΒΑ-
5) ΡΑΧΩ

Translation:

1) To the lord Bal Amun and
2) to our lady Thinith, Fane Bal,
3) which vowed Sosipatros, the son
4) of Zopyros. He heard his voice [and]
5) blessed him.

Remarks:

This Greco-Punic text is from Constantine (ancient Cirta) in Algeria. This text was found among many Punic and Neo-Punic texts, and it must be much earlier than the Latino-Punic texts. However, it shows some similarities in spelling with the latter. As the text itself contains the well-known Punic votive formula (cf. Constantine N 42 supra, et passim), its interpretation is not difficult, and comparison with Punic and Neo-Punic texts using vowel-letters, sheds light on their phonetic value. The formula closely follows texts such as El-Hofra 153:

1) *l*^{ɔ}*dn lb*^{c}*l ḥmn*
2) *wlrb*^{c}*tn tnt*
3) *p*^{c}*n*^{ɔ} *b*^{c}*l nd*^{c}*r*
4) *grskn bn* ^{c}*bd-*
5) ^{ɔ}*mn š*^{c}*mn [ql*^{ɔ} *brk*^{ɔ}*]*

Here we will limit ourselves to only a few remarks (cf. the detailed commentary by RÖLLIG, *KAI* a.l.). One sees that the guttural consonants no longer seem to have been a phonetic reality (i.e. *βαλ*, *αμουν*, *σαμο*). Of interest is the transcription of Punic *k* with χ, which corresponds to the use of *ch* in the Latino-Punic texts, e.g. *thychleth* (Wadi Umm el-Agerem LP 2), *Chyrdid* (Bir ed-Dreder LP 2, re. Libyan KRDD), *Masauchan* (Wadi Umm el-Agerem LP 2, re. Libyan MSKN), and note e.g. *Chinidial* (*CIL* viii 5217) with its Libyan parallel KNDIL and Neo-Punic *kndy*^{c}*l* (Guelma N 3). The rendition of the other tenues (Neo-Punic *p*, *t*) is also similar, namely *φ* (cf. Latino-Punic *fel* (e.g. Breviglieri LP 1 et passim) and *θ* (e.g. *mynşyfth* Wadi Umm el-Agerem LP 2 et passim; spellings such as *tribynvs* Bir ed-Dreder LP 1 and *centenari* Breviglieri LP 1, are probably based on Latin conventions). Also of interest is the consequent use of *υ* (>Latin *y*) to transcribe the schwa (comp. *ρυβαθων* with *ryb mşir* in Bir ed-Dreder LP 2). *ου* consequently renders /*ū*/, cf. e.g. *qwl*^{ɔ} (Guelma N 19). Of interest is the spelling -*θων* of the pronominal suffix 1 pl. c. in *ρυβαθων* (the plate reads *o*, the cross-bar seems to have been forgotten). One would expect a form with a final vowel (cf. *PPG* §112, p.67), which seems to have been apocopated.

Mention should be made of El-Hofra 3 GR./*KAI* 176, a Greek translation of the same dedicatory formula:

1) ΚΡΟΝΩΙ ΘΕΝ-
2) ΝΕΙΘ ΦΕΝΗ Β-
3) ΑΛ ΕΘΥΣ(ΕΝ Α-
4) ΛΚΙΜΗΔΗ(Σ)

5) ΚΑΙ ΕΠΗΚ(ΟΥ-)
6) ΣΕ)ΤΗ(Ν ΦΩΝΗΝ ?)

The text is indeed a Greek calque of the Punic, and *Bal Amun* is equated with *Chronos* (Latin *Satvrnus*; cf. LIPIŃSKI 1995: 256ff.), although *Thinith* (Greek *Artemis*, cf. *KAI* 53; Roman *Diana*, cf. *idem* 199-215, esp. 205f.) and her title are transcribed, the syncretism was probably not a reality at Constantine at this time. Note the varying transcription of *θενειθ φενη βαλ* in the Greek text vs. *θινιθ φανη βαλ* in the transcribed text. Possibly *θενειθ* renders probably /*θənīθ*/, while *θινιθ* is rendering /*θiniθ*/, due to vowel harmony.

Appendices

Neo-Punic Glossary

ᵓb n. FATHER, sg. abs. Hr. Gen Rieime N 1, sg. + suff. 3 sg. m. *ᵓbyᵓ* Wadi el-Amud N 1, + suff. 3 pl. m. *ᶜbnᵓm* Wadi el-Amud N 2, pl. + suff. 3 sg. m. *ᵓbtm* Lepcis Magna N 19, pl. + suff. 3 pl. m. *ᵓbᶜthm* Hr. Brirht N 1

ᵓbn n. STONE, sg. abs. Djebel Massoudj 1, Hr. Sidi Khalifat N 1, Hr. Bou Atfan N 2, Ksiba Mraou N 3, *ᶜbn* Dougga N 3, 4, Guelma N 1, 3, 4, 9, Kef Bezioun N 1, 2, Ksiba Mraou N 1, pl. abs. *ᵓbnm* Bordj Helal N 1

ᵓgᵓdr PN, Berber, Sabratha N 16

ᵓdn n. LORD, sg. abs. Breviglieri N 1; Lepcis Magna N 10, 17, Bir bou Rekba N 1, Hr. Maktar N 1, 39, 77, 112, Hr. Medeine N 1, Tunisia OU N 2, 7, 13, Constantine N 7, 10, 23, 28, 42, *ᶜdn* Guelma N 19, 22

ᵓdnbᶜl PN, Semitic, Hr. Medeine N 1, Tunisia OU N 7, Constantine N 23, S. Antioco N 3

ᵓdr adj. GREAT, MIGHTY, m. sg. abs. Bir Tlelsa N 1, cstr. Lepcis Magna N 16, 19, f. sg. abs. *ᶜdrt* Ain Zakkar N 1, pl. cstr. *ᵓdrᵓ* Lepcis Magna N 19

ᵓdrbᶜl PN, Semitic, Hr. Maktar N 77, Tunisia OU N 7, Constantine N 42

ᵓw conj. OR, Hr. Medeine N 1

ᵓwtnᵓ PN, Latin, AVITANNUS ? Hr. Maktar N 76

ᵓzrm n. in the combination *mlk ᵓzrm* of uncertain meaning, *mlk ᵓšrm* Guelma N 19, 22

ᵓḥ n. BROTHER, + suff. 3 sg. m. *ᵓḥyᵓ*, Lepcis Magna N 2

ᵓḥr adj. OTHER, Lepcis Magna N 2 (used adverbially ?)

ᵓḥr prep. AFTER, Cherchel N 1

ᵓyᵓṣdn PN, Berber ? / Semitic ?, Wadi el-Amud N 1

ᵓyknᶜ PN, Berber, Hr. Maktar N 76

ᵓynḥ PN, Semitic ? Tirekbine N 1

ᵓyspn PN, Berber, Hr. Medeine N 1

ᵓl PN, Semitic, the god EL, Lepcis Magna N 10

ᵓl dem. pl. THESE, Bir Bou Rekba N 1, *ᵓlᵓ* Bordj Helal N 1

ᵓlm n. sg (pl. tantum ?) GOD, Breviglieri N 1

ᵓln n. GOD, pl. abs. *ᵓlnm* Bir bou Rekba N 1, *ᶜlnm* Hr. Maktar N 76, cstr. *ᶜlᵓnᵓ*, El-Amruni N 1

ᵓlpqy GN, Berber ?, LEPCIS, Lepcis Magna N 19

ᵓlt n. GODDESS, sg. abs *ᵓlt* S. Antioco N 3

ᵓltbrš PN, Berber, Altiburus, Hr. Medeine N 1

ᵓm n. sg. cstr. MOTHER, Lepcis Magna N 4, sg. + suff. 3 sg. m. *ᵓmm* Wadi el-Amud N 1, Cherchel N 1

ᵓmdrn PN, Berber ? Memphis N 1

ᵓmn PN, Semitic ? Breviglieri N 1

ᵓmtbᶜlhṣry PN, Semitic, Lepcis Magna N 24

ᵓnkn PN, Berber, Bir Bou Rekba N 1

ᵓsp v. nif. TO BE COLLECTED, perf. 3 pl. *nᶜspᵓ* Ksiba Mraou N 3

ᵓpkn PN, Berber ? Memphis N 1

ᵓpšn PN, Berber, Bir Bou Rekba N 1

ᵓqylᵓ PN, Latin, AQUILA, Hr. Brirht N1

ᵓrbᶜ num. FOUR, Bir bou Rekba N 1

ᵓrbᶜm num. FORTY, Ksiba Mraou N 1

ᵓrbᶜt num. FOUR, + suff. 3 pl. m. *ᵓrbtnm* Wadi el-Amud N 1

ᵓrṣ n. EARTH, COUNTRY, sg. abs. Lepcis Magna N 10, 16, 19, pl. cstr. *ᵓrṣt* Djebel Massoudj 1

ᵓrš PN, Semitic, Bir bou Rekba N 1, Hr. Medeine N 1; Tunisia OU N 7, Cherchel N 2

ʾršm PN, Semitic, Wadi el-Amud N 1, 2, Hr. Maktar N 39, Hr. Maktar N 76

ʾš n. MAN, HUSBAND, sg. abs. Lepcis Magna N 2, Cherchel N 1, Ksiba Mraou N 1, *hyš* Guelma N 19

ʾšt n. WOMAN, WIFE, sg. abs. *ʾšt* Cherchel N 1, Guelma N 22, cstr. *ʾšt* Lepcis Magna N 44, 54, *ʿšt* Hr. Sidi Khalifat N 1, + suff. 3 sg. m. *ʿštʾ*, El-Amruni N 1, *ʾšty* Wadi el-Amud N 1, *ʾštm* Guelma N 1, 3, Kef Bezioun N 1

ʾt prep. WITH, to Lepcis Magna N 18, Bir bou Rekba N 1

b prep. IN, Breviglieri N 1; Lepcis Magna N 2, 10, 18 et passim

bʾr n. GRAVE, TOMB Wadi el-Amud N 1

bdmlqrt PN, Semitic, Lepcis Magna N 17, Hr. Bou Atfan N 2

bdʿlqrt PN, Semitic, Lepcis Magna N 5

bdʿštrt PN, Semitic, Bir bou Rekba N 1, Carthage N 5, Constantine N 10, Melilla N 1

bwʾ v. qal TO COME, perf. 3 pl. *bʾ* Bir bou Rekba N 1

bll PN, Berber ? Hr. Medeine N 1

bn n. SON, sg. cstr., Memphis N 1 et passim; + suff. 3 sg. m. *ʾbny* Wadi el-Amud N 1, *bnʾ* S. Antioco N 3, *bʿnm* Qalat Abi s-Siba N 2, pl. cstr. *bnʾ* Breviglieri N 1; Lepcis Magna N 19, + suff. 3 sg. m. *bnyʾ* Lepcis Magna N 6, *bnʾm* Wadi el-Amud N 1, + suff. 3 pl. m. *bʿnm*, El-Amruni N 1; *bn bn* grandson, Lepcis Magna N 18

bnʾ n. BUILDING, sg. abs. Bir Bou Rekba N 1

bny v. qal TO BUILD, perf. 3 sg. m. *bnʾ* Lepcis Magna N 10, *bʿnʾ* Hr. Djerou N 1, *bʾnʾ* Breviglieri N 1, f. *bʿnʿ* El-Amruni N 1, *bnʾ* Djebel Mansour N 1, inf. *bnʾt* S. Antioco N 3, part. m. pl. abs. *bʿnym* Djebel Mansour N 1

bʿl n. CITIZEN, sg. cstr. Djebel Mansour N 1, pl. cstr. *bʿl* Bir bou Rekba N 1, *bʿlʾ* Djebel Mansour N 1, Hr. Maktar N 39, 77, 112, Hr. Meded N 21

bʿl PN, Semitic, epithet of a god > divine name, Sabratha N 16, Ain Zakkar N 1, Bir Tlelsa N 1, Hr. Maktar N 1, Tunisia OU N 7, Constantine N 23, 54, Tirekbine N 1

bʿl ḥmn PN, Semitic, deity, Hr. Maktar N 39, 77, 112, Hr. Meded N 21, Hr. Medeine N 1, Tunisia OU N 2, 13, Constantine N 10, 28, 42, *bʿl ʿmn* Constantine N 7, *bʿl mn* Guelma N 19, 22

bʿlḥnʾ PN, Semitic, Bir Bou Rekba N 1

bʿlyḥy PN, Semitic, Pantelleria N 1

bʿlyn PN, Semitic, Kef Bezioun N 1, 2

bʿlytn PN, Semitic, Lepcis Magna N 18, Constantine N 7, Guelma N 19

bʿlpdʾ PN, Semitic, Carthage N 5

bʿlšlk PN, Semitic, Lepcis Magna N 4, Bir Tlelsa N 1, Hr. Maktar N 39, 112

bʿnwk PN, Berber, Dougga N 3 (*bʿ[n]-wk*), 4 (*bʿn̊k*).

bqy PN, Latin, BOCCIUS, Lepcis Magna N 29

brṭʾ PN, Latin, BRUTUS, Djebel Mansour N 1

bryʾt n. of unknown meaning, Lepcis Magna N 2

brk v. qal TO BLESS, perf. sg. 3 m. + suff. 3 sg. m. *brkʾ* Lepcis Magna N 10, Hr. Maktar N 1, Tunisia OU N 2, 7, Constantine N 7, 10, 28, 42, + suff. 3 sg. f. *brkʾ* Tunisia OU N 13, + suff. 3 pl. m. *brkm* Hr. Maktar N 39, 77, 112, Hr. Medeine N 1, Hr. Meded N 21, impf. 2 pl. m. + suff. 3 sg. m. *tbrkyʾ* Constantine N 54, part. m. sg. abs *brk* blessed, Dougga N 3, 4, Teboursouk N 5

brk PN, Semitic, Hr. Maktar N 77, Hr. Medeine N 1; Constantine N 10

brkbʿl PN, Semitic, Hr. Maktar N 76, Hr. Maktar N 112, Kef Bezioun N 1

brkt PN, Semitic, Lepcis Magna N 4, Guelma N 9

bšm n. PERFUME, sg. abs. Bir Tlelsa N 1

bt n. DAUGHTER, sg. cstr., Lepcis Magna N 4, Tarhuna N 1, Hr. Sidi Khalifat N 1, Tunisia OU N 13, Cherchel N 1, Kef Bezioun N 1

bt n. HOUSE, FAMILY, sg. abs. *bt*, Lepcis Magna N 18; pl.° suff. 3 sg. m. *bt*$^{\supset}$*y* Breviglieri N 1 (uncertain interpretation)

g$^{\supset}$*ml*$^{\supset}$ PN, Latin, GEMELLUS, Hr. Maktar N 76

ggm PN, Berber, Hr. Medeine N 1

gdsn PN, Berber, Bir Bou Rekba N 1

gwṭ^{c}*l* PN, Berber, Qalat Abi s-Siba N 1

gwmz^{c}*l* PN, Berber, Ksiba Mraou N 1

gzr PN, Berber, Hr. Medeine N 1

gṭm PN, Berber, Arseu N2

gnn v. yiph. TO REPAIR ? perf. 3 sg. m. *ygn* Lepcis Magna N 18

g^{c}*tyṭ* PN, Berber, Wadi el-Amud N 1

g^{c}*dy* PN, Latin, GADAEUS, Hr. Brirht N 1

g^{c}*d*^{c}*y* PN, Latin, GADAEUS, Hr. Brirht N 1

g^{c}*wd* PN, Berber, Dougga N 3, 4

g^{c}*y* PN, Latin, GAIUS, Lepcis Magna N 18, Hr. Maktar N 76, Tunisia OU N 7, Guelma N 9

g^{c}*l* GN, Djebel Mansour N 1

g^{c}*r*^{c}*p* PN, Berber ? Tarhuna N 1

g^{c}*tydn* PN, Berber, Wadi el-Amud N 1

grmlkt PN, Semitic, Sousse N 1

dbr n. MATTER, AFFAIR, pl. cstr. dbr$^{\supset}$ Lepcis Magna N 18

dḥ$^{\supset}$ n. ABLUTION, Sabratha N 16

dl prep. WITH, Qalat Abi s-Siba N 1

dmṭry PN, Greek, Δεμετριος, Pompei N 1

dr n. FAMILY, sg. + suff. 3 sg. m. *dr*$^{\supset}$ Hr. Gen Rieime N 1, Qalat Abi s-Siba N 1, + suff. 3 sg. f. *dr*$^{\supset}$ Cherchel N 1

d^{c}*t* n. sg. KNOWLEDGE, Lepcis Magna N 16, 19

h article, *h* El-Amruni N 1; Lepcis Magna N 1, 4 et passim

hy pron. SHE, Hr. Maktar N 76

hlk n. PASSER-BY, sg. abs. $^{\supset}$*lk* Qalat Abi s-Siba N 1

hm^{c}*nt* PN, Berber ? Djebel Mansour N 1

hnkt adv. HERE, Kef Bezioun N 1, 2, *ḥn*^{c}*kt* Qalat Abi s-Siba N 2

w copula, AND, passim

w$^{\supset}$*sp*^{c}*sy*^{c}*n*$^{\supset}$ PN, Latin, VESPASIANUS, Lepcis Magna N 19

wrwsn PN, Berber, Hr. Medeine N 1

z dem. sg. Lepcis Magna N 17, Guelma N 1, 4, Kef Bezioun N 1, 2

zbḥ v. TO SACRIFICE, qal perf 3 sg. masc. *z*^{c}*b*$^{\supset}$ Guelma N 19

zbḥ n. SACRIFICER, sg. abs. Lepcis Magna N 16, 19; Hr. Medeine N 1

zbr n. some sort of metal VESSEL, pl. abs. *zbrm* Bir bou Rekba N 1

zw$^{\supset}$*sn* PN, Berber, Guelma N 1

zwṭ PN, Berber, Wadi el-Amud N 1

z^{c}*zbl* PN, Berber, Hr. Medeine N 1

z^{c}*lgm* PN, Berber, Hr. Medeine N 1

z^{c}*nn* PN, Berber, Ain el-Kebch N 1

zr^{c} n. SEED, PROGENY, sg. abs. Hr. Maktar N 76

ḥbb yiph. TO LOVE, part. sg. m. *mḥb* Lepcis Magna N 16, 19

ḥbr n. COLLEAGUE, pl. + suff. 3 pl. m. *ḥbrnm* Hr. Medeine N 1

ḥdš v. pi. TO RENEW, perf. 3 sg. m. *ḥydš* Bir Tlelsa N 1

ḥwy v.qal TO LIVE, perf. 3 sg. m. *ḥw*$^{\supset}$ Hr. Gen Rieime N 1, Hr. Bou Atfan N 2, ^{c}*w*$^{\supset}$ Guelma N 4, Kef Bezioun N 2, Qalat Abi s-Siba N 1, 2, ^{c}*wh* Hr. Brirht N 1, f. *ḥw*$^{\supset}$ Djebel Mansour N 1, Kef Bezioun N 1, Ksiba Mraou N 1, ^{c}*w*$^{\supset}$ Guelma N 1, ^{c}*w*^{c} Hr. Brirht N 1, Hr. Sidi Khalifat N 1, Guelma N 3, Ksiba Mraou N 3

ḥy adj. LIVING, sg. cstr. *ḥy* Cherchel N 2, pl. abs. *ḥym* Cherchel N 2

ḥyt n. LIFE, sg. cstr. Wadi el-Amud N 1, + suff. 3 sg. m. *ḥytm* Lepcis Magna N 19, + suff. 3 pl. m. *ḥytnm* Wadi el-Amud N 1

ḥym n. LIVE, LIVING, pl. abs. Cherchel N 1

ḥmlk PN, Semitic, Bir Bou Rekba N 1

ḥmlkt PN, Semitic, Lepcis Magna N 16, Djebel Mansour N 1, Hr. Maktar N 76, Constantine N 28, S. Antioco N 3

ḥmšm num. FIFTY, *ḥmšm* Djebel Mansour N 1, Cherchel N 1, ^{c}*mšm* Qalat Abi s-Siba N 1

ḥmšm wšlš num. FIFTY-THREE, Lepcis Magna N 17

ḥn n. GRACE, sg. abs. *ḥn* Constantine N 23

ḥn$^{\supset}$ PN, Semitic, Lepcis Magna N 10, 18

ḥnbʿl	PN, Semitic, Lepcis Magna N 6, 16, 44, Constantine N 23
ḥsm	PN, Berber ? Hr. Djerou N 1
ḥš	interjection, ALAS, Wadi el-Amud N 1
ḥtm	v. qal TO SEAL, TO COMPLETE, perf. 3 sg. m Lepcis Magna N 18.
ḥtmlqrt	PN, Semitic, Sousse N 1
ṭbḥpy	PN, Berber, TAPAFI, Lepcis Magna N 16
ṭhrt	n. PURITY, sg. abs. Cherchel N 1
ṭybry	PN, Latin, TIBERIUS, Lepcis Magna N 19
ṭyṭyʿ	PN, Latin TITIA, Tunisia OU N 2
ṭnʾ	v. pi. TO ERECT, perf. 3 sg. m. *ṭnʾ* Tarhuna N 1, Djebel Massoudj 1, Cherchel N 1, *ṭynʾ* Ksiba Mraou N 1, S. Antioco N 3, *ṭnyʾ* Qalat Abi s-Siba N 2, *ṭnʿ* Guelma N 9, Lepcis Magna N 17, Teboursouk N 5, pu. TO BE ERECTED, perf. 3 sg. f. *ṭnʾ* Dougga N 3, 4, Guelma N 1, Kef Bezioun N 1, 2, Ksiba Mraou N 1, *ṭʿnʾ* Hr. Bou Atfan N 2, *ṭʿnʿ* Hr. Sidi Khalifat N 1, Guelma N 3, 4, Ksiba Mraou N 3, pl. *ṭnʾ* Bordj Helal N 1
yʾ	vocative part. O, Qalat Abi s-Siba N 1
yʾly	PN, Latin, IULIUS, Tunisia OU N 7
yd	n. HAND, pl. cstr. *ydʾ* Hr. Maktar N 76
ygwʿkny	PN, Berber, Bordj Helal N 1
yhbʿt	PN, Berber, Hr. Maktar N 76
ywbzʿlʿn	PN, Berber, El-Amruni N 1
ywrḥtn	PN, Berber, Hr. Djerou N 1
ywrʿtʿn	PN, Berber, El-Amruni N 1
yzrm	PN, Berber, Hr. Medeine N 1
yksltn	PN, Berber, Hr. Medeine N 1
yl	PN, Latin, IULIUS, Guelma N 9
yll	v. pu. TO BE REGRETTED, part. sg. abs. ? *myll* Cherchel N 2
yll	PN, Berber, Hr. Medeine N 1
ym	n. DAY, sg. abs. Dougga N 3, 4, Teboursouk N 5
ymrr	PN, Berber, Wadi el-Amud N 1
ynkdʿsn	PN, Berber, Wadi el-Amud N 1
ystʿtʿn	PN, Berber, Hr. Sidi Khalifat N 1
yʿsktn	PN, Berber, Hr. Maktar N 39
yʿsmzgr	PN, Berber, Hr. Medeine N 1
yʿstʾn	PN, Berber, Hr. Medeine N 1
yʿrtn	PN, Berber, Guelma N 4
ypk	PN, Berber, Tunisia OU 13
ypš	PN, Berber, Bir bou Rekba N 1
yptʿn	PN, Berber, Hr. Maktar N 76, Guelma N 3
yrḥ	n. MONTH, sg. cstr. Bir bou Rekba N 1, Hr. Medeine N 1
yrnʿbt	PN, Berber, Ain el-Kebch N 1
yrʿtʿn	PN, Berber, Hr. Maktar N 112
yšdʾ	PN, Berber, Bir bou Rekba N 1
ytn	v. qal TO GIVE, perf. 3 sg. m. *ytn* Hr. Aouin N 1, 3 pl. *ytnʾ* Lepcis Magna N 19, *yʿtnʾ* Hr. Maktar N 76
ytn	n. PRESENTATION, Hr. Maktar N 76
ytn	PN, Semitic, Constantine N 28
k	conjunction, BECAUSE, Lepcis Magna N 10, *kʿ* Hr. Maktar N 39, 77, 112, Tunisia OU N 2, Constantine N 42, *kh* Tunisia OU N 7, *kʾ* Hr. Medeine N 1; Constantine N 10
kṭʿ	word of unknown meaning, Delos N 1
khn	n. PRIEST, pl. abs *khnm* Bir bou Rekba N 1; Hr. Medeine N 1
khnt	n. PRIESTESS, sg. abs. *knt* Ain Zakkar N 1, Djebel Mansour N 1
kwlb	n. COLUMN ?, pl. abs. *kwlbm* Hr. Maktar N 76
kwn	v. qal TO BE, perf. 3 sg. f. *knʿ* Ain Zakkar N 1, 3 pl. *knʾ* Bir Bou Rekba N 1, Hr. Maktar N 76, impf. 3. sg. f. *tkn* Teboursouk N 5, inf. cstr. *kn*, Lepcis Magna N 2
ky	? conj. BECAUSE, Hr. Maktar N 76
kyw	PN, Berber ?, Dougga N 3, 4
kynʾ	PN, Berber ? Teboursouk N 5
kl	n. sg. cstr. ALL, COMPLETE, Lepcis Magna N 2, 19, Hr. Maktar N 76
klbʾ	PN, Semitic, Constantine N 54
km	prep. AS, Bir Tlelsa N 1, Hr. Maktar N 76
kmr	n. PRIEST, sg. / pl. cstr. Hr. Medeine N 1
kndyʿl	PN, Berber, Guelma N 3
knzrmn	PN, Berber, Hr. Medeine N 1
knsʾʿn	PN, Berber, Hr. Medeine N 1
knṣwlʿt	n. (< Latin) CONSULATE, Hr. Maktar N 76
knrdʿt	PN, Berber, Bordj Helal N 1

knš PN, Berber ? Hr. Medeine N 1

knttʾ PN, Berber ? Memphis N 1

ks n. BOWL, sg. cstr. Sabratha N 16

kʿs v. qal (?), meaning unknown, perf. 3 : sg. m. Lepcis Magna N 18

krr name of a month, Hr. Medeine N 1

ktb v. WRITE, PRESCRIBE, nif. TO BE PRESCRIBED part. f. sg. abs. *nktbt* Cherchel N 1

ktb n. DOCUMENT, sg. cstr. *ktʿb* Bir Tlelsa N 1

ktbt n. DOCUMENT, sg. cstr. Lepcis Magna N 18

l prep., FOR, El-Amruni N 1 et passim, + suff. 3. sg. m. *lʾ* Cherchel N 2, Constantine N 50, Guelma N 9, Qalat Abi s-Siba N 2, *lm* Teboursouk N 5, + suff. 3 sg. f. *lʾ* Cherchel N 1, Ksiba Mraou N 1

lʾ part., O !, Sabratha N 17

lbwʿ PN, Berber, Hr. Medeine N 1

lwby nisbe adj. LIBYAN, pl. abs. *lwbym* Breviglieri N 1

lwqy PN, Latin, LUCIUS, Breviglieri N 1

lylʿy PN, Berber, Hr. Medeine N 1

lmb prep. DURING, BY, compound prep. *l* + *m* + *b*, Lepcis Magna N 6, 18, 19

lʿmyʿ PN, Latin, LAMIA, Breviglieri N 1

lpy compound prep., ACCORDING TO, Lepcis Magna N 19

lpny compound prep. BEFORE, Lepcis Magna N 19

lpny derived adj. FRONTAL, sg. abs. Bir bou Rekba N 1

lqy PN, Latin, LUCIUS, Hr. Maktar N 76

mʾ pron. interr. / rel. WHAT, WHICH, *mʾ* Tarhuna N 1, Wadi el-Amud N 2, Hr. Djerou N 1, *mh* Tunisia OU N 2

mʾgmʿ PN, Berber, Hr. Medeine N 1

mʾs n. MERIT, pl. cstr. *mʾsʾ* Lepcis Magna N 19, pl./ sg., + suff. 3 sg. m. *mʾsm* Lepcis Magna N 19.

mʾš n. STATUE, sg. abs. *mʾš* Lepcis Magna N 17, S. Antioco N 3, sg. cstr. *mʾš* Breviglieri N 1.

mʾtm wʾrbʿm du. abs. TWO HUNDRED AND FORTY, Djebel Massoudj 1

mbyw PN, Berber, Hr. Medeine N 1

mgnm PN, Semitic, Guelma N 22

mgr PN, ? Pompei N 1

mddm GN, Berber ? always preceded by the article, *hmdm* Hr. Meded N 21

mdty nisbe adj. MEDEDIAN, FROM MIDIDI, m. sg. abs. *mdty* Dougga N 4, *mdyty* Dougga N 3

mhr adj. QUICK, f. sg. abs. *mhrt* Cherchel N 1

mwt v. qal TO DIE, perf. 3 sg. f. *mtʿ* Ain Zakkar N 1

mzbḥ n. ALTAR, sg. abs. *mzbḥ* Lepcis Magna N 19, Bir Tlelsa N 1

mzrḥ n. ASSEMBLY, sg. abs. *mzrḥ* Hr. Medeine N 1; *mzrʾ* Hr. Maktar N 76

mḥy n. LIFE, sg. + suff. 3 sg. m. *mḥyʾ*, Lepcis Magna N 6

mḥz n. FORUM, sg. abs. *mḥz* Lepcis Magna N 18

mḥnt n. sg. ARMY, *rb mḥnt*, consul, Breviglieri N 1

mṭḥ n. PLASTERING, sg. abs. *mṭḥ* Bir bou Rekba N 1

my pron. interrog. or relat., WHO, Lepcis Magna N 19

myṭb n. APPROBATION, pl. cstr. *myṭbʾ* S. Antioco N 3

mylkʿtn PN, Semitic ? Guelma N 19

mkwsn PN, Berber, Djebel Massoudj 1, Cherchel N 2

mkpr n. EXPIATION, sg. + suff. 3 sg. *mkprm* Teboursouk N 5

mktrm GN, Berber ? Mactar, always preceded by the article, *hmktʿrm* Hr. Maktar N 39, 77, *hmktʿrym* Hr. Maktar N 112

mlk v. qal TO REIGN, inf. cstr. + suff. 3 sg. m. *mlkm* Djebel Massoudj 1

mlk n. KING, sg. abs. *mlk* Cherchel N 2

mlk n. certain type of SACRIFICE, sg. cstr. Guelma N 19

mlkt n. WORK sg. abs. *mlkt* Lepcis Magna N 1, Bir Tlelsa N 1, cstr. Bir Bou Rekba N 1, + suff. 3 sg. m. *mlktm* Lepcis Magna N 18, 19

mmlkt n. KING, sg. abs. *mmlkt* Djebel Massoudj 1

mndkn PN, Berber, Bir bou Rekba N 1

mnwl^{ɔ} PN, Latin, MANULUS, Guelma N 9

msygr^{c}n PN, Berber, Hr. Maktar N 39

mshb^{ɔ} PN, Berber, Hr. Medeine N 1

msy^{c}ln PN, Berber, Bordj Helal N 1

msyr^{c}n PN, Berber, Hr. Maktar N 39

mskr PN, Berber ? Bir Bou Rekba N 1

msly^{c}n PN, Berber, Hr. Sidi Khalifat N 1

mslm PN, Berber ? Hr. Gen Rieime N 1

m^{c}grs^{c}n PN, Berber, Hr. Maktar N 76

m^{c}ksm^{ɔ} PN, Latin, MAXIMUS, Hr. Maktar N 76

m^{c}kšm^{ɔ} PN, Latin, MAXIMUS, El-Amruni N 1

m^{c}ll PN, Berber, Guelma N 3

m^{c}nkl^{c}t PN, Berber, Guelma N 4

m^{c}syr PN, Berber, Hr. Maktar N 112

m^{c}smk^{c}t PN, Berber, Hr. Maktar N 76

m^{c}snk^{c}w PN, Berber, Breviglieri N 1

m^{c}ṣwkn PN, Berber, Wadi el-Amud N 1

m^{c}qr PN, Berber ? Lepcis Magna N 2, 18

m^{c}qryn^{ɔ} PN, Latin, MACRINUS, Kef Bezioun N 2, Holt N 1

m^{c}rg^{c}ryṭ^{c} PN, Latin, MARGARITA, Lepcis Magna N 52

m^{c}rwz^{ɔ} PN, Berber, Hr. Maktar N 39

m^{c}ryš PN, Berber, Hr. Medeine N 1

m^{c}rq^{ɔ} PN, Latin, MARCUS, Bir Tlelsa N 1

m^{c}rqy PN, Latin, MARCIUS, Hr. Aouin N 1

mp^{c} PN, Semitic, name of a month, Bir bou Rekba N 1

mṣbt n. STELE, sg. abs. *mṣbt* Pantelleria N 1, *mnṣbt* Tarhuna N 1, Wadi el-Amud N 2, Hr. Djerou N 1, Cherchel N 1, Qalat Abi s-Siba N 1

mṣly nisbe adj. MASSYLIAN, sg. abs. Wadi el-Amud N 1

mqdš n. SANCTUARY, sg. abs. *mqdš* S. Antioco N 3, Hr. Medeine N 1, cstr. *mqdš* Breviglieri N 1; *myqdš* Cherchel N 2, pl. abs. *mqdšm* Bir bou Rekba N 1, Hr. Medeine N 1

mqm n. PLACE, sg. abs. *mqm* Lepcis Magna N 1, Ksiba Mraou N 3, *m^{c}q^{ɔ}m* Lepcis Magna N 18

mqnt n. CATTLE, PROPERTY, sg. abs. *mqnt* Bir Tlelsa N 1, *mqn^{ɔ}t* Wadi el-Amud N 1

mqrty nisbe adjective, Lepcis Magna N 5

mrṣ n. MILE (or comparable indication of distance) pl. abs. *mrṣm* Djebel Massoudj 1

mš^{c}rt PN, Berber, Ain Zakkar N 1

mt^{ɔ}by nisbe adjective, El-Amruni N 1

mtnb^{c}l PN, Semitic, Hr. Gen Rieime N 1, Lepcis Magna N 17, Hr. Maktar N 76, 112, *mtnbl* Guelma N 1

mt^{c}t PN, Berber, Qalat Abi s-Siba N 1

mtnt n. GIFT, sg. abs. *mtnt* Teboursouk N 5

nbl n. certain type of VESSEL, pl. cstr. *nbl* Bir bou Rekba N 1.

nglby nisbe adj. sg. abs. Wadi el-Amud N 1

ngry nisbe adj. sg. abs. Qalat Abi s-Siba N 1

ndr v. qal TO VOW, perf. 3 sg. m. *ndr* Sabratha N 16, Hr. Maktar N 1, Tunisia OU N 7, Constantine N 7, 23, 28, 42, *n^{c}dr* Tunisia OU N 2, 3 pl. *ndr^{ɔ}* Hr. Medeine N 1, *n^{c}dr^{ɔ}* Hr. Meded N 21

ndr n. VOW, sg. abs. *ndr* Hr. Maktar N 1, Hr. Medeine N 1, Tunisia OU N 7, 13, Arseu N 2, Constantine N 7, 23, 28, 54 *nd^{c}r* Hr. Meded N 21

ny^{c}ṭmn PN, Berber or Egyptian ? divine name, Hr. Medeine N 1

nymr^{c}n PN, Berber, Wadi el-Amud N 2

nmrsy nisbe adj. sg. abs. Ain el-Kebch N 1

ns^{ɔ} v. qal TO ELEVATE, part. pass.pl. abs. *ns^{ɔ}m* Hr. Maktar N 76

nskt n. CAST IRON, sg. abs. Bir bou Rekba N 1

nsmrn PN, Berber, Hr. Medeine N 1

n^{c}m adj. PLEASANT, m. sg. abs. *n^{ɔ}m* Dougga N 3, 4, *nm* Teboursouk N 5, f. sg. abs. *n^{c}mt* Cherchel N 1

n^{c}mtgd^{ɔ} PN, Semitic, Lepcis Magna N 54

n^{c}mtpm^{ɔ} PN, Semitic, Lepcis Magna N 44

npš mt see sub Hr. Gen Rieime N 1

npṯhn PN, Berber, Djebel Mansour N 1

nṣb v. qal TO ERECT, perf. 3 sg. m. *nṣb* Ain Zakkar N 1

nš^{ɔ} v. qal TO LIFT UP, TO PRESENT, perf. 3 sg. m. *n^{ɔ}s^{ɔ}* Guelma N 22

ntn v. nif. TO BE GIVEN, perf. 3 pl. *nntn* Bir bou Rekba N 1 *s$^{\supset}$wr$^{\supset}$* PN, Latin, SEVERUS, Hr. Maktar N 76

s$^{\supset}$lwl PN, Berber ? Kef Bezioun N 1

sbg PN, Berber, Hr. Medeine N 1

sbq v. qal TO STOP, im: sg. m. *sbq* Qalat Abi s-Siba N 1

ṣdn adj. FREED, f. sg. abs. *ṣdt* Hr. Sidi Khalifat N 1

sw^{c}w$^{\supset}$ PN, Latin ? SUAVUS (a non-existing name !), Hr. Maktar N 76

sys$^{\supset}$y PN, Berber, Ksiba Mraou N 3

skr n. MEMORIAL, REMEMBRANCE, sg. cstr. *skr* Cherchel N 1, Qalat Abi s-Siba N 2, *sk^{c}r* Qalat Abi s-Siba N 1

slky GN, SULCIS, S. Antioco N 3

slkny PN, Berber, Hr. Maktar N 76

slpqy PN, Latin, SULPICIUS, Lepcis Magna N 64

s^{c}byn$^{\supset}$ PN, Latin, SABINUS, Lepcis Magna N 20

s^{c}ldy$^{\supset}$ PN, Berber, Hr. Maktar N 77

sp n. BOWL, BASIN, pl. abs. *spm* Bir bou Rekba N 1.

srwy PN, Latin, SERVIUS, Lepcis Magna N 64

st dem. sg. Breviglieri N 1, Lepcis Magna N 10, Ksiba Mraou N 3, Qalat Abi s-Siba N 1, S. Antioco N 3

^{c}bd v. qal TO USE, inf. cstr.Lepcis Magna N 19

^{c}bd$^{\supset}$ PN, Semitic, Cherchel N 2

^{c}bd$^{\supset}$šmn PN, Semitic, Cherchel N 1

^{c}bn v. qal TO BURY, nif. TO BE BURIED, perf. 3 sg. m. *n^{c}bn* Kef Bezioun N 2, f. *n^{c}bn^{c}* Kef Bezioun N 1

^{c}br n. CEREALS, sg. abs. Bir Tlelsa N 1

^{c}bdmlqrt PN, Semitic, Lepcis Magna N 6, 10, Hr. Aouin N 1, Hr. Maktar N 76, Hr. Medeine N 1, Constantine N 42, Pantelleria N 1

^{c}gt n. CAKE, sg. abs. *^{c}g^{c}* Bir Tlelsa ZN 1

^{c}dyt PN, Berber ? Ain Zakkar N 1

^{c}wṭh PN, Berber, Hr. Sidi Khalifat N 1

^{c}wṭp^{c}tn PN, Berber, Hr. Djerou N 1

^{c}wy^{c}ny PN, Latin, AVIANIUS, Bir Tlelsa N 1

^{c}zrb^{c}l PN, Semitic, Delos N 1, Hr. Medeine N 1; Cherchel N 1

^{c}zrm n. sg. ? abs. some type of OFFERING, Lepcis Magna N 16, 19

^{c}ṭrt n. CROWN, sg. abs. Qalat Abi s-Siba N 1

^{c}yg$^{\supset}$ PN, probably Berber, Lepcis Magna N 2

^{c}ykn^{c} PN, Berber, Hr. Maktar N 77

^{c}yly PN, Latin, AELIUS, Breviglieri N 1

^{c}ṭrt n. CORNICE, sg. abs *^{c}ṭrt* Hr. Maktar N 76

^{c}ksndr^{c} n. (< Greek) EXEDRA, sg. abs. *^{c}ksndr^{c}* Lepcis Magna N 10

^{c}l prep. TOGETHER WITH, OVER, ON, El-Amruni N 1; Lepcis Magna N 1, Bir Bou Rekba N 1, Djebel Massoudj 1, Hr. Maktar N 76, Hr. Medeine N 1, Qalat Abi s-Siba N 1, S. Antioco N 3

^{c}ly v. qal TO GO UP, TO ENTER, perf. 3 sg. m. *^{c}l$^{\supset}$* Lepcis Magna N 18; yif. TO OFFER Hr. Medeine N 1 (highly uncertain)

^{c}lm n. ETERNITY, sg. abs. *$^{\supset}$wlm* Hr. Gen Rieime N 1, Qalat Abi s-Siba N 2, *$^{\supset}$lm* Qalat Abi s-Siba N 1

^{c}lt n. HOLOCAUST, sg. abs. Hr. Medeine N 1

^{c}lt prep. INTO, OVER, Bir bou Rekba N 1; Hr. Medeine N 1

^{c}m n. PEOPLE, sg. abs. *^{c}m* Lepcis Magna N 19

^{c}md n. COLUMN, pl. abs. *^{c}mdm* Lepcis Magna N 18

^{c}sly^{c}n PN, Berber, Wadi el-Amud N 1

^{c}sr wšb^{c} num. SEVENTEEN, Bir bou Rekba N 1

^{c}sr wšmn num. EIGHTTEEN, Ain Zakkar N 1

^{c}srm w$^{\supset}$ḥt num. f. TWENTY-ONE, Djebel Masoudj 1

^{c}srm wḥmš num. TWENTY-FIVE, *$^{\supset}$srm w^{c}ms* Guelma N 3

^{c}srm wšb^{c} num. TWENTY-SEVEN, Kef Bezioun N 2

^{c}pwl$^{\supset}$y PN, Latin, APULEIUS, El-Amruni N 1

^{c}ṣm n. BONE, REMAIN, pl. cstr. *^{c}ṣm$^{\supset}$* Sousse N 1, pl. + suff. 3 sg. f. *^{c}ṣmy^{c}* Ksiba Mraou N 3

^{c}qptn PN, Berber, Constantine N 42

^{c}rpt n. PORTICO, sg. abs. *^{c}rpt* Lepcis Magna N 10, pl. abs. *ḥrp$^{\supset}$t* Breviglieri N 1

ʿršqs PN, (<Persian ?) Hr. Maktar N 76

ʿt n. TIME, sg. cstr. *ʿt* Hr. Maktar N 39, 77, 112

pʾrtnʿtʾ PN, Latin, FORTUNATUS, Hr. Maktar N 76

pwdnš PN, Latin, PUDENS, El-Amruni N 1

pnṭnʾ PN, Latin, FONTANUS, Guelma N 22

pʾdy n. (< Latin) PODIUM, sg. abs. *pʾdy* Lepcis Magna N 19

pḥln PN, Berber, Hr. Brirht N 1

plkš PN, Latin, FELIX, Hr. Brirht N 1

plʿwṭʾ PN, Latin, PLAUTUS, Lepcis Magna N 64

pnm n. pl. FACE, in the divine epithet of Tinnit, *pn bʿl*, face of Bal, Bir bou Rekba N 1, *pnʾ bʿl* Tirekbine N 1, *pʿn bʿl* Constantine N 42, *pʿnʾ bʿl* Constantine N 54, Tirekbine N 1

ps n. TABLET, sg. abs. *pʿs* Qalat Abi s-Siba N 1

pʿbyt PN, Berber ? Tarhuna N 1

pʿwstʾ PN, Latin, FAUSTUS, Hr. Maktar N 76

pʿl v. qal TO DO, TO MAKE, perf. 3 sg. m. Lepcis Magna N 2, 16, 19, Cherchel N 1, 2, + suff. 3 sg. m. *pʿlʾ* Lepcis Magna N 6; *pʿlm* Wadi el-Amud N 1, 3 pl. *pʿl* Bir bou Rekba N 1, *pʿlʾ* Wadi el-Amud N 2, *phlʾ* Hr. Brirht N1, inf. cstr. Lepcis Magna N 18, nif. TO BE MADE, perf. 3 sg. m. *npʿl* Hr. Maktar N 76, f. *nplʾ* Wadi el-Amud N 1, 3 pl. *npʿl* Bir bou Rekba N 1

pʿlt n. WORK, sg. abs. *pʿlt* Hr. Maktar 76

pʿšksʿt PN, Berber, Hr. Maktar N 112

prmh PN, Latin, PRIMUS / FIRMUS ? Hr. Sidi Khalifat N 1

prnkn PN, Berber, Bir bou Rekba N 1

ṣdnt n. FREEDWOMAN, sg. abs. *ṣdt* Hr. Sidi Khalifat N 1

ṣywk PN, Berber, Wadi el-Amud N 1

ṣywʿn n. TOMB MONUMENT, sg. abs. *ṣywʿn* Cherchel N 1

ṣlm n. LIKENESS, IMAGE, sg. abs. *ṣlm* Bir Tlelsa N 1

ṣpy v. qal TO WATCH, TO SEE, part. m. sg. abs. *ṣp* Hr. Medeine N 1

ṣpt n. TOGA WITH PURPLE STRIPE, sg. (or pl. ?) abs. *ṣpʾt* Lepcis Magna N 19

qbr n. GRAVE, TOMB, sg. abs. *qbr* Pantelleria N 1, *qbʿr* Hr. Gen Rieime N 1, *qbʾr* Wadi el-Amud N 1

qdš hit: TO CONSECRATE FOR ONESELF, per. 3 sg. m. Bir Tlelsa N 1, yiph. TO CONSECRATE, perf. 3 sg. m. *ʾyqdš* Breviglieri N 1, Lepcis Magna N 10, 16, Bir Tlelsa N 1

qwdrʿtʾ PN, Latin, QUADRATUS, Hr. Maktar N 76

qwynṭʾ PN, Latin, QUINTUS, Tarhuna N 1, Ksiba Mraou N 3; *qynṭʾ*, Hr. Aouin N 1

ql n. VOICE, sg. + suff. 3 sg. m. *qlʾ* Lepcis Magna N 10, Hr. Maktar N 1, Tunisia OU N 2, 7, Arseu N 2, Constantine N 7, 10, 23, 28, 42, Tirekbine N 1, *qwlʾ* Guelma N 19, *qlm* Sabratha N 16, Teboursouk N 5, *qly* Guelma N 22, + suff. 3 sg. f. *qlʾ* Tunisia OU N 13, + suff. 3 pl. m. *qlm* Hr. Maktar N 39, 77, 112, Hr. Meded N 21, Hr. Medeine N 1

qlʿʾʿy PN, Latin, CLAUDIUS, Lepcis Magna N 4; *qlʿʾy* Lepcis Magna N 5

qlr PN, Latin, CELER, Djebel Mansour N 1

qny v. qal, TO CREATE, TO OWN, part. sg. m. cstr. *qn* Lepcis Magna N 10

qmdʾ PN, Latin, COMMODUS, Lepcis Magna N 18

qnʾm pron. SOMEONE, PERSON, Lepcis Magna N 2, Cherchel N 2

qʿnddʾ PN, Latin, CANDIDUS, Lepcis Magna N 10

qrʾ v. qal TO READ, impf. 3 sg. m. *yqrʾ* Qalat Abi s-Siba N 1

r abbrev. OFFICE or official function, Hr.Maktar 39, 77, 112

rʾdybtʾ PN, Latin REDEMTUS, Tunisia OU N 2

rʾmʿnʿ PN, Latin, ROMANA, Hr. Maktar N 76

rʾsṭṭytʾ PN, Latin, RESTITUTUS, Hr. Maktar N 76

rʾps PN, Latin, RUFUS, Lepcis Magna N 16

rʾš n. HEAD, pl. cstr. *ršʾ* S. Antioco N 3

rb adj. GREAT, as noun PRESIDENT, f. as a divine epithet LADY, m. sg. abs *rb* Breviglieri N 1, Hr. Maktar N 39, 77, cstr. *rb* Breviglieri N 1, f. sg. abs. *rbt* S. Antioco N 3

rbd v. qal / piel TO PAVE, 3 : sg. m. *rbd* Lepcis Magna N 18.

rgʿṭʾ PN, Latin, ROGATUS, Djebel Mansour N 1, Guelma N 9

rds n. of unknown meaning, Lepcis Magna N 2

rwpʾ PN, Latin, RUFUS, Djebel Mansour N 1

rydʿy PN, Latin (?), RIDEUS, El-Amruni N 1

rpʾ v. qal TO HEAL, part. sg. abs. *rpʾ* Hr. Aouin N 1, *rbʾ*, Lepcis Magna N 4, 5; pl. abs. *rʾpʾm*, Manes, El-Amruni N 1

š marker or relativity, El-Amruni N 1, Bir Tlelsa N 1, *ʾš* Breviglieri N 1, Lepcis Magna N 18, Wadi el-Amud N 1, Bir bou Rekba N 1, Djebel Massoudj 1, Hr. Maktar N 1 et passim.

šʾwʾwʾrʾ PN (misspelling), Latin, SEVERUS, El-Amruni N 1

šblt PN, Semitic ? Guelma N 3, Ksiba Mraou N 1

šbʿm num. SEVENTY, Kef Bezioun N 1

šbʿt n. ABUNDANCE ?, sg. abs. *šbʿt* Hr. Maktar N 76

šbʿm wḥmš num. SEVENTY-FIVE, *šbʿm wḥmš* Hr. Bou Atfan N 2, *šbʿm wʿmš* Guelma N 1

šbʿm wšbʿ num. SEVENTY SEVEN, Ain Zakkar N 1

šd n. AREA, TERRITORY, sg. / pl. cstr. *šd* Breviglieri N 1

šdby PN, uncertain origin, Lepcis Magna N 17

šdrpʾ PN, Semitic, Lepcis Magna N 17

šhqndʿ PN, Latin, SECUNDA, Hr. Brirht N 1

šṭwʿn PN, Berber, Hr. Medeine N 1

šṭmn PN, Berber, Hr. Medeine N 1

šlk v. pi. TO SAVE, part. sg. abs./cstr. *mšlk* Lepcis Magna N 19

šlm PN, Semitic, Constantine N 54

šm n. NAME, sg. cstr. *šm* Lepcis Magna N 18, Qalat Abi s-Siba N 1

šmnm wḥmš num. EIGHTY-FIVE, Ksiba Mraou N 3

šmnšš num. SIXTY-EIGHT, Hr. Gen Rieime N 1

šmnm num. EIGHTY, Cherchel N 1

šmʿ v. qal TO HEAR, perf. 3 sg. m. *šmʿ* Lepcis Magna N 10, Hr. Maktar N 1, 39, 77, 112, Hr. Medeine N 1, Tunisia OU N 2, 7, 13, Constantine N 7, 10, 23, 28, 42, *šmʾ* Hr. Meded N 21, Guelma N 22, Tirekbine N 1, *šʿmʾ* Teboursouk N 5, Guelma N 19, impf. 3 sg. m. *yšmʾʾ* Arseu N 2

šnm num. TWO, Bir bou Rekba N 1

šnt n. YEAR, sg. abs. *št* Djebel Massoudj 1, Cherchel N 1, cstr. *št* Breviglieri N 1, Bir Bou Rekba N 1, Hr. Medeine N 1; Hr. Aouin N 1, Constantine N 54, pl. abs. *šnt* Cherchel N 1, Guelma N 1, Kef Bezioun N 1, Ksiba Mraou N 1, Qalat Abi s-Siba N 2, *šʿnt* Ain Zakkar N 1, Djebel Mansour N 1, Hr. Brirht N 1, Guelma N 3, 4, Kef Bezioun N 2, Qalat Abi s-Siba N 1, *šʿnʾt* Hr. Brirht N 1, *šʿnwt* Ksiba Mraou N 3

šsyʿt PN, Berber, Hr. Medeine N 1

šʿṭr PN, Latin, SATUR, Djebel Mansour N 1

šʿṭry PN, Latin, SATURIUS, Hr. Brirht N 1

šʿsydwʿsn PN, Berber, Breviglieri N 1

špṭ v. qal TO REIGN, part. sg. m. abs. Lepcis Magna N 16, pl. m. abs. *špṭm* Lepcis Magna N 17, Bir Bou Rekba N 1, Hr. Medeine N 1; Hr. Aouin N 1

špṭ PN, Semitic, Malta N 1

špʿr word of unknown meaning, Breviglieri N 1

šṣp PN, uncertain origin, Constantine N 7

šql yiph. TO ADORN ?, part. sg. m. *myšql* Lepcis Magna N 16, 19

šqln PN, Berber, Cherchel N 1

šqndʿ PN, Latin, SECUNDA, Hr. Brirht N 1

šrm PN, Semitic ? Constantine N 54

ššm wd num. SIXTY-ONE, Guelma N 4

ššm wḥmš num. SIXTY-FIVE, *ššm wʿmš* Qalat Abi s-Siba N 2

ššm wšnm num. SIXTY-TWO, Lepcis Magna N 17

ššm wšš num. SIXTY-SIX, *šyšm wšʾš* Hr.Brirht N 1

t object marker, Lepcis Magna N 10, 18 et passim, *ʾt* Sabratha N 16, Guelma N 19

tʾr n. plan, sg. + suff. 3 sg. m. *tʾrm* Lepcis Magna N 16, Bir Tlelsa N 1

tbbʿ PN, Berber, Guelma N 1

tbrsn PN, Berber, Hr. Medeine N 1

tzʿbš PN, Berber, Tunisia OU N 13

tḥt prep. INSTEAD OF, UNDER, Breviglieri N 1

tynb PN, Berber, Hr. Maktar N 76

tm n. sg. COMPLETENESS, *btm* 'in completeness, completely, at someones own expense', Breviglieri N 1, Lepcis Magna N 10, 16, 18, 19, Tarhuna N 1, Bir Tlelsa N 1, Hr. Djerou N 1

tm adj. sg. f. *tmt* complete, Lepcis Magna N 16, 19, *tmʾ* Wadi el-Amud N 1

tnsmt GN, Berber, Bir bou Rekba N 1

tnt PN, Semitic, name of a female deity, *tnt* Ain Zakkar N 1, Constantine N 54, *tnyt* Tirekbine N 1

tsdt PN, Berber, Qalat Abi s-Siba N 1

tʿwnt PN, Berber, Cherchel N 1

tʿnbrʿ PN, Berber, El-Amruni N 1

tʿṣmt n. STRENGTH, HEROISM, sg. abs. Qalat Abi s-Siba N 1

tprʿt PN, Berber, Hr. Sidi Khalifat N 1

tṣʾt n. sg. EXPENSE, + suff. 3 sg. m. *tṣʾtm* Breviglieri N 1, Lepcis Magna N 10, Hr. Djerou N 1, *tṣty* Wadi el-Amud N 1

tškʿt GN, Berber, Djebel Massoudj 1

Latino- and Greco-Punic Glossary

N.B. Verbs are generally listed by their historical roots, otherwise lexemes are listed alphabetically including vowels (note that LP σ follows s). Words marked with a * are derived forms.

a- article, Gasr el-Azaiz LP1, Ghirza LP1

**ab* n. sg., FATHER, + prefix *l-* and suff. 3 m. pl. *labunom* Wadi Umm el-Agerem LP1; pl., PARENTS, + prefix *ly-* and suff. 3 sg. f. *lybytha* (with vowel reduction) Ghirza LP1, + prefix *ly-* and suff. 3 sg. m *lobvthem* Gasr el-Azaiz LP1, (with vowel reduction) *lybythem* Zliten LP1

abdvsmvn PN, Semitic, Sirte LP5

αδουν n., LORD, sg. abs., El-Hofra GP1

alide PN, Latin, ALIDUS, Sirte LP8

amice Name, Latin, AMICUS, Lepcis Magna LP3

amonis PN, Semitic?, Sirte LP11

aniboni PN, Semitic, Sirte LP1

anobal PN, Semitic, Wadi Umm el-Agerem LP1, LP2

apvpvrus PN, ?, Sirte LP 10

ars n. ARTISAN, sg. rectum Bir Shmech LP1

brk v. qal TO BLESS, perf 3 sg. m. + suff. 3 sg. m. *βαραχω* El-Hofra GP1

bal n. FOREMAN, PERSON IN CHARGE, sg. cstr. *bal ars* Bir Shmech LP1, *bal ysrim* Lepcis Magna LP3

βαλ αμουν DN, Semitic deity, El-Hofra GP1

bibi PN, Berber, Gasr Doga LP1

birich PN, Semitic, Sirte LP12

bvr n. GRAVE, TOMB Zliten LP1

by- prep., IN, Bir ed-Dreder LP1, Breviglieri LP1, Wadi Umm el-Agerem LP2

byn n. SON, sg. cstr., Bir ed-Dreder LP2, LP4, LP9, LP14, Wadi Umm el-Agerem LP2, Zliten LP1, *βυν* El-Hofra GP1, *bn* Bir ed-Dreder LP1; sg. + suff. 3 sg. m. *binim* Bir Shmech LP1, Gasr Doga LP1; pl. cstr. *byne* Wadi Umm el-Agerem LP2; pl. + copula, prefix and suff. 3 sg. masc. *vlybanem* Gasr el-Azaiz LP1

byth n. DAUGHTER, sg. cstr., Ghirza LP1

cecili PN, Latin, CAECILIUS, Breviglieri LP1

centenari n. (<Latin), FORTIFIED FARM, Breviglieri LP1; *centeinari* Bir Shmech LP1

chaross v.? qal 3 sg. m. TO LAY THE FOUNDATION and/or TO DEDICATE Wadi Umm el-Agerem LP1

chyrdid PN, Berber, Bir ed-Dreder LP2

dasama PN, Berber, Bir Shmech LP1

dinario n. (<Latin, abl.?), COIN, MONEY, Wadi Umm el-Agerem LP2

dvniad PN, Berber, Gasr el-Azaiz LP1

felioth n. CRAFTSMANSHIP? Lepcis Magna LP1

fillyth n. DEED, ACTIVITY Wadi Uaeni LP1

flabivs PN, Latin, FLAVIUS Bir ed-Dreder LP 14, *flavi* Bir ed-Dreder LP1; *flabi* Bir Shmech LP1; *flav* (abbrev.) Wadi Uaeni LP1

θινιθ DN, Semitic deity, El-Hofra GP1

ḥwy v. qal TO LIVE, perf. 3 sg. m. *avo* Sirte LP1, LP2, LP3, LP7<!>, LP8, LP11, LP12, *av* (abbrev.?) Sirte LP5, Wadi Uaeni LP1(2x); perf. 3 sg. f. *ava* Sirte LP4, LP6; *ave* pro *avo*? Nawalia LP1

hoc dem. sg. (<Latin) Wadi Uaeni LP1

**iad*	n. HAND, pl./du. or +suff. 3 sg. m. Lepcis Magna LP1
iarnvhan	PN, Berber, Bir ed-Dreder LP14
isachv	PN, Berber, Bir ed-Dreder LP4
isicvarlvl	PN, Berber, Bir ed-Dreder LP9
isigvari	PN, Berber, Bir ed-Dreder LP14
ivlivs	PN, Latin, IULIUS Bir ed-Dreder LP2; *iv* (abbrev.) Wadi Uaeni LP1
iylul	PN, Berber, Wadi Umm el-Agerem LP2; *iyllul* Wadi Umm el-Agerem LP1
kalli	PN, Berber?, Sirte LP12
**κουλ*	n. voice, sg. + suff. 3 sg. m. *κουλω* El-Hofra GP1
licini	PN, Latin LICINIUS Zliten LP1
ly-	prep., FOR, Gasr el-Azaiz LP1, Ghirza LP1, Lepcis Magna LP3, Nawalia LP1, Zliten LP1(2x), *λυ-* El-Hofra GP1(2x); *li-* (vowel harmony) Gasr Doga LP1, Zliten LP1; *l-* (before a vowel) Gasr el-Azaiz LP1, Wadi Umm el-Agerem LP1, *λ-* El-Hofra GP1; +suff. 3 sg. m. *lo* Nawalia LP1
macarcvm	PN, Berber, Bir ed-Dreder LP1
machrvς	PN, Berber, Bir ed-Dreder LP1
macrine	PN, Latin, MACRINUS, Bir Shmech LP1
marci	PN, Latin, MARCIUS, Breviglieri LP1
masavchan	PN, Berber, Wadi Umm el-Agerem LP1, LP2
masthalvl	PN, Berber, Bir ed-Dreder LP2
maσicama	PN, Berber, Bir ed-Dreder LP4
memoria	n.(<Latin), MEMORIAL, FUNERARY MONUMENT, Ghirza LP1
mercuri	PN, Latin, MERCURIUS, Sirte LP2
mia	PN, Latin?, Wadi Uaeni 1
mylthe	PN, Berber?, Lepcis Magna LP3; *milth.n* Wadi Umm el Agerem LP1
mṣir	n. GUARD, sg. rectum Bir ed-Dreder LP2
mv	rel. pron., WHAT, WHICH, Breviglieri LP1, Ghirza LP1(2x); *ymv* (after a consonant cluster) Gasr Doga LP1, Nawalia LP1
myft	n. COMMAND, sg. cstr., Bir ed-Dreder LP1
mynṣyfth	n. MEMORIAL, FUNERARY MONUMENT, (STELE), Gasr Doga LP1<!>; Nawalia LP1, Wadi Umm el-Agerem LP2
mythicsin	PN, Berber?, Lepcis Magna LP3
mythvmbal	PN, Semitic, Nawalia LP1
mythvnilim	PN, Semitic, Gasr Doga LP1
ndr	v. qal TO VOW, perf. 3 sg. m. *ναδωρ* El-Hofra GP1
nṣb	v. yiph. TO ERECT, perf. 3 sg. m. *uṣeb* Bir ed-Dreder LP 1; *inṣeb* Gasr Doga LP1
nasif	PN, Berber, Ghirza LP1, Wadi Umm el-Agerem LP2
naṣiba	n. FORTIFIED FARM, Gasr el-Azaiz LP1
osilim	PN, Semitic?, Gasr el-Azaiz LP1
$p^{c}l$	v. qal, TO DO, TO MAKE, perf. 3 sg. m. *fel* Gasr el-Azaiz LP1, Gasr Doga LP1, Nawalia LP1, Zliten LP1, +suff. 3 sg. m. *felo* Zliten LP1; perf. 3 sg. f. *fela* Ghirza LP1(2x); perf. 1 sg. c. *felthi* Breviglieri LP1; perf. 3 pl. m. Bir Shmech LP1, Wadi Umm el-Agerem LP1, LP2
piso	PN, Latin, PISO Zliten LP1
rogate	PN, Latin, ROGATUS, Lepcis Magna LP1
ryb	n., m. COMMANDER, CHIEF, sg. cstr. *rb mṣir* Bir ed-Dreder LP2; f. LADY, +prefix *λυ-* and suff. 1 pl. com. *ρυβαθων*, El Hofra GP1
$šm^{c}$	v. qal TO HEAR, perf. 3 sg. m. *σαμω* El-Hofra GP1
sabare	PN, Berber, SABARRUS, Bir Shmech LP1
saicham	PN, Berber, Bir ed-Dreder LP1
sanv[th]	n. pl. abs. YEARS *sanvth* Nawalia LP1, Sirte LP5, LP11; *sanvt* Sirte LP7; *sanv* Sirte LP1, LP2, LP9, Wadi Uaeni LP1(2x), Zliten LP1; *s* (abbrev.) Sirte LP12
sarvnv	PN, Berber?, Zliten LP1
**snim*	num. TWO, +prefix *l- lisnim* Zliten LP1
σωσιπατρος	PN, Greek, El-Hofra GP1
syṣan	PN, Berber, Wadi Umm el-Agerem LP1; *sysan* Gasr el-Azaiz LP1
σonmon	PN/title?, Berber, Bir ed-Dreder LP1

σy- marker of relativity, Bir Shmech LP1; *ys* Gasr el-Azaiz LP1, *υς* El-Hofra GP1; *sit* Sirte LP12

thanubda PN, Berber, Wadi Umm el-Agerem LP2

thualath PN, Berber, Ghirza LP1

thy object marker, Zliten LP1

thychleth n. EXPENSE Wadi Umm el-Agerem LP2

tribvnvs n. (<Latin), TRIBUNE, Bir ed-Dreder LP4; *tribynys* Bir ed-Dreder LP1; *trybvnvs* Bir ed-Dreder LP14

φανε βαλ divine epithet of *Θινιθ*, El-Hofra GP1

vdrvna PN, Berber, Gasr el-Azaiz LP1

vy- copula, AND, Bir Shmech LP1, Wadi Umm el-Agerem LP1(2x), LP2, Zliten LP1(2x); *v-* Gasr el-Azaiz LP1 (2x), Gasr Doga LP1, Wadi Umm el-Agerem LP2; *ου* El-Hofra GP1

yriraban PN, Berber, Bir ed-Dreder LP1, LP9

ysrim num. TWENTY, Lepcis Magna LP3

**ysth* n. WOMAN, WIFE, +copula, prefix and suff. 3 sg. m. *vylysthim* Zliten LP1

ζοπυρος PN, Greek, El-Hofra GP 1

Overview of Neo-Punic Inscriptions

Texts given in bold type are to be found in the present collection.

EGYPT

Memphis
N 1

GREECE

Delos
N 1

LIBYA

El-Amruni
N 1

Bir Gebira
N 1 *IPT* 81

Breviglieri
N 1

Bu Khemmàsc
N 1 *IPT* 6

Hr. Gen Rieime
N 1

Lepcis Magna
N 1
N 2
N 3 *IPT* 11
N 4
N 5
N 6
N 7 *IPT* 15
N 8 *IPT* 16
N 9 *KAI* 130; *IPT* 17
N 10
N 11 *KAI* 131; *IPT* 19
N 12 *KAI* 132; *IPT* 68
N 13 *KAI* 120; *IPT* 21
N 14 *KAI* 122; *IPT* 22
N 15 *KAI* 123; *IPT* 23
N 16
N 17
N 18
N 19
N 20
N 21 *KAI* 125; *IPT* 30
N 22 *IPT* 32
N 23 *IPT* 91
N 24
N 25
N 26 *IPT* 35
N 27 *IPT* 36
N 28 *IPT* 37
N 29
N 30 *IPT* 39
N 31 *IPT* 40
N 32 *IPT* 41
N 33 *IPT* 42
N 34 *IPT* 43
N 35 *IPT* 44
N 36 *IPT* 45
N 37 *IPT* 46
N 38 *IPT* 47
N 39 *IPT* 48
N 40 *IPT* 49
N 41 *IPT* 50
N 42 *IPT* 51
N 43 *IPT* 52
N 44
N 45 *IPT* 54
N 46 *IPT* 55
N 47 *IPT* 56
N 48 *IPT* 57
N 49 *IPT* 58
N 50 *IPT* 59
N 51 *IPT* 60
N 52
N 53 *IPT* 62
N 54
N 55 *IPT* 64

N 56 *IPT* 65
N 57 *IPT* 66
N 58 *IPT* 67
N 59 *IPT* 69
N 60 *IPT* 70
N 61 *IPT* 71
N 62 *IPT* 72
N 63 *IPT* 73
N 64
N 65 *IPT* 75
N 66 *IPT* 84
N 67 *IPT* 92

Misurata Marina
N 1 *IPT* 96

Al Qusbat
N 1

Sabratha
N 1 *IPT* 1
N 2 *IPT* 2
N 3 *IPT* 3
N 4 *IPT* 4
N 5 *IPT* 82A
N 6 *IPT* 82B
N 7 *IPT* 82C
N 8 *IPT* 82D
N 9 *IPT* 82E
N 10 *IPT* 82F
N 11 *IPT* 82G
N 12 *IPT* 82H
N 13 *IPT* 82I
N 14 *IPT* 82J
N 15 *IPT* 82K
N 16
N 17
N 18 GARBINI 1987a
N 19 GARBINI 1987a

Saniat ben Howedi
N 1 GARBINI 1986: 18a
N 2 GARBINI 1986: 18b

Sàmet el-Crèma
N 1 *IPT* 80

Taglit
N 1 GARBINI 1986: 18c

Tarhuna
N 1

Tripoli
N 1 *IPT* 5A
N 2 *IPT* 5B
N 3 *IPT* 87
N 4 *IPT* 88
N 5 *IPT* 6
N 6 *IPT* 7
N 7 *IPT* 8
N 8 *IPT* 83
N 9 *IPT* 89
N 10 *IPT* 90

Wadi el-Amud
N 1
N 2
N 3 *IPT* 78

Zaiuet el-Mahgiub
N 1 *IPT* 93
N 2 *IPT* 94
N 3 *IPT* 95
N 4 *IPT* 85

TUNISIA

Ain Barchouch
N 1 GHAKI 1985: 177

Ain Zakkar
N 1

Arg el-Ghazouani
N 1 FANTAR 1975b: 269
N 2 FANTAR 1975b: 269

Bir Bou Rekba
N 1

Bir Tlelsa
N 1

Bordj Bou Chateur
N 1 CINTAS 1951: 79

Bordj Helal
N 1

Bou Grara
N 1 DUSSAUD 1915: cxcv

Carthage
N 1 *CIS* 174
N 2 *CIS* 580
N 3 *CIS* 842
N 4 *CIS* 942
N 5
N 6 *CIS* 2992; *KAI* 94
N 7 *CIS* 3244
N 8 *CIS* 3245
N 9 *CIS* 3246
N 10 *CIS* 3247
N 11 *CIS* 3248
N 12 *CIS* 3249
N 13 *CIS* 3250

N 14 *CIS* 3251
N 15 FERRON-PINARD, 1960-1961: 152-153

Djebel Mansour
N 1

Djebel Massoudj
1

El-Djem
N 1 *RÉS* 941

Dougga
N 1 *RÉS* 563
N 2 GHAKI 1994: 35
N 3
N 4
N 5 CHABOT 1916: 123-126
N 6 CHABOT 1916: 127

Gabes
N 1 TEMPLE1835, ii: 133, 321

Hammam Derradji
N 1 GARBINI 1986: 62
N 2 FEVRIER 1965-1966: 229

Hr. Aouin
N 1

Hr. el-Bled
N 1 DUSSAUD 1925: cclii

Hr. Brirht
N 1

Hr. Djebbara
N 1 DUSSAUD 1923: lxxix
N 2 DUSSAUD 1923: lxxix-lxxx

Hr. Djerou
N 1

Hr. Guergour
N 1 SZNYCER 1983
N 2 *KAI* 143
N 3 CHABOT, *Punica* ix 3
N 4 *KAI* 144
N 5 CHABOT, *Punica* ix 5
N 6 CHABOT, *Punica* ix 6
N 7 CHABOT, *Punica* ix 7
N 8 CHABOT, *Punica* ix 8
N 9 GARBINI 1974b: 27
N 10 CHABOT, *Punica* ix 10

Hr. Hammam Zouakra
N 1 *RÉS* 780 (cf. *RÉS* 782)

Hr. Kanefir
N 1 *RÉS* 363

Hr. Kasbat
N 1 CHABOT 1924: 162-164

Hr. Kasbat
N 2 CHABOT 1938-1940: 397-399

Hr. Maktar
N 1
N 2 MENDLESON 2003: 38
N 3 MENDLESON 2003: 38
N 4 CHABOT, *Punica* xii 5
N 5 CHABOT, *Punica* xii 6
N 6 CHABOT, *Punica* xii 7
N 7 MENDLESON 2003: 37
N 8 MENDLESON 2003: 38
N 9 MENDLESON 2003: 40
N 10 CHABOT, *Punica* xii 11
N 11 CHABOT, *Punica* iv A 5, *id.* xii, 18
N 12 MENDLESON 2003: 39
N 13 CHABOT, *Punica* xii 14
N 14 CHABOT, *Punica* xii 15
N 15 CHABOT, *Punica* xii 16
N 16 CHABOT, *Punica* xii 17
N 17 MENDLESON 2003: 48
N 18 CHABOT, *Punica* xii 19; *KAI* 133
N 19 MENDLESON 2003: 48
N 20 CHABOT, *Punica* xii 22
N 21 CHABOT, *Punica* xii 23
N 22 CHABOT, *Punica* xii 24
N 23 CHABOT, *Punica* xii 25
N 24 MENDLESON 2003: 47
N 25 CHABOT, *Punica* xii 27
N 26 CHABOT, *Punica* xii 28
N 27 CHABOT, *Punica* xii 29
N 28 CHABOT, *Punica* xii 30
N 29 CHABOT, *Punica* xii 31
N 30 CHABOT, *Punica* xii 32
N 31 CHABOT, *Punica* xii 33
N 32 CHABOT, *Punica* iv A 6
N 33 CHABOT, *Punica* iv A 7
N 34 CHABOT, *Punica* iv A 8
N 35 CHABOT, *Punica* iv A 9; *KAI* 152
N 36 CHABOT, *Punica* ii, 2; id., xii, 36
N 37 MENDLESON 2003: 39
N 38 CHABOT, *Punica* ii, 3
N 39
N 40 CHABOT, *Punica* iv A 2
N 41 CHABOT, *Punica* iv A 3
N 42 SZNYCER 2000: 45-47
N 43 CHABOT, *Punica* xv, 2
N 44 CHABOT, *Punica* xv, 3
N 45 CHABOT, *Punica* xv, 4
N 46 CHABOT, *Punica* iv B 7
N 47 PICARD 1954, tab. cxx, Cb 1025
N 48 PICARD 1954, Cb 1024

N 49 CHABOT, *Punica* iv D3
N 50 CHABOT, *Punica* iv D4
N 51 CHABOT 1916: 130
N 52 PICARD 1954, tab. cxx, Cb 1022
N 53 CHABOT, *Punica* v, 1
N 54 *KAI* 153
N 55 CHABOT, *Punica* iv E 7
N 56 *KAI* 148
N 57 *KAI* 149
N 58 *KAI* 150
N 59 CHABOT, *Punica* iv E 11
N 60 *RÉS* 165
N 61 *RÉS* 166
N 62 CHABOT, *Punica* iv E 14
N 63 *KAI* 151
N 64 *KAI* 145
N 65 *KAI* 146
N 66 *KAI* 147
N 67 JONGELING 1984: 8
N 68 CHARLES-PICARD 1943-1945: 481
N 69 PICARD 1945: 196
N 70 FEVRIER 1952a: 111-112
N 71 FEVRIER 1952a: 112-113
N 72 FEVRIER 1952a: 113
N 73 FEVRIER 1952b: 144
N 74 FEVRIER 1952b: 144
N 75 FEVRIER & FANTAR 1965: 45-49
N 76
N 77
N 78 BISI 1972, tav. vi
N 79 FÉVRIER 1958-1959: 31
N 80 BISI 1978: 43
N 81 PICARD 1954, tab. cxvii, Cb 1011 c12
N 82 PICARD 1954, tab. cxxii, Cb 1032 d2
N 83 PICARD 1954, tab. cxiii, Cb 994 d6
N 84 PICARD 1954, tab. cxi, Cb 986 d9
N 85 PICARD 1954, tab. cxxi, Cb 1026 d11
N 86 *Karthago* 8, pl. xv C
N 87 PICARD 1954, tab. cxvi, Cb 1008 d13
N 88 PICARD 1954, tab. cxvi, Cb 1007 d 14
N 89 PICARD 1954, tab. cxv, Cb 1005 d23
N 90 PICARD 1954, tab. cxvi, Cb 1006 d24
N 91 PICARD 1954, tab. cxi, Cb 988 d29
N 92 PICARD 1954, tab. cxii, Cb 993 d30
N 93 VATTIONI 1996: 77
N 94 *Karthago* 8: 1957, pl.xv E
N 95 PICARD 1954, tab. cxviii, Cb 1016 d39
N 96 PICARD 1954, tab. cx, Cb 984 d40
N 97 PICARD 1954, tab. cxxi, Cb 1028 d 41
N 98 PICARD 1954, tab. cxix, Cb 1020 d45
N 99 PICARD 1954, tab. cxxii, Cb 1033 d46
N 100 PICARD 1954, tab. cxviii, Cb 1017 d50
N 101 PICARD 1954, tab. cxii, Cb 991 d51
N 102 PICARD 1954, tab. cxi, Cb 989 d55
N 103 PICARD 1954, tab. cviii, Cb 977 d 58
N 104 PICARD 1954, tab. cxxi, Cb 1029 d 59
N 105 JONGELING 1999: 84
N 106 PICARD 1954, tab. cix, Cb 980 d 62
N 107 PICARD 1954, tab. cxxiii, Cb 1035 d68
N 108 PICARD 1954, tab. cxii, Cb 990
N 109 PICARD 1954, tab. cix, Cb 981
N 110 JONGELING 1999: 82
N 111 BISI 1978: 42-43, 64
N 112
N 113 PICARD 1954, tab. cix, Cb 979 d 57
N 114 PICARD 1954, tab. cx, Cb 983
N 115 PICARD 1954, tab. cx, Cb 985
N 116 PICARD 1954, tab. cxi, Cb 987
N 117 PICARD 1954, tab. cxii, Cb 992
N 118 PICARD 1954, tab. cxiii, Cb 995
N 119 PICARD 1954, tab. cxiii, Cb 996
N 120 PICARD 1954, tab. cxiii, Cb 997
N 121 PICARD 1954, tab. cxiv, Cb 998
N 122 PICARD 1954, tab. cxiv, Cb 1000
N 123 PICARD 1954, tab. cxiv, Cb 1001
N 124 PICARD 1954, tab. cxv, Cb 1003
N 125 PICARD 1954, tab. cxxiii, Cb 1034
N 126 *Karthago* 8: pl. xiv a
N 127 *Karthago* 8: pl. xv G
N 128 PICARD 1954, tab. cxix, Cb 1021
N 129 VATTIONI 1984: 667-668
N 130 VATTIONI 1984: 667-668

Hr. Meded
N 1 SZNYCER 1986: 7, 1
N 2 SZNYCER 1986: 9, 2
N 3 SZNYCER 1986: 10, 3
N 4 SZNYCER 1986: 10-11, 4
N 5 SZNYCER 1986: 11, 5
N 6 SZNYCER 1986: 13, 6
N 7 SZNYCER 1986: 13, 7
N 8 SZNYCER 1986: 13, 8
N 9 SZNYCER 1986: 15, 9
N 10 SZNYCER 1986: 15, 10
N 11 SZNYCER 1986: 15: 17,11
N 12 SZNYCER 1986: 17, 12
N 13 SZNYCER 1986: 17-18, 13; *KAI* 155
N 14 SZNYCER 1986: 18: 20,14
N 15 SZNYCER 1986: 22, 18; *KAI* 156
N 16 SZNYCER 1986: 22, 17; *KAI* 157
N 17 SZNYCER 1986: 20-21, 16; *KAI* 158
N 18 SZNYCER 1986: 23, 19
N 19 SZNYCER 1986: 20, 15
N 20 FANTAR 1986: 26, 1
N 21
N 22 FANTAR 1986: 28, 3
N 23 FANTAR 1986: 28-30, 4
N 24 FANTAR 1986: 33: 35, 1

N 25 Fantar 1986: 35-36, 2
N 26 Fantar 1999: 58
N 27 Ferjaoui 1989: 56
N 28 Ferjaoui 1989: 57

Hr. Medeine
N 1
N 2 *KAI* 160

Hr. Merah
N 1 Garbini 1986: 60-61

Hr. Oum Guerguer
N 1 Ghaki 1985: 172f.

Hr. Sidi Khalifat
N 1
N 2 Fevrier 1959-1960a: 61-63

Hr. Zian
N 1 *RÉS* 558

Ksar Lemsa
N 1 Fevrier 1968b: 226: 228
N 2 Fevrier 1968b: 228

Ksar Toual Zouamel
N 1 Fevrier 1946-1949: 252, 1
N 2 Fevrier 1946-1949: 252, 2
N 3 Fevrier 1946-1949: 253, 3

Ksour
N 1 Clermont-Ganneau 1924

Ksour Abd el-Melek
N 1 Chabot, *Punica* xx, 1
N 2 Chabot, *Punica* xx, 2
N 3 Chabot, *Punica* xx, 3
N 4 Chabot, *Punica* xx, 4
N 5 Fevrier 1968b: 224

Metameur
N 1 Chabot, *Punica* xxi
N 2 Berger 1889e: 86

Sidi Ahmed el-Hachmi
N 1 *RÉS* 306

Sidi Ali Belkassem
N 1 *RÉS* 938
N 2 *RÉS* 939A
N 3 *RÉS* 939C
N 4 *RÉS* 939D

Sousse
N 1
N 2 *RÉS* 944
N 3 *RÉS* 945
N 4 *RÉS* 946
N 5 *RÉS* 947A
N 6 *RÉS* 947B
N 7 *RÉS* 947C
N 8 *RÉS* 948
N 9 *RÉS* 949
N 10 *RÉS* 950A
N 11 *RÉS* 950B
N 12 *RÉS* 950C
N 13 *RÉS* 950D
N 14 *RÉS* 951
N 15 *RÉS* 952
N 16 *RÉS* 953
N 17 Dussaud 1914: 343, 1
N 18 Dussaud 1914: 343-344, 2
N 19 Dussaud 1914: 344, 3
N 20 Dussaud 1914: 344, 4
N 21 Dussaud 1914: 344-345, 5
N 22 Dussaud 1914: 345, 6
N 23 Dussaud 1914: 346, 8
N 24 Dussaud 1914: 346, 9
N 25 Dussaud 1914: 346f., 10f.
N 26 Dussaud 1916 : 163-165
N 27 Chabot 1941-1942: 399a
N 28 Chabot 1941-1942: 399b
N 29 Chabot 1941-1942: 400
N 30 Chabot 1941-1942: 400
N 31 Berger 1889: 31; *RÉS* 906
N 32 Berger 1884: 168

Tatahouine
N 1 *RÉS* 237, 1857

Teboursouk
N 1 Chabot, *Punica* xix
N 2 *RIL* 12
N 3 Fantar 1974: 397
N 4 Fantar 1974: 401
N 5
N 6 Fantar 1974: 407
N 7 Fantar 1974: 408
N 8 Fantar 1974: 409
N 9 Fantar 1974: 410
N 10 Fantar 1974: 411
N 11 Fantar 1974: 412
N 12 Fantar 1974: 413-414
N 13 Fantar 1974: 414
N 14 Fantar 1974: 415
N 15 Fantar 1974: 416a
N 16 Fantar 1974: 416b
N 17 Fantar 1974: 417a
N 18 Fantar 1974: 417b
N 19 Fantar 1974: 418a
N 20 Fantar 1974: 418b
N 21 Fantar 1974: 419a

Utica
N 1 Ferron 1975: 235-236, 275-276, 412
N 2 Ferron 1975: 242 & : 275, 428

Zaghouan
N 1 *RÉS* 598

Tunisia OU
N 1 SZNYCER 2000
N 2
N 3 MENDLESON 2003: 37
N 4 JONGELING 1984: 9
N 5 MENDLESON 2003: 38
N 6 MENDLESON 2003: 42
N 7
N 8 MENDLESON 2003: 37-38
N 9 MENDLESON 2003: 39
N 10 MENDLESON 2003: 39
N 11 MENDLESON 2003: 48
N 12 EUTING 1871: 33
N 13
N 14 MENDLESON 2003: 39
N 15 MENDLESON 2993: 39f.
N 16 CHABOT, *Punica* xvii, 12
N 17 CHABOT, *Punica* xxiii
N 18 FANTAR 1972
N 19 BISI 1978: 69-70
N 20 LEMAIRE 1994: 71-72
21 LEMAIRE 1994: 73-74

ALGERIA

Ain el-Kebch
N 1

Ain Youssef
N 1 DERENBOURG 1876: 175-179; *CIL* viii 4636

Arseu
N 1 SCHRÖDER 1869: 265, xxix 5
N 2

Bedja
N 1 CHABOT, *Punica* xii, 18b

Cap Djinet
N 1 *KAI* 170

Cherchel
N 1
N 2
N 3 DUSSAUD 1924: cxlvi

Constantine
N 1 JUDAS 1860-1861, pl 5, xi
N 2 CHABOT, *Punica* xviii/i 3
N 3 CHABOT, *Punica* xviii/i 7
N 4 CHABOT, *Punica* xviii/i 12
N 4bis CHABOT, *Punica* xviii/i 15
N 5 CHABOT, *Punica* xviii/i 17
N 6 CHABOT, *Punica* xviii/i 18
N 7
N 8 LEVY 1864: 76, 19
N 9 CHABOT, *Punica* xviii/i 22
N 10
N 11 CHABOT, *Punica* xviii/i 29
N 12 CHABOT, *Punica* xviii/i 30
N 13 CHABOT, *Punica* xviii/i 31
N 14 CHABOT, *Punica* xviii/i 32
N 15 CHABOT, *Punica* xviii/i 33
N 16 CHABOT, *Punica* xviii/i 34
N 17 CHABOT, *Punica* xviii/i 36
N 18 CHABOT, *Punica* xviii/i 39
N 19 LEVY 1864: 77
N 20 CHABOT, *Punica* xviii/i 43
N 21 CHABOT, *Punica* xviii/i 44
N 22 CHABOT, *Punica* xviii/i 45
N 23
N 24 CHABOT, *Punica* xviii/i 55
N 25 CHABOT, *Punica* xviii/i 57
N 26 CHABOT, *Punica* xviii/1 59
N 27 *SPC* 73
N 28
N 29 *SPC* 96
N 30 *SPC* 113
N 31 *SPC* 126
N 32 *SPC* 78
N 33 *SPC* 127
N 34 *SPC* 135
N 35 *SPC* 79
N 36 *SPC* 64
N 37 *SPC* 89
N 38 *SPC* 104
N 39 *SPC* 42
N 40 *SPC* 84
N 41 *SPC* 65
N 42
N 43 *SPC* 70
N 44 *SPC* 82
N 45 *SPC* 60
N 46 CHABOT, *Punica* xviii/iii, 1
N 47 SCHRÖDER 1869: 263, xxviii
N 48 CHABOT, *Punica* xviii/iii 3
N 49 CHABOT, *Punica* xviii/iii 4
N 50
N 51 *KAI* 163
N 52 *EH* 10
N 53 *EH* 11
N 54
N 55 *EH* 23
N 56 *KAI* 164
N 57 *EH* 29
N 58 *EH* 30
N 59 *EH* 36

N 60 *EH* 49
N 61 *EH* 66
N 62 *EH* 72
N 63 *EH* 73
N 64 *EH* 84
N 65 *EH* 90
N 66 *EH* 91
N 67 *EH* 96
N 68 *EH* 98
N 69 *EH* 104
N 70 *EH* 241
N 71 *EH* 263
N 72 *EH* 267
N 73 *EH* 268
N 74 *EH* 269
N 75 *EH* 270
N 76 *EH* 271
N 77 *EH* 272
N 78 *EH* 273
N 79 *EH* 274
N 80 *EH* 275
N 81 *EH* 276
N 82 *EH* 277
N 83 *EH* 278
N 84 *EH* 279
N 85 *EH* 280
N 86 *EH* 281

Dellys
N 1 DUSSAUD 1917: 161-163

Gouraya
N 1 *RÉS* 1979
N 2 *RÉS* 1980
N 3 *RÉS* 1981
N 4 *RÉS* 1982
N 5 *RÉS* 1983
N 6 *RÉS* 1984
N 7 *RÉS* 1985
N 8 *RÉS* 1986
N 9 *RÉS* 1987
N 10 *RÉS* 1988
N 11 *RÉS* 198bis
N 12 *RÉS* 1989
N 13 *RÉS* 1990
N 14 *RÉS* 1991
N 15 *RÉS* 1992
N 16 *RÉS* 1993
N 17 *RÉS* 1994
N 18 *RÉS* 1995
N 19 *RÉS* 1996
N 20 *RÉS* 1997
N 21 *RÉS* 1998
N 22 *RÉS* 1999
N 23 *RÉS* 2000

Guelma
N 1
N 2 CHABOT, *Punica* xi, 2
N 3
N 4
N 5 CHABOT, *Punica* xi, 5
N 6 CHABOT, *Punica* xi, 6
N 7 *KAI* 166
N 8 CHABOT, *Punica* xi, 8
N 9
N 10 CHABOT, *Punica* xi, 10
N 11 CHABOT, *Punica* xi, 11
N 12 CHABOT, *Punica* xi, 12
N 13 CHABOT, *Punica* xi, 13
N 14 CHABOT, *Punica* xi, 14
N 15 CHABOT, *Punica* xi, 15
N 16 CHABOT, *Punica* xi, 16
N 17 CHABOT, *Punica* xi, 17
N 18 CHABOT, *Punica* xi, 18
N 19
N 20 CHABOT, *Punica* xi, 20
N 21 CHABOT, *Punica* xi, 21
N 22
N 23 CHABOT, *Punica* xi, 23
N 24 CHABOT, *Punica* xi, 24
N 25 CHABOT, *Punica* xi, 25
N 26 CHABOT, *Punica* xi, 26
N 27 CHABOT, *Punica* xi, 27
N 28 CHABOT, *Punica* xi, 28
N 29 CHABOT, *Punica* xi, 29
N 30 CHABOT, *Punica* xi, 30
N 31 CHABOT, *Punica* xi, 31
N 32 CHABOT, *Punica* xi, 32
N 33 CHABOT, *Punica* xi, 33
N 34 CHABOT, *Punica* xi, 34
N 35 CHABOT, *Punica* ix, 9b; *Punica* xi, 35
N 36 CHABOT, *Punica* xi, 36
N 37 CHABOT, *Punica* xi, 37
N 38 CHABOT, *Punica* xi, 38
N 39 CHABOT, *Punica* xi, 39
N 40 *RIL* 657

Hr. Bou Atfan
N 1 CHABOT, *Punica* x 1
N 2

Kef Bezioun
N 1
N 2

Kef Smaar
N 1 CADENAT 1972: 40

Khallik
N 1 LEVY 1856: 26-27

Kheneg
N 1 BERTHIER & LEGLAY 1958: 25-27a
N 2 BERTHIER & LEGLAY 1958: 25-27b
N 3 BERTHIER & LEGLAY 1958: 25-27c

Ksiba Mraou
N 1
N 2 CHABOT, *Punica* xiv, 2
N 3
N 4 CHABOT, *Punica* xiv, 4
N 5 CHABOT, *Punica* xiv, 5
N 6 CHABOT, *Punica* xiv, 6
N 7 CHABOT, *Punica* xiv, 7
N 8 CHABOT, *Punica* xiv, 8
N 9 CHABOT 1934-1935: 203
N 10 CHABOT 1934-1935: 203-204

Oran
N 1 GARBINI 1986: 69

Oudjel
N 1 *RÉS* 783

Qalat Abi s-Siba
N 1
N 2

Siga
N 1 HORN-RÜGER 1979: 546

Souk Arrhas
N 1 CHABOT, *Punica* ix, 6b

Tiffech
N 1 JONGELING 1986: 251-252

Tirekbine
N 1

MOROCCO

Banasa
N 1 *IAM* 14
N 2 *IAM* 15

Melilla
N 1
N 2 RUIZ CABRERO 1998: 55-56

Thamusida
N 1 *IAM* 12
N 2 *IAM* 13

Volubilis
N 1 *IAM* 5
N 2 *IAM* 6
N 3 *IAM* 7
N 4 *IAM* 8
N 5 *IAM* 9
N 6 *IAM* 10
N 7 *IAM* 11
N 8 EL-KHAYARI 2000

Morocco OU
N 1 *IAM* 19
N 2 *IAM* 20
N 3 *IAM* 21

MALTA

Malta
N 1 *ICO* Malta Np 2
N 2 *ICO* Malta Np 3
N 3 *ICO* Malta Np 4
N 4 *ICO* Malta Np 5
N 5
N 6 *ICO* Malta Np 7
N 7 *ICO* Malta Np 8
N 8 *ICO* Malta Np 9
N 9 *ICO* Malta Np 9
N 10 *ICO* Malta Np 10
N 11 *ICO* Malta Np 10
N 12 *ICO* Malta Np 11
N 13 *ICO* Malta Np 12
N 14 *ICO* Malta Np 13
N 15 *ICO* Malta Np 13
N 16 *ICO* Malta Np 14
N 17 *ICO* Malta Np 15
N 18 *ICO* Malta Np 16
N 19 *ICO* Malta Np 17
N 20 *ICO* Malta Np 18
N 21 *ICO* Malta Np 19
N 22 AMADASI 1969: 75
N 23 AMADASI 1972: 126
N 24 AMADASI 1972: 127
N 25 AMADASI 1972: 127
N 26 AMADASI 1972: 127
N 27 AMADASI 1973: 94
N 28 AMADASI 1973: 94

PANTELLERIA

Pantelleria
N 1

SICILY

Favignana
N 1 BISI 1969

Grotta Regina
N 1 COACCI POLSELLI-AMADASI-TUSA 1979: 45 (29A)

N 2 *idem* 1979: 60 (40)
N 3 *idem* 1979: 77-78 (58)
N 4 *idem* 1979: 45 (64)

Palermo
N 1

Sicily OU
N 1 *ICO* Sicilia Npu 2
N 2 ROCCO 1971: 17

ITALY (mainland)

Pompei
N 1
N 2 GARBINI 1986: 19b
N 3 GARBINI 1986: 19c
N 4 GARBINI 1986: 19d

Rome
N 1

SARDINIA

Antas
N 1 FANTAR 1969: 91

Cagliari
N 1 *ICO* Sardegna Np 4

Capo di Pula
N 1 *ICO* Sardegna Np 3

Chia
N 1 *KAI* 173

S. Antioco
N 1 *ICO* Sardegna Np 1
N 2 *ICO* Sardegna Np 2
N 3
N 4 *ICO* Sardegna Np 6
N 5a PILI 1990: 12-13
N 5b PILI 1990: 12-13

Tharros
N 1 *ICO* Sardegna Np 9
N 2 *ICO* Sardegna Np 10

Villaperucciu
N 1 *ICO* Sardegna 11

SPAIN

Ibiza
N 1 *ICO* Spagna Np 2
N 2 *ICO* Spagna Np 3

Malaga
N 1 SZNYCER 1985, 57-59
N 2 SZNYCER 1985, 57-59

Villaricos
N 1 CHABOT 1932-1933: 501

Spain OU
N 1 *ICO* Spagna Np 1

WALES

Holt
N 1

Overview of Latino- and Greco-Punic Inscriptions

Texts given in bold face are discussed in the present collection. Texts in [], have been interpreted as belonging to the Latino-Punic corpus, inappropriately in our opinion; texts in {} too have been seen as Latino/Greco-Punic, although we cannot identify a word in any language; + indicate ostraca (cf. also AMADASI 1990b)

LIBYA

Bir ed-Dreder
LP 1
LP 2
LP 3 *IRT* 886c
LP 4
LP 5 *IRT* 886e
LP 6 *IRT* 886f
LP 7 *IRT* 886g
LP 8 cf. GOODCHILD 1954
LP 9
LP 10 cf. GOODCHILD 1954
LP 11 cf. GOODCHILD 1954
LP 12 cf. GOODCHILD 1954
LP 13 *IRT* 886j
LP 14
LP 15 cf. GOODCHILD 1954
LP 16 cf. GOODCHILD 1954
LP 17 cf. GOODCHILD 1954
LP 18 cf. GOODCHILD 1954
LP 19 cf. GOODCHILD 1954
LP 20 cf. GOODCHILD 1954
LP 21 cf. GOODCHILD 1954

Bir el-Uaar
LP 1 *IRT* 865

Bir Scedeua
LP 1 *IRTS* 20

Bir Shmech
LP 1

Breviglieri
LP 1
{ LP 2 *IRT* 877a}

Bu Njem
+LP 1 MARICHAL 1992, 240

Dukakra
LP 1 *LA 1*: 46

Fasciet el-Habs
LP 1 *IRT* 894

Gasr el-Azaiz
LP 1

Gasr Bugar
LP 1 *LA 1*: 54

Gasr Doga
LP 1

Gasr Isawi
[Latin1 VATTIONI 1976, 550]

Gasr Suq el-Oti
{LP 1 *IRT* 890}

Gasr el-Ureia
LP 1 *IRT* 892

Gasr Zugesh
{LP 1 *IRT* 878}

Ghadames
{LP 1 VATTIONI 1976, 553}

Gheria el-Gharbia
LP 1 VATTIONI 1976, 554

Ghirza
LP 1
{LP 2 *IRTS* 21}
{LP 3 VATTIONI 1976, 553}

Lepcis Magna
LP 1
LP 2 *IRT* 826
LP 3
LP 4 *IRT* 671
GP 1 *SM* 6: 45ff.

Libya OU
LP 1 *IRT* 828
LP 2 unpublished

Miragen Ngosta
LP 1 *LA* 1: 54

Nawalia
LP 1

Al-Qusbat
LP 1 *IRT* 879

Silin
+LP 1 unpublished
+LP 2 unpublished

Sirte
LP 1
LP 2
LP 3
LP 4
LP 5
LP 6
LP 7
LP 8
LP 9
LP 10
LP 11
LP 12

Wadi el-Amud
+LP 1 unpublished
+LP 2 unpublished
+LP 3 unpublished
+LP 4 unpublished

Wadi Beni Musa
LP 1 *LA* 1: 45
LP 2 *LA* 1: 45

Wadi Chanafes
LP 1 unpublished
LP 2 905 (?)

Wadi Ghalbun
LP 1 unpublished

Wadi Uaeni
LP 1 *IRT* 873

Wadi Umm el-Agerem
LP 1
LP 2

Zliten
LP 1

ALGERIA

El-Hofra
GP 1
GP 2 *KAI* 177

Henchir Smala
{LP 1 *RIL* 665}

TUNISIA

Carthage
GP 1 VATTIONI 1976, 536

SYRIA

Wasta
GP 1 *KAI* 174

Bibliography

ADAMS, J.N., 2003: *Bilingualism and the Latin language*. Cambridge.

ADAMIK, T., 1987: Romaniane vivat –Bemerkungen zum Gebrauch des Vokativs und zur afrikanischen Latinität. In: J. HERMAN (ed.), *Actes du Ier Colloque international sur le latin vulgaire et tardif (Pécs, 2-5 septembre 1985)*, Tübingen, 1-9.

DELGADO, J. Á., 1964: *Inscripciones Libicas de Canarias, Ensayo de interpretación Líbica.* Tenerife.

AMADASI GUZZO M.G., 1967: *Le iscrizioni Fenicie e Puniche delle Colonie in Occidente.* [Studi Semitici 28] Rome.

–, 1969: Le iscrizoni puniche. In: A. M. BISI – M. G. GUZZO AMADASI - V. TUSA, *Grotta Regina i, Rapporto Preliminare della Missione congiunta con la Soprintendenza alle Antichità della Sicilia Occidentale.* [Publicazioni del Centro di Studio per la civiltà Fenicia e Punica 4, Studi Semitici 33] Roma, 39-62.

–, 1972, Le iscrizoni puniche e neo puniche. In: *Missione Archeologhica Italiana a Malta, Raporto Preliminare della Campagna 1969.* [Publicazioni del Centro di Studio per la civiltà Fenicia e Punica 9, Serie Archeologica 18] Roma, 121-127.

–, 1973: Le iscrizoni puniche. In: *Missione Archeologhica Italiana a Malta, Raporto Preliminare della Campagna 1970.* [Publicazioni del Centro di Studio per la civiltà Fenicia e Punica 13, Serie Archeologica 20] Roma, 87-94.

–, 1979: Osservazioni sull'iscrizione Tripol. 32. *SM* 11: 27-35.

–, 1979-1984: *my* pronom relatif en Punique. *GLECS* 24-28: 31-37.

–, 1983a: Osservazioni su alcune iscrizioni di Lepcis. In: *Atti del I Congresso internazionale di Studi fenici e punici,* vol. 3, Rome, 789-796.

–, 1983b: Una grande famiglia di Lepcis in rapporto con la ristrutturazione urbanistica della città (I sec. A. C. - I sec. D. C.). In: *Architecture et Société, de l'Archaïsme Grec à la fin de la République Romaine, Actes du colloque international organisé par le Centre national de la recherche scientifique et l'École française de Rome* (= Collection de l'École Française de Rome, vol. 66), Rome, 377-385.

–, 1990a: *Iscrizioni Fenicie e Puniche in Italia*. Rome.

–, 1990b: Stato degli studi sulle iscrizioni latino-puniche della Tripolitania. *AR* 7: 101-108.

–, 1992: Varia Phoenicia. *RSF* 20: 95-104.

–, 1995. More on the Latin personal names ending with *–us* and *–ius* in Punic. In: Z. ZEVIT et al. (edd.), *Solving Riddles and Untying Knots. Biblical and Semitic Studies in Honor of J. C. Greenfield.* Winona Lake, 495-504.

–, 2002: Le iscrizioni del tofet: osservazioni sulle espressioni di offerta. In: WAGNER–RUIZ CABRERO 2002: 93-119.

–, 2003: I sostantivi fenici *'ab* e *'aḥ*. In P. MARRASINI et al. (edd.), *Semitic and Assyriological Studies Presented to P. Fronzaroli by Pupils and Colleagues*. Wiesbaden, 13-26.

BARKER, G. et al. (edd.), 1996: *Farming the Desert. The UNESCO Libyan Valleys Archaeological Survey*. [2 vols.] Paris-Tripoli-London.

BARTOCCINI, C. R., 1926: *Le antichità della Tripolitania.* Milan.

–, 1927: Rinvenimenti vari di interesse archeologico in Tripolitania (1920-1925). *AI* 1: 213-248.

–, 1928: Scavi e rinvenimemti in Tripolitania nagli anni 1926-1927. *AI* 2: 187-200.

BEGUINOT, F., 1949: Di alcune iscrizioni in caratteri latini e in lingua sconosciuta trovate in Tripolitania. *RSO* 24: 14-19.
BENZ, F. L., 1972: *Personal Names in the Phoenician and Punic Inscriptions*. [Studia Pohl 8] Rome.
BERGER, P., 1884: [Note]. *Revue Archéologique* 3/4: 168.
–, 1887: [Note], *JA* 8-9: 294.
–, 1889: [Deux inscriptions néo-puniques trouvées aux environs de Kesseur Métameur]. *CRAIBL* 1889: 85-86.
–, 1895: Le mausolée d'El-Amroun. *Revue Archéologique* 3: 71-83.
–, 1908: [Rapport]. *BAC* 1908: 166-168.
–, - CAGNAT, R. 1899: L'inscription trilingue d'Henchir Alaouin. *CRAIBL* 1899: 48-54.
BERLINER, A., 1916: Le mois intercalaire de calendrier punique. *RevAss* 13: 55-61.
BERTHIER, A. - R. CHARLIER, 1955: *Le sanctuaire punique d'El-Hofra à Constantine*. Paris.
BERTINELLI ANGELI, M. G., 1969: Termini Romani, pubblici e sacri, in epigrafi 'latino-libiche.' In: *Studi di storia antica in memoria di L. De Regibus*, Genova 1969. 217-224.
BERTRANDY, F. – M. SZNYCER, 1987: *Les stèles Puniques de Constantine*. Paris.
BISI, A. M., 1969: Iscrizione neo-punica inedita da Favignana. *AION* 19: 555-558, tav. i.
–, 1972: Le stele neo-puniche del Museo Nazionale di Napoli. *AION* 32: 135-150.
–, 1976: Su un gruppo di stele neo-puniche del British Museum. *RSF* 4: 23-40, tav. i- v.
–, 1978: A proposito di alcune stele del tipo della Ghorfa al British Museum. *Aaf* 12: 21-88.
BISI INGRASSIA, A. M., 1977: A proposito di alcune iscrizioni puniche su anfore di Pompei. *Quaderni di cultura materiale* 1: 151-153.
BORHY, L., 1989: The rank indicator role of the names Flavius and Iulius for prefects on the Tripolitanus limes (remarks on Late Roman frontier defence in Tripolitania). *AArchH* 41: 151-157.
BROGAN, O., 1976-77: Some ancient sites in Eastern Tripolitania. *LA* 13-14: 93-129.
–, - J. M. REYNOLDS, 1960: Seven new inscriptions from Tripolitania. *PBSR* 28: 51-54.
–, –, 1964: Inscriptions from the Tripolitanian hinterland. *LA* 1: 43-46.
–, –, 1984: Latin Inscriptions. In: BROGAN - SMITH 1984: 160-263.
–, - D. J. SMITH, 1984: *Ghirza: a Libyan Settlement in the Roman Period*. Tripoli.
BROWN, P., 1967: *Augustine of Hippo. A Biography*. London
–, 1968: Christianity and local culture in late Roman Africa. *JRS* 58: 85-95
CAGNAT, R. – A. MERLIN – L. CHATELAIN, 1923: *Inscriptions latines d'Afrique*. Paris.
CHABOT, J.-B., 1916: Sur deux inscriptions puniques et une inscription latine d'Afrique. *CRAIBL* 1916: 246.
–, 1916-1917: *Punica*: i-v, *JA* xi/vii: 77ff., vi-x, ib: 443ff., xi, *JA* 1916, xi/viii: 483ff., xii, *JA* 1917, xi/ix: 145ff., xiii-xviii, *JA* 1917, xi/x: 5ff., xix-xxv, *JA* 1918, xi/xi: 249ff.
–, 1932-1933: [Communication]. *BAC* 1932-1933: 447-449.
–, 1936-1937: [Communication]. *BAC* 1936-1937: 170-171.
–, 1940-41: *Recueil des inscriptions libyques*. [3 vols.] Paris.
–, 1943-1945: Note sur l'inscription punique d'une borne-limite découverte en Tunisie, *BAC* 1943-1945: 64-67.
CHARLES-PICARD, G., 1943-1945: Rapport sur l'activité du Service des Antiquités et Arts de la Tunisie du 1er juillet au 31 octobre 1945. *BAC* 1943-1945: 474-482.
CLERMONT-GANNEAU, C., 1900: Le *Mazrah* et les curiae ou ordines carthaginois dans le Tarif des sacrifices de Marseille et dans les inscriptions néo-puniques de Maktar et d'Altiburos, *RAO* 3: 22-40 (cf. *CRAIBL* 1898: 348-368).
COACCI POLSELLI, G., 1978: Per un corpus delle iscrizioni latino-puniche. In: *Atti del'I Convegno Italiano sul vincino oriente antico*. Rome, 231-241.
–, 1979: A proposite di alcune iscrizioni Latino-Puniche. *SM* 11:37-49.`
–, - M. G. GUZZO AMADASI – V. TUSA 1979: Le iscrizoni puniche, *Grotta Regina ii, Rapporto della Missione congiunta con la Soprintendenza alle Antichità della Sicilia Occidentale*. [Publicazioni del Centro di Studio per la civiltà Fenicia e Punica 19, Studi Semitici 52] Roma, 39-62.

COLLINGWOOD, R.G. - R.P. WRIGHT, 1995: *The Roman inscriptions of Britain, Vol. ii, Instrumentum domesticum*, ed. by S. S. FRERE et al., fasc. viii: *Graffiti on coarse pottery* ..., Gloucester.

COOKE, G. A., 1903: *A Textbook of North-West Semitic Inscriptions*. Oxford.

COX, M. G., 1988: Augustine, Jerome, Tyconius and the *lingua punica*. *SO* 64: 83-105.

CUMONT 1926: [Communication]. *Rivista della Tripolitania* 2: 158, 165-167.

CUNCHILLOS J.-L. - J.-A. ZAMORA, ²2000: *Gramática Fenicia Elemental*. Madrid.

DEMATHUISIEULX, H., 1904: *Nouvelles archives des missions scientifiques* 12. Paris.

DERENBOURG, J., 1876: Inscription bilingue de Ain-Youssef. *RevArch* 2: 175-179.

DI VITA-EVRARD, G., 1998: [Note in ELMAYER 1998: 131].

–, 2002-2003[2004]: Sur deux inscriptions votives «bilingues» de Sabratha et de Lepcis Magna. *Aaf* 38-39: 315-324.

DESSAU, H., 1892-1916: *Inscriptiones Latinae Selectae*. [3 vols.] Berlin.

DONNER, H. – W. RÖLLIG, ²1966-69: *Kanaanäische und Aramäische Inschriften mit einem Beitrag von O. Rössler*, 3 vols. Wiesbaden.

–, –, ⁵2002: *Kanaanäische und Aramäische Inschriften. Band 1. 5., erweiterte und überarbeitete Auflage*. Wiesbaden.

DUSSAUD, R., 1914: Trois stèles votives néopuniques de Dougga. *BAC* 1914: 44-45.

–, 1917: Inscriptions néopuniques d'Algérie et de Tunisie. *BAC* 1917: 161-167.

–, 1921: Rapport sur une inscription néo-punique. *BAC* 1921: 259-260.

–, 1923: [Deux textes néopuniques funéraires ... de Djama]. *BAC* 1923: 79-80.

–, 1924: [Fragment néopunique découvert à Cherchel]. *BAC* 1924: 146.

–, 1925: [Sur une inscription néopunique, Henchir-el-Bled]. *BAC* 1925: 252.

EL-KHAYARI, A., 2000: Une stèle funéraire portant une inscription néopunique découverte dans le temple C à Volubilis. *Semitica* 50: 55-68.

ELMAYER, A. F., 1983: The reinterpretation of Latino-Punic inscriptions from Roman Tripolitania. *LS* 14: 86-95.

–, 1984: The reinterpretation of Latino-Punic inscriptions from Roman Tripolitania. *LS* 15: 93-105.

–, 1985: The 'centenaria' of Roman Tripolitania. *LS* 16: 77-84.

–, 1997: *Tripolitania and the Roman Empire (B.C. 47-A.D. 235)*. [Series No. 8] Tripoli.

–, 1998: A Latino Punic funerary inscription from Nawailia (Tarhuna). *LA* n.s. 4: 129-132.

EUTING, J., 1871: *Punische Steine*. St.-Petersburg (= *Mémoires de l'Académie Impériale des Sciences de St.-Pétersbourg*, viie série, tome 17, nº 3).

FANTAR, M., 1972: Une inscription exposée au Musée d'Utique. *Les Cahiers de Tunisie* 20: 9-15.

–, 1974: Stèles anépigraphes et stèles à inscriptions néopuniques. *MAIBL* 16: 379-431.

–, 1986: Nouvelles stèles a épigraphes néopuniques de Mididi. *Semitica* 36: 25-42.

–, 1993: *Carthage. Approche d'une civilisation.* [2 vols.] Tunis.

FERCHIOU, N., 1989: Le mausolée de Q. Apuleus Maxssimus à El Amrouni. *PBSR* 57: 47-76.

–, 1996: Une épitaphe néopunique d'une grande prêtresse de Cérès provenant de `Ayin Zakkar (Tunisie). *Semitica* 46: 25-35.

FERJAOUI, A., 1989: Nouvelles inscriptions néopuniques de Mididi. *Bulletin des Travaux de l'Institut d'Archéologie et d'Art de Tunis* 3: 55-61.

FERRON, J., 1975: *Mort-dieu de Carthage*. Paris.

–, - M. E. AUBET, 1974: *Orants de Carthage*. Paris.

–, - M. PINARD, 1960-1961: Les fouilles de Byrsa (suite). *CB* 9: 152-253, nº 456.

FEVRIER, J. G., 1949a: À propos de Baᶜal Addir. *Semitica* 2: 21-28.

–, 1949b: L'inscription Punico-Libyque de Maktar. *JA* 237: 85-91.

–, 1951: L'inscription funéraire de Micipsa. *RA* 45: 138-150.

–, 1952a: L'inscription néopunique Cherchell i. *RHR* 141 (n.s. 61): 19-25.

–, 1952b: 'Fils adoptif' en punique, *GLECS* 6 (1951-1954): 12-13.

–, 1953a: La prononciation punique des noms propres latins en *–us* et en *–ius*. *JA* 241: 465-471.

–, 1953b: Un sacrifice d'enfant chez les Numides. In: *Mélanges Isidore Lévy, AIPHOS* 13: 161-171.

–, 1954: La borne de Micipsa. *BAC* 1951-1952: 116-120.
–, 1955-1956: [review of BERTHIER-CHARLIER 1952]. *BAC* 1955-1956: 152-159.
–, 1955: Épitaphe néopunique d'une prêtresse. *Semitica* 5: 63-64.
–, 1956: Les découvertes épigraphiques puniques et néopuniques depuis la guerre. In: *Studi orientalistici in onore di G. Levi Della Vida* [Pubblicazioni dell'Istituto per l'Oriente 52], Rome, 281-284.
–, 1958-1959: Paralipomena Punica. *CB* 8: 25-31.
–, 1959-1960: Deux inscriptions néopuniques. *Karthago* 10: 61-66.
–, 1960: Essai de reconstitution du sacrifice Molek. *JA* 248:167-187.
–, 1961: Textes puniques et néopuniques relatifs aux testaments. *Semitica* 11: 5-8.
–, 1964-1965: À propos de l'épitaphe néopunique d'une prêtresse. *Mélanges de Carthage* (=*CB* 10): 93-95.
–, 1971a: Le waw conversif en punique. In: *Hommages à A. Dupont-Sommer*. Paris, 193-194.
–, 1971b: Une mention des cursores dans un texte dit latino libyque. *BAC* n.s. 7: 225-227.
–, & M. FANTAR 1965: Les nouvelles inscriptions monumentales néo-puniques de Mactar, *Karthago* 12:45-59, pl. i-iii.
–,. – L. GALAND – G. VAJDA 1966: *Inscriptions Antiques du Maroc*. Paris.
FREND, W., 1942: A note on the Berber background in the life of Augustine. *JTS* 43: 179-181.
–, 1952: *The Donatist Church. A movement of protest in Roman North Africa*. Oxford.
FRIEDRICH, J., 1957: Punische Studien. *ZDMG* 107: 295-298.
–, - W. RÖLLIG, 1970: *Phönizisch-Punische Grammatik*. [Analecta Orientalia 46] Rome.
–, –, 1999: *Phönizisch-Punische Grammatik. 3. Auflage, neu bearbeitet von Maria Giulia Amadasi Guzzo unter Mitarbeit von Werner R. Meyer*. [Analecta Orientalia 55] Rome.
GALAND, L., 1990: Le libyque et les études sémitiques. *Semitica* 38: 121-124.
GANDOLPHE, P., 1999: Notes d'épigraphie africaine. In: L. CAGNI (ed.), *Biblica et Semitica. Studi in memoria di Francesco Vattioni*. Naples, 217-234.
GARBINI, G., 1967: Un'iscrizione «latino-punica» dall'Algeria? *AION* 17: 69-72.
–, 1968: Note di epigrafia punica iii. *RSO* 43: 5-17.
–, 1974: Dieci anni di epigrafia punica nel Magreb (1965-1974). *SM* 6: 1-36.
–, 1976: Epigrafia punica nel Magreb – 1975-1976. *SM* 8: 11-24.
–, 1978: Epigrafia punica nel Magreb (1977-1978). *SM* 10: 1-12.
–, 1983: Nuovi documenti di epigrafia punica. *Epigraphica* 45: 102-107.
–, 1986[1987]: Venti anni di epigraphia punica nel Maghreb (1965-85). *RSF* 14 (supplemento).
–, 1992: Nota sulla neopunica di Tarhuna. *RSF* 20: 105-106.
GELB, I., 1929-1930: La mimazione e la nunazione nelle lingue semitiche. *RSO* 12: 217-265.
GESENIUS, W., 1837: *Scripturæ linguæque Phoeniciæ monumenta quotquot supersunt*. Leipzig.
–, -F. BUHL (ed.), [16]1915: *Wilhelm Gesenius' Hebräisches und Aramäisches Handwörterbuch über das Alte Testament*. Leipzig.
GHAKI, M., 1985: Textes libyques et puniques de la haute vallée de l'Oued El Htab. *REPPAL* 1: 172-177.
–, 1994: Épigraphie libyque et punique à Dougga (TBGG), in: M. KHANOUSSI & L. MAURIN (edd.), *Dougga* (Thugga) *Études Épigraphiques*, Paris, 27-45.
GOODCHILD, R. G., 1949: Some inscriptions from Roman Tripolitania. *Reports and Monographs* 2: 29-35.
–, 1950a: The Latino-Libyan inscriptions of Tripolitania. *AJ* 30: 135-144.
–, 1950b: The Limes Tripolitanus II. *JRS* 40: 25-40 = GOODCHILD 1976: 35-45.
–, 1951: Roman sites on the Tarhuna plateau of Tripolitania. *PBSR* 19:43-77 =GOODCHILD 1976: 72-106.
–, 1954: La necropoli Romano-Libica di Bir ed-Dréder. *QAL* 3: 91-107 =GOODCHILD 1976: 59-71.
–, 1976: *Libyan Studies. Selected Papers of the Late R. G. Goodchild, edited by J.M. Reynolds*. London.
GORDON, C. H., 1968: Northwest Semitic texts in Latin and Greek letters. *JAOS* 88: 285-289.

GRAHAME, M., 1998: Rome without Romanization: cultural change in the pre-desert of Tripolitania (first-third centuries AD). *OJA* 17: 93-111.
GRATWICK, A. S., 1971: Hanno's Punic speech in the Poenulus of Plautus. *Hermes* 99: 25-45.
HÄBERL, C. G., 2000: *The language of the inscriptions at Bir ed-Dréder*. Cambridge (Mass.), (Unpublished seminar paper, Harvard University).
HALFF, G., 1963-1964: L'onomastique punique de Carthage: répertoire et commentaire. *Karthago* 12: 63-146.
HARRIS, Z. S., 1936: *A Grammar of the Phoenician Language*. [AOS 8]. New Haven.
HAYNES, D. E. L., ^{3}1965: *An Archaeological and Historical Guide to the pre-Islamic Antiquities of Tripolitania*. London.
HOFTIJZER, J., 1961: Notes sur une épitaphe en écriture néopunique. *VT* 11: 344-348.
–, 1963: Liste des pierres et moulages à textes Phéniciens/Puniques du Musée des Antiquités à Leyde. *OML* 44: 89-98.
–, - K. JONGELING, 1995: *Dictionary of the North-West Semitic Inscriptions*. (2 vols.) [HdO 21] Leiden.
JEAN, C.-F. – J. HOFTIJZER, 1965: *Dictionnaire des inscriptions sémitiques de l'ouest*. Leiden.
JONGELING, K., 1984: *Names in Neo-Punic Inscriptions*. Groningen (Thesis Groningen).
–, 1986: Remarks on Some Punic Texts. *VO* 6: 249-254.
–, 1988: The name element BRK in Latin epigraphical sources. *VO* 7: 223-241.
–, 1989: A remark on a votive text from Constantine *KAI* 162. *SEL* 6: 127-134.
–, 1994: *North-African Names from Latin Sources*. Leiden.
–, 1996a: 'I wrote forty-three characters.' *DS-NELL* 2: 69-80.
–, 1996b: A few remarks on some Neo-Punic Texts. *DS-NELL* 2: 157-167.
–, 1997: The Neo-Punic text from Ain Zakkar. *DS-NELL* 3: 39-44.
–, 1999: A note on the inscription H. Maktar N 39. *DS-NELL* 4: 81-85.
–, 2003: Use of Vowel Letters in Neo-Punic Texts from Guelma. *DS-NELL* 5: 117-136.
–, 2004: A Remark on Late Punic Syntax. *DS-NELL* 6: 41-46.
–, - R. M. KERR, 2002: A personal Phoenico-Punic Dictionary. *Orientalia* 71: 173-81.
–, –, 2003[2005]: The Grammar of Krahmalkov's Phoenicians.*Folia Orientalia* 39:193-201.
JUDAS, A. C., 1860-61: Mémoire sur 19 inscriptions numidico-puniques. *Annuaire*.
KERR, R. M., 2003: The grapheme *y* in transcribed late Punic. *DS-NELL* 5: 137-156.
–, 2005: North African *centenaria* and Hebrew נְצִיבִים. *Bibel und Babel* 2 [forthcoming].
KOSSMANN, M., 1999: Essai sur la phonologie du proto-berbère. [Grammatische Analysen Afrikanischer Sprachen 12] Cologne.
KRAHMALKOV, C. R., 1969: Observations on the affixing of Possessive Pronouns in Punic. *RSO* 44: 181-186.
–, 1970: Studies in Phoenician and Punic grammar. *JSS* 15: 181-188.
–, 1972: Comments on the vocalisation of the suffix pronoun of the third feminine singular in Phoenician and Punic. *JSS* 17: 69-75.
–, 1973: A reinterpretation of the Neo-Punic inscription IRT 889 from Roman Tripolitania. *JAOS* 93: 61-64.
–, 1974: The object pronouns of the third person of Phoenician and Punic. *RSF* 2: 39-43.
–, 1975: Two Neo-Punic Poems in Rhymed Verse. *RSF* 3:169-205.
–, 1976: A Neo-Punic shaft tomb inscription from Roman Tripolitania. In L. L. ORLIN (ed.), *Michigan Oriental Studies in Honor of George G. Cameron*. Ann Arbor, 58-59.
–, 1978: A Punic punning epitaph. *RSF* 6: 27-30.
–, 1979a: On the third feminine singular of the perfect in Phoenician-Punic. *JSS* 24: 25-28.
–, 1979b: The Neo-Punic dedication of the Mausoleum of Iyllul. *RSF* 7: 175-179.
–, 1988: Observations on the Punic monologues of Hanno in the Poenulus. *Orientalia* 57: 55-66.
–, 1993: The third feminine plural possessive pronoun in Phoenician-Punic.*JNES* 52:37-41.
–, 1994a: Notes on Tripolitanian-Neopunic. *JAOS* 114: 453-56.
–, 1994b: 'When he drove out Yrirachan': A Phoenician (Punic) poem. *BASOR* 294: 69-82.
–, 2000: *A Phoenician-Punic Dictionary* [OLA 90] Louvain.
–, 2001: *A Phoenician-Punic Grammar* [HdO 54] Leiden.

LALOMIA, M. R., 1974: Iscrizione punica in caratteri greci sulla base di una parasata dell'arco di Marco Aurelio a Leptis Magna. *SM* 6: 45-50.
LANDAU, W. Frhr. v., 1903: *Beiträge zur Altertumskunde des Orients iii, Die Stele von Amrith – Die neuen phönicischen Inschriften*. Leipzig.
LEMAIRE, A., 1994: Nouvelle Inscription néo-punique sur jarre. *RSF* 22: 71-74, tab. ii-iv.
LEVI DELLA VIDA, G., 1927: Le iscrizioni neopuniche della Tripolitania. *Libya* 1 (*Rivista della Tripolitania* 3): 91-116.
–, 1929: *AI* 4: 186-87.
–, 1938: Il Teatro Augusteo di Leptis Magna secondo le ultime scoperte e un'iscrizione bilingue in Latini e Neo-Punico ii, *AI* 6: 104-109.
–, 1940: A Neopunic Inscription in England. *JAOS* 60: 578-579.
–, 1942: The Phoenician God Satrapes. *BASOR* 87: 29-32.
–, 1944: 'El 'Elyon in Genesis 14: 18-20. *JBL* 63: 1-9.
–, 1949: Iscrizioni neopuniche di Tripolitania. *RANL* 8: 399-412.
–, 1951: The Neo-Punic dedication of the Ammonium at Ras el-Haddagia. *PBSR* 19: 65-68 =GOODCHILD 1976: 93-96.
–, 1963: Sulle iscrizioni «latino-libiche» della Tripolitania. *OA* 2: 65-94.
–, 1964a: Le iscrizioni neopuniche di Wadi el-Amud. *LA* 1: 57-63.
–, 1964b. Recension of DONNER-RÖLLIG ([1]1962-1964). *RSO* 39: 295-314.
–, 1965: Parerga neopunica. *OA* 4: 59-62.
–, 1967a: Su una bilingue latino-punica da Leptis Magna. *Atti dell'Academia delle Scienze di Torino* 1967: 395-409.
–, 1967b: Qualche osservazione a *AIUON, n.s.*, 16, 37-55. *AION* 17: 257-266.
–, 1970: Punico *mu* pronome interrogativo e relativo. In: *Mélanges M. Cohen*. Paris.
–, - M. G. AMADASI GUZZO 1987: *Iscrizioni Puniche della Tripolitania (1927-1967)*. [Monografie di Archeologia Libica 22] Rome.
LEVY, M. A., 1857: *Phönizische Studien, Zweites Heft*. Breslau.
–, 1864: *Phönizische Studien, Drittes Heft*. Breslau
–, 1870: *Phönizische Studien, Viertes Heft*. Breslau.
LIDZBARSKI, M., 1898: *Handbuch der nordsemitischen Epigraphik nebst ausgewählten* Inschriften. [2 vols.] Weimar.
–, 1902: *Ephemeris für semitische Epigraphik* i, 1900-1902. Gießen.
–, 1908: *Ephemeris für semitische Epigraphik* ii, 1903-1908. Gießen.
–, 1915: *Ephemeris für semitische Epigraphik* iii, 1909-1915. Gießen.
LIPIŃSKI, E., 1995: *Dieux et déesses de l'univers phénicien et punique*. [OLA 64] Louvain.
MACMULLEN, R., 2000: *Romanization in the time of Augustus*. New Haven.
MANFREDI, L.-I., 1995: *Monete Puniche, Repertorio Epigrafico e Numismatico delle Leggende Puniche*. [Bolletino di Numismatica, Monografia 6] Roma.
MARCY, G., 1936: *Les inscriptions libyques bilingues de l'Afrique du Nord*. [Cahiers de la Société Asiatique, première série, v] Paris.
MARICHAL, R., 1992: *Les ostraca de Bu Njem*. [Suppléments de LA 7] Tripoli.
MASSON, O., 1977: Libyca, v. Inscriptions libyques au Musée du Louvre. *Semitica* 27: 41-45.
MAZZA, F., 1983: A proposito di une iscrizione neopunica dipinta su anfora. *OA* 22: 61-65.
MENDLESON, C., 2003: *Catalogue of Punic Stelae in the British Museum*. [The British Museum Occasional Papers No. 98] London.
MILLAR, F., 1968: Local Cultures in the Roman Empire: Libyan, Punic and Latin in Roman Africa. *JRS* 58: 126-134.
MÓCSY, A., 1964: Der Name Flavius als Rangbezeichnung in der Spätantike. In: *Akte des IV. Internationalen Kongresses für griechische und lateinische Epigraphik*. Vienna, 256-263.
NAVEH, J., 1966: The scripts of two ostraca from Elath. *BASOR* 183: 27-30.
OATES, D., 1954: Ancient settlement in the Tripolitanian Gebel, II: The Berber period. *PBSR* 22: 91-117.
PECKHAM, J. B., 1968: *The Development of the Late Phoenician Scripts*. Cambridge (Mass.).
PICARD, G., 1945: La basilique funéraire de Julius Piso à Mactar. *CRAIBL* 1945: 185-212.

–, 1954: *Catalogue du Musée Alaoui*. [2 vols.] Tunis.
PILI, F., 1990: Iscrizione Neopunica e bollo Punico inediti. *Speleologia Sarda* 75: 11-16.
REYNOLDS, J. M., 1951: Some inscriptions from Lepcis Magna. *PBSR* 19: 118-121.
–, 1955: Inscriptions of Roman Tripolitania: a supplement. *PBSR* 23: 124-147.
–, 1958: Three inscriptions from Ghadames in Tripolitania. *PBSR* 26: 135-136.
–, - J. B. Ward Perkins 1952: *Inscriptions of Roman Tripolitania*. London.
ROSCHINSKY, H. P., 1979: Die Mikiwsan-Inschrift aus Cherchel. In: H. G. HORN & C. B. RÜGER, *Die Numider, Reiter und Könige nördlich der Sahara*, Köln-Bonn, 111-116.
–, 1988: Punische inschriften zum MLK-Opfer und seinem Ersatz. In: *Texte aus der Umwelt des Alten Testaments*, Band 2, Gütersloh, 606-620.
ROSSI, M. - G. GARBINI, 1976-1977[1983]: Nuovi documenti epigrafici dalla Tripolitania romana, *LA* 13-14: 7-19.
RUIZ CABRERO, L. A., 1998: Dos graffiti púnicos de Melilla (antigua Rusaddir - España). *SEAP* 17: 55-65.
SCHRÖDER, P., 1869: *Die phönizische Sprache. Entwurf einer Grammatik*. Halle (reprint Wiesbaden 1979).
SEGERT, S., 1976: *A Basic Grammar of Phoenician and Punic*. Munich.
SHIFMAN, I., Sh. 1965: Epigrafi eskie zametki. 2. 'Me evoj' kamen' iz rajona Maktara (Tunis). *KSINA* 86 (Istorija i filologija Bli nego Vostoka): 122-124.
SZNYCER, M., 1963-66: Les inscriptions dites «latino-libyques.» *GLECS* 10: 97-104.
–, 1977a: Le texte néopunique de la bilingue de Bordj Hellal. *Semitica* 27: 47-57.
–, 1977b: Antiquités et épigraphie nord-sémitiques (1975-1976). *Annuaire de l'école Pratiques des Hautes études,* ive section, 109: 177-186.
–, 1980: Observations sur l'inscription néo-punique de Bir Tlelsa. *Semitica* 30: 33-41.
–, 1982[1988]: Observations sur deux inscriptions néo-puniques de Tripolitaine récemment publiée. *BAC* n.s. 18: 195-197.
–, 1983: Deux inscriptions funéraires néopuniques de Henchir Guergour (Masculula). *Semitica* 33: 51-57.
–, 1985: Trois graffites puniques et néopuniques de Malaga. *Semitica* 35: 57-59.
–, 1994: À propos de la stèle néopunique de Tarhuna en Tripolitaine Romaine. In: Y. LE BOHEC (ed.), *L'Afrique, la Gaule, la religion à l'époque romaine. Mélanges à la mémoire de Marcel Le Glay*, [Collection Latomus 226] Bruxelles: 27-33.
–, 1998: Une inscription néopunique de la région de Maktar conservée au British Museum de Londres. *Semitica* 48: 41-59.
–, 2000: Inscriptions néopuniques conservées au musée de Copenhague. *Semitica* 50: 41-54.
TEIXIDOR, J., 1964-1980: *Bulletin d'épigraphie sémitique (1964-1980)*. [Bibliothèque Archéologique et Historique 127] Paris 1986.
TEMPLE, G. T., 1835: *Excursions in the Mediterranean, Algiers and Tunis*. [2 vols.] London.
THACKER, T. W. - R. P. WRIGHT, 1955: A new interpretation of the Phoenician graffito from Holt, Denbighshire. *Iraq* 17: 90-91.
VAN DEN BRANDEN, A., 1969: *Grammaire phénicienne*. Beirut.
–, 1972: L'iscrizione neopunica *KAI* 162. *B&O* 14: 195-200.
–, 1973: Il sacrificio umano presso i Punici. *B&O* 15: 197-208.
–, 1974: Inscription de Guelat bou Sba. *RSF* 2:145-146.
–, 1977: L'inscription néopunique Février-Fantar B de Mactar. *RSF* 5: 55-65.
VÁRHELYI, Z., 1998: What is the evidence for the survival of Punic culture in Roman North Africa? *AAH* 38: 391-403.
VASSEL, E., 1920: Sur l'orthographe punique du nom de Thinissut. *BAC* 1920: 475-477.
VATTIONI, F., 1966: Appunti sulle iscrizioni puniche tripolitane. *AION* 16: 37-55.
–, 1968: Note feniche. *AION* 18: 71-73.
–, 1971: Tripolitana 1 et Tobie, iii, 6. *RB* 78: 242-246.
–, 1976: Glosse Puniche. *Augustinianum* 16: 505-555.
–, 1980-1981: La bilingue latina e neopunica di El-Amrouni. *Helikon* 20-21: 293-299.
–, 1993a: Varia semitica – VII. *AION* 53: 464-467.

–, 1993b: La radice *šb^c*, «giurare», in neopunico. *AION* 53: 451-454.
–, 1993c: Le iscrizioni di Ghirza (Tripolitania). *AION* 53: 455-458.
–, 1994: Mididi e le sue epigrafi. *SEL* 11: 113-128.
–, 1995: Varia Semitica xxvi, un altro testo neopunico da Maktar. *AION* 55: 110-111.
VOLTERRA, E., 1952: L'adozione testamentaria ed un'iscrizione latina e neopunica della Tripolitania. *RAL* ser, 8,7: 175-188.
WAGNER, C. G. – L. A. RUIZ CABRERO, (edd.) 2002: *El Molk como Concepto del Sacrificio Púnico y Hebreo y el Final del Dios Moloch. Edición Bilingüe Alemán-Español del famoso libro de O. Eissfeldt ampliada con artículos de actualización de E. Acquaro, Mª G. Amadasi, A. Ciasca y E. Lipiński*, Madrid.

Neo-Punic Paleographic Chart

Transcription
Punic
Constantine
Breviglieri
Guelma
H. Brirht
Cherchel
Al-Qusbat
H. Maktar
Hebrew
ʾ b g d h w z ḥ ṭ y k l m n s ʿ p ṣ q r š t
א ב ג ד ה ו ז ח ט י כ ל מ נ ס ע פ צ ק ר ש ת